ca
917.94
D
Decker, Peter
  Diaries of the author.

c.1

Decker, Peter, 1822-1888.
   The diaries of Peter Decker:
overland to California in 1849 and
life in the mines, 1850-1851. Edited
by Helen S. Giffen. Georgetown,
Calif., Talisman Press, 1966.
   338 p. illus., 2 fold. maps (1
col.) port.   24 cm.

"Original manuscript diaries in the
collection of Society of California
Pioneers, San Francisco."

(Cont'd on next card)

PKT   880528   880525   RPL
F000130   DB /XXX   A*   87-B23174
                              66-27366//r86

THE DIARIES of PETER DECKER

*Overland to California in 1849
and Life in the Mines, 1850-1851*

PETER DECKER

THE DIARIES of PETER DECKER

Overland to California in 1849 and Life in the Mines, 1850-1851

[ORIGINAL MANUSCRIPT DIARIES IN THE COLLECTION OF
SOCIETY OF CALIFORNIA PIONEERS, SAN FRANCISCO.]

EDITED BY

Helen S. Giffen

THE TALISMAN PRESS
Georgetown, California   1966

Contents

Foreword

The Decker Diaries have been a part of the manuscript collection of The Society of California Pioneers for twenty-three years, having been presented to them by member Elliot McAllister, grandson of Peter Decker, in April, 1942. Dr. Ralph Bieber of Washington University, in St. Louis, Missouri, an authority on overland diaries of the 1840's, considers the 1849 diary of Peter Decker one of the outstanding records of 1849.

The journals and miscellaneous notes kept by Peter Decker are as follows:

Diary, April 4, to November 5, 1849, from Columbus, Ohio, to Sacramento.

Journal, March 18 to July 22, 1850, begun at Vernon, California, and kept on the Yuba River.

Journal, July 22 to September 3, 1850, "Notes on the South Yuba."

Journal, September 24 to November 11, 1850, Nevada, California.

Journal, November 11 to January 30, 1851, Nevada, California.

Journal, January 30 to May 30, 1851, Nevada, California.

Journal, January 27 to February 13, 1853, Parks Bar and Trip East.

Journal, February 13 to 25, 1853, further notes on trip east.

Journal, May 26 to June 4, 1853, Columbus, Ohio, and start for California.

Journal, June 18 to July 13, 1853, Return voyage and Parks Bar.

Notes on Mountain Trip, January, 1854.

Notes on Goodyears Bar, August, 1851.

Miscellaneous Notes, September, 1854.

Notes, "My night after leaving Rich Bar, Feather River, October, 1855."

Journal, May 29 to June 22, 1857, Inland Journey from Portland, Oregon, to Marysville, California.

Journal, "Trip to Los Angeles and a partial description of Yosemite, July to October, 1857."

Journal, "Closing Notes on Los Angeles October 7-11, 1857."

Notes, "Trip to Yreka and Siskiyou County, May, 1871."

As will be seen by the foregoing list, Decker's contribution to the record of events during the 1850's was considerable. The intent of the editor has been to publish the overland journal and the California journals through May 30, 1851. This decision was based upon two considerations. The first was the continuity of the journals through the date of May 30, 1851. After that date the continuity is sparse and fragmentary. The second consideration was in terms of the broad historical interest of the journals to the cutoff date. After that, while the historical interest is no less real, it is of a more regional type, and the interest clearly centers upon what may be termed regional history.

Wherever a personal name appears in Decker's Diaries an effort has been made by the editor to supply additional identification when such is possible. In every instance it was not possible to do so, due to a complete lack of information and data. When such is the case, no footnote appears by the personal name. When such instances occurred, diaries of the other forty-niners were checked, biographical index files at the Society of California Pioneers and the California State Library, together with contemporary printed accounts of departures of overland parties printed in the New York *Herald* for 1849. In a few instances the 1850 Census of California was also checked. Insofar as some 22,000 people were on the overland trail to California in 1849—a far larger migration than previous years—the reader will understand that it is

not possible to identify every personal name that Decker
set down.

One of the richest experiences of a professional historian is to annotate the recollections, reminiscences and
diaries of someone who has participated in the building
of a new country. It leads one down winding paths and
along devious routes that converge at last upon the particular bit of information that is desired to amplify and
clarify some statement or passage which the original
writer has either left unclear or failed to sufficiently describe. To say the least, the editing of the Decker Diaries
has been a most satisfying effort, and I am deeply grateful for the fresh fields of exploration it has revealed.

No historian is sufficient unto himself. He must rely
upon the help of others to expand his own knowledge.
Therefore, I wish to acknowledge the aid of the Bancroft
Library of the University of California, The California
State Library, Miss Thelma Neaville, Librarian of the
Marysville Public Library, the Librarian of the Ohio
State Library, Librarian of the Ohio Historical Society,
Yale University for the use of the Ware Map, Dale
Morgan of the Bancroft Library, and various others who
have contributed bits and pieces of information pertinent
to the annotations in this book.

Particular thanks is due to Messrs. Elliot, Decker G.
and Breck P. McAllister for permission to reprint the
diaries of their grandfather, and especially to Elliot Mc-
Allister for furnishing family letters and other material.

HELEN S. GIFFEN

SAN FRANCISCO, CALIFORNIA
SEPTEMBER, 1966

FRONTIER FORT

Introduction

I

THE YEAR 1849 witnessed the beginning of the greatest westward migration this country had ever experienced. It was also the year of the greatest number
of amateur literary efforts to eventually find their way
into the archives of historical societies, libraries, and
other repositories, not to mention the vast number that
may still repose in attics and basements perhaps forever
lost to posterity. The diaries, letters and reminiscences
of the forty-niners who traveled to the gold country of
California by sail and by prairie schooner add up to an
impressive total never before or since equalled.

Dale Morgan, in his editing of *The Overland Diary of
James A. Pritchard,* (Denver, 1959) has undertaken to
list the diaries that were kept by those going to California,
Oregon and Utah via South Pass in 1849. It is an impressive list and bears out the fact that it was not those
with literary talent alone who were impelled to record
their impressions of this great westward march. Probably

11

the travellers coming via Panama, and around the Horn were equally prolific in setting down their experiences.

Why should these manuscripts be so carefully preserved, even though many have scant literary merit? Primarily their value lies in the fact that they reconstruct for us a picture of a great mass movement of humanity bound together by a single purpose, to find gold, and whose collective determination changed completely the face of California, the West, and even the course of history. Reading through these often tattered pages we experience once again, through the eyes of the beholder, scenes and events so new to the men and women leaning over the rail of a ship, or peering from the high seat of a prairie schooner, that they were, at times, over-awed by the breadth of the world they had set out to conquer by peaceful means.

Peter Decker, one of this great crowd of migrating humanity, was a prolific diarist. A man of education, he was possessed with a more than average facility with words. As a young man in Columbus, Ohio, Decker went to school at Covert's Academy. He had the good fortune to have there as one of his instructors Lorenzo Sawyer, a lawyer who was to join the emigration to California in 1850, where he became a United States Circuit Judge. It is quite possible that some of Decker's ability with words came from his early association with Judge Sawyer. Their paths were to cross again in California, when both would be residents of Nevada City. Decker was twenty-six years old when he started from Columbus, Ohio, to make the long journey across the plains. Born November 22, 1822, on Manada Creek, West Hanover, Pennsylvania, he was the son of Michael Decker, a farmer. When Peter was sixteen the Decker family left Pennsylvania to settle in Columbus, Ohio, where the elder sons, Charles and Augustus, had already established a thriving mercantile business. Peter's early training in merchandising was to stand him in good stead. He clerked in the family store in Columbus during his school days, and after graduation he joined full-time with his brothers in the firm of A. S. Decker and Brothers.

A young man with few financial problems, a bachelor with no serious romantic attachments, and with a youthful hankering for adventure, it is not surprising that the news of the gold discovery in California should stir in him the desire to be up and away and to try his fortune in a new country. To reach this mecca required not only courage and physical stamina, but resourcefulness and imagination. It was his ability to envision a future beyond the rigors of the westward journey that prompted him to make the momentous decision to travel to California.

On February 15, 1849, an article appeared in the Columbus *Ohio State Journal,* announcing that a company known as the "Columbus and California Industrial Association" had been formed with the stated intention "for operating in the gold regions in California." John Walton was listed as president, J. G. Canfield listed as vice-president, Peter Decker as secretary, and G. Q. McColm listed as treasurer. Five directors were also listed together with a constitution consisting of seventeen articles. On April 2, 1849, the *Journal* announced the departure of the Association, comprised of a company of thirty young men —"ten wagons and 40 mules, and is well supplied with equipage, provisions and arms. In organization it is divided into five messes, with one director in each. Leaving Columbus, they pass thro' Xenia to Cincinnati, thence by water to Independence, in Missouri, beyond which the particular route is not determined upon."

In another column of the *Journal,* the editor wishes farewell to the young adventurers, and waxed poetic: "Impelled more by a desire for adventure than by a love of riches, a large number of young men of the city and neighborhood have this day bid adieu to their families and friends, to the sweets of society and appliances of civilization, and taken their departure for that country where the setting sun gilds with its rays mountains rich in the precious metals, and streams whose shining sands are impregnated with yellow gold." All over Ohio—as elsewhere—newspapers reported the departure of companies for the California gold fields. The editor of the *Ohio Statesman* estimated by the end of the year that some twenty thousand Ohioans had departed for the new El Dorado. For most Ohio companies the overland route was preferred, but a substantial number chose the long sea route via Cape Horn, while others sailed to Panama and crossed the Isthmus.

"In coming to California," Decker wrote in the preface to his Diary, "I left Columbus, Ohio by stage to Springfield thence by rail to Cincinnati. There I took a S[team]-boat and enroute touched at various places on both sides of the Rivers Ohio, Mississippi and Missouri, so that our landings were in Kentucky, Indiana, Illinois, & Missouri." Once arrived at St. Joseph, Peter wrote a letter to his sisters Catherine and Sarah under date of April 27, 1849:

Dear Sisters—

As time and opportunity are not favorable for writing I will say but a few words here and refer to my lengthy letter to Charles for particulars concerning my journey and situation thus far. A kind of providence has favored me with the best of health and enjoyment far better than I anticipated ... I am now fourteen hundred miles from home ... and have but started on my journey toward the setting sun—the far west— ... I know of nothing to send you excepting a few wild flowers that grow around our camp ... the flowers I send grew on Indian territory and gave the appearance of a cultivated garden to the woods. We are encamped four miles from the town of St. Joseph .... The town has about 2000 inhabitants and but one church. Some of the people seem very kind but many are of the 'baser sort'. I think ladies are scarce here. I have seen but two or three in town, and they had no charms for me ... We are encamped on the west side of the Missouri River on a fine bottom ... enclosed by beautiful bluffs or hills ... From the top of these hills are stretched out the rolling gently undulating prairies stretched out as far as the eye can reach ... Near us is encamped the Delaware Company among which are two young men who are Methodists (Mr Allen and Mr Bodly) ... There are a great variety of birds among the trees by

our camp . . . I have wished you were here to listen to their gleeful
songs at break of day and at twilight. Sarah and Catherine, there
is pleasure even here in the wilderness which cities afford not . . .
I have not felt like returning as yet although I would gladly associate with kind friends from whose Society I am separated . . .

> Affectionately yours,
> PETER DECKER

The Delaware Company which Decker mentions took
its name from the town of Delaware, in Ohio, and among
its members were the brothers Joshua D. Breyfogle and
Charles C. Breyfogle. Their cousin, Charles Breyfogle,
was a member of the Columbus California Industrial
Association, and the two companies traveled in close
proximity all the way to California. Joshua kept a diary
on his westward travels and references to it have been
made in the notes to Decker's Diary.

From St. Joseph, Decker's company crossed the Missouri River and "were in the Indian country extending
to the Pacific Ocean. Going west we crossed the Little
and Big Blue Rivers—or creeks, and passed through the
N.E. corner of what is now Kansas, into Nebraska to
Fort Kearny on the Platt River. Following the South
Platt to about where Julesburg now is, crossing a small
point (probably) of the N.E. corner of Colorado, thence
into Nebraska again toward the North Platt & to Fort
Laramie in what is now Wyoming."

From Fort Kearny on May 14, Decker wrote a letter
to his father in Columbus, describing his experiences on
the overland trail. Decker's father apparently sent Peter's
letter to the editor of the *Ohio State Journal;* unfortunately, the editor summarized the letter rather than
printing it verbatim. The summary appeared in the
Journal on July 14, 1849:

FROM THE PLAINS.

We have seen a letter from P. Decker, a member of one of the
Columbus companies of California emigrants, to his father, in this
city, dated May 14th, at Fort Kearny, in the Pawnee country. The
letter gives an interesting description of the incidents of travel
across the plains, by this hardy company of adventurers. They

are in advance of the great body of emigrants which is now on its
way to the land of golden promise. The letter describes the mode
of travel—the splendid sights which the wide green rolling prairies
constantly exhibit, the herds of deer and antelopes with which the
expanse is enlivened, the passage of fire sweeping over the vast
plains, the solitary grave by the road side, the primitive cooking
of the camp, the first encounter with Indians, the manner in which
the rivers are passed—by lowering the wagons with ropes, the
fishing, hunting and hardships of the emigrant's life, its rough
cheer and its independent spirit. He recommends the St. Joseph
route as preferable to any other, states that the travellers by the
Independence track were forced to throw away much of their
equipage in order to lighten their loads, and speaks of the primitive manner in which the emigrants in advance send messages to
those in the rear, by writing upon trees, bones, the horns of gigantic
elk which lie scattered along the road, or upon cards placed in
conspicuous positions. The company is in excellent health and
spirits—have had good luck, comparatively few hardships, and
have every prospect of a speedy and prosperous journey.

The trail took them over South Pass to Fort Hall
on the Snake River, a branch of the Lewis Fork of the
great Columbia, then on to the Great Falls, then into
Utah, Nevada, and to the Humboldt River, following
it down to the Humboldt Sink. To reach the Carson
River the company crossed the Forty Mile Desert—one
of the most difficult crossings on the overland route—
then through Carson Pass over the Sierra and into California. The company arrived at Sutter's Fort on August
9, 1849.

If one were to read all the diaries kept by those who
negotiated the hazardous trails to California there would
be found a certain similarity. By common accord, and
certainly by no predestined plan, these travellers were
primarily concerned with rain, wind, heat, cold, sickness,
and all the other physical aspects of their trek across the
plains. Time was another important factor. The hour
of breaking camp, the "nooning" and the setting up of
a new camp for the night — these hours were usually
meticulously recorded as well as daily temperatures. To
us, in this age of swift transportation these items have
little meaning, but they were of infinite importance at

the time, and most useful as guides to others contemplating a similar trip across the plains.

The Company traveled from Sutter's Fort to Coloma and disbanded there on August 17. It was at Coloma that Decker first saw miners at work and he remarked on the hard labor required to sink a hole. Of the gold discovery site itself—the famous sawmill was working while Decker was there—Decker wrote: "It is here that the curious gaze upon the place marked by a lofty pine where Marshall first discovered the glittering and seducing gold which has, by its magic words caused towns and cities to spring up in a day and peopled the secret recesses of the mountain wilds of California. It was at Coloma that man first realized the ideal."

With the Company disbanded, each man went his separate way—or formed partnerships—and turned his attention to locating a claim. Decker was given the Company flag and closed the books of the Association. Part of the Company left for the Mokelumne Diggings, others left for the middle fork of the American River. Decker wrote: "Thus our company scatter over this land to seek each his fortune & some of us may meet not again." Decker and T. J. Price returned to Sacramento.

It was during that time Decker was in Sacramento— the last days of August, 1849—that reports of an extremely rich gold strike in the Trinity River began to circulate. As the following letter suggests, these reports were patently exaggerated. They were to prove the death of many a forty-niner and extreme hardship to many another—Decker and his companions included—by luring them to a remote wilderness at an unfavorable time of the year, that time referred to generally by the miners as the "sickly season." Hearing the rumors, Decker, Price, and a few other Ohio companions joined with a group of Yorkers in Sacramento to make for the Trinity River mines. This was to be the first exploration of that wild region by miners, and Decker was in the vanguard of those to arrive there. Conditions in that area were ex-

tremely difficult. The hardships and sickness Decker
and his companions endured there were far worse than
anything experienced on the overland trail. It is this
part of Decker's Diary that graphically describes the
ordeal of the miner. The following letter by Andrew
Bradbury, who was himself in the Trinity River area
at approximately the same time as Decker's party, was
printed in the New York *Tribune,* March 22, 1850. It
is printed here because it provides an excellent back-
ground and description of the Trinity River "humbug."

CORRESPONDENCE OF THE TRIBUNE.

SAN FRANCISCO, Jan. 11, 1850

MR. EDITOR: In the letter of your correspondent, BAYARD
TAYLOR, of Oct. 1st, I find the following passage:

"I lately saw a letter from a merchant in San Francisco in
which he says:—There is good news from Trinity River; gold is
very plenty and provisions scarce. *We shall make a great raise on
the loads I have sent there.*"

The italicising is mine and that passage lets out the secret of a
humbug the most rascally, and at the same time the most successful of any that ever fell under my notice. The merchants of Sacramento, together with an interested party at Losson's Ranche—
are the guilty ones in this imposition.

The facts are these: Gold having been discovered on the Trinity
River, some Oregonians coming through with a lot of Indians,
crossed over to that river in June and July, and with the profits
of their Indian labor accumulated a good deal of gold. What one
white man had obtained with the labor of a dozen Indians, was
reported as the product of one man's labor. The Sacramento
merchants took up the story in good earnest, and in a few weeks
common report had it that the richest gold deposits yet discovered
were on Trinity River, where any man could dig $100 per day,
and from that to $2,000. To every man who could be gulled by this
story, some merchant would sell two mules, provisions for three
months, mining tools, &c., &c. Thousands of emigrants were coming in at Losson's, and here the same game was played upon them
with even better success.

I was on my way to Oregon when I first heard these exaggerated
reports. I turned aside, crossed the coast range, and landed on
Trinity in the first part of September. There were then not over
fifty white men on the river, and of these less than a dozen were
at work. The remainder were either sick or looking in vain for

a place where they could make an ounce a day. Our party of six were all taken sick and remained so for three weeks. We sold our provisions to the Oregonians, the only men who were making anything. The "victims" began to pour in rapidly, and when we left there were several hundred on the river. Three-fourths of them were sick, and the other fourth prospecting and cursing Losson or the Sacramento merchants who had deceived them, or the Indians who had stolen their horses.

To get to Trinity River from Sacramento City, it is necessary to travel up the Valley of the Sacramento about 200 miles, then cross the coast range some 40 or 50 miles. The trail across the mountain is the worst ever traveled by any horse, mule, donkey or camel. At least one pack mule in ten is lost in crossing, by tumbling down some precipice. Out of six our party lost two.

Eight miles from the Sacramento River are Redding's Diggings (dry). Here a few men did well last Spring. Fifty men might each probably average an ounce a day during the rainy season. That is the whole extent of these mines, and yet by the success of this humbug, this mine with Trinity River have come to be designated as the "Upper Mines," and all the old diggings as the "Lower Mines." The proportion of the former to the latter is about as one to a thousand; and yet 10,000 men have gone up to Winter in the "Upper Mines," and with the anticipation, too, of making their fortunes before Spring. We met, in coming down, 355 teams between Redding and the mouth of the Juba, with from three to eight men attached to each. Many were induced to turn back by the representations of those they met, and many others were only going up to Redding's to sell their provisions.

That this a good country for a robust enterprising man, who has nothing to bind him to home, I will not deny. But by these exaggerated reports of new and rich discoveries, thousands are induced to come here who should have staid at home, and who are destined to a most woful disappointment. The "gold fever" runs sufficiently high of itself, and I can but consider those letter-writers as exceedingly culpable, who are constantly inflaming it by presenting the bright, and often a false, side of the picture....

Yours truly,
ANDREW BRADBURY.

From some fragmentary notes Decker wrote it appears that when he returned to Sacramento he was in poor health and financially depleted. He had met in Sacramento two men, Williamson and John J. Rogers, father and son. Together they traveled up the Sacramento

River to the recently established town of Fremont, located on the west bank of the Sacramento opposite the mouth of the Feather River, where Decker hoped he might regain his health. "Circumstances of being an invalid threw me on the hospitable Fremont," Decker later wrote. "On this spot I set my foot an invalid with scarcely a dollar or a friend as a resource. The log hut in which in company with 6 or 8 ladies (bless them) I spent my first Christmas in California, is not now standing. It sheltered me in weakness from the storms without, while it almost made me forget the adversity within. Here I rec'd the first glad tidings, welcome news from home." During this period from October, 1849 to March, 1850, Decker did not keep a diary.

In the spring of 1850 reports of rich strikes on the bars of the South Yuba dominated the news from the Northern Mines. Decker undoubtedly heard these reports, and on March 19, his health improved, he set out with the two Rogers for the South Yuba River. They traveled via present-day Nevada City, and descended to the south fork of the Yuba a few miles below what is today the town of Washington. They set up camp on Irishman's Bar, a location not to be found on any map, and one of the many short-lived camps destined for oblivion. Decker's experiences in this locality are covered in his diaries from March, 1850 to May, 1851.

About the time Decker and his companions arrived at the South Yuba, the number of miners at work on the bars numbered approximately 750. They had gathered in from numerous places waiting for the water to fall, to turn the river, and prospect their claims. Dams and canals were constructed at great expense in those days. The success of working in the banks—such as the modest success Decker had, for a time, working both the banks and bars—gave encouragement to the undertaking. But when the river was turned the unsatisfactory results at once depopulated the area. Goods of all kinds immediately fell in price and almost any article could be had

at the scene of recent activity for half what it would sell
for in nearby Nevada City. The price of active claims
also collapsed. The large anticipations that had been
formed of fortunes covered by the river vanished and
with them the crowd of miners that had made the woods
and canyons echo with life. This general disappointment
notwithstanding, Decker himself met with modest success.
During June and part of July, he averaged about $40.00
a day, and on some days he took out as much as $80.00.

One experience common to all gold seekers was the
feeling of being removed by vast distances from their
homes and families. There in the remote canyons and
hills, this often took the form of loneliness, and the only
link with those back in the East was an infrequent letter
from home. Failing that, the miner would himself write
letters to those back home, often complaining that too
few letters came to him. To Decker and his companions
on the South Yuba, this situation was made even more
difficult, as only one Express Company delivered letters
to the area, and those deliveries were infrequent. Otherwise it was necessary to pick up letters at Nevada City,
some twenty miles distant. To send a letter, miners often
entrusted their mail to miners who were about to depart
California for the East. Decker's letter to his sister Sarah,
bearing the date of August 18, 1850, South Yuba River,
California, expresses his melancholy over not receiving
letters from home:

Dear Sister:

I have the pleasure of setting down in good health and comparative contentment to say a few words to you by letter, which
is a great satisfaction to me ... The fact that we are separated
by a great portion of the American Continent seldom occurs to me
in my frequent thoughts of you and the rest of our folks. When
I think of the near four thousand miles that separate us and the
weakly condition you may be in ... I feel an interest in your
welfare and happiness that at times gives me real anxiety.

I have looked for a letter from you this long time but have
received none, and you can imagine that I have but little news
from you or any of my acquaintances as I have received but two

letters from the States, one from brother Charles and one from brother Augustus. But I have not neglected to write to you all and I hope you have received all my letters from which you will have learned my history in California pretty well . . . I had the good luck to get a Columbus paper a few days ago in which I see the marriage of Miss Cloud published . . . I suppose of course that nearly all of the young ladies of my acquaintance are no more enjoying a life of 'single blessedness' . . . There are some of us old bachelors that expect some day to return home and hope to find a few of the same sort left for us . . . I expect to send this to the States by a friend Mr. Lippard.

Enclosed you will find a small specimen of gold which I dug myself. These pieces are worn here in their natural shape on Breast Pins and made into finger rings . . . I have specimens too large to send in a letter.

While he was frequently beset by temporary ailments caused by working long hours in the cold mountain streams, Decker found the life of a miner tolerable. He was sometimes discouraged by lack of success in his mining ventures, and like many of his companions, he pursued trails that led to rumored rich "strikes," only to return to Irishman's Bar, richer in experience if not in gold. His companion, John J. Rogers, who mined with Decker on the South Yuba, wrote in the *Miner's Transcript* of Nevada City, in 1888, of one incident which was indicative of miner's luck:

Decker and I were among the first men to go to Poor Man's Creek as far as the forks and a little above. At least there was not a man working on it as far as we went or was a prospect hole to be seen . . . While we were eating lunch on a large projection into the creek I saw a piece of gold and afterwards creviced up several dollars. Decker came back to the place with a rocker and worked two days . . . He made $10 a day. We were doing much better than that on Irishman's Bar and we never went back to the creek again. [This afterwards was known as one of the richest gold producing streams tributary to the South Yuba.] . . . We went down to Nevada City. In the fall we hired a man to help sink a few shafts in the Kiota diggings . . . Those were the richest diggings I ever saw in California. A man named Truesdell . . . an old acquaintance took me down in his mine which was twelve to fifteen feet deep and for about eight inches of the bottom dirt on the bedrock I could see as much gold as dirt. He washed a pan of it in my presence. I was perfectly astonished. He told me afterwards it contained $900 and I had no reason to doubt it.

It was September 2, 1850 when Decker and Rogers packed their gear and trudged three miles to the summit of Washington Ridge from which they proceeded to Nevada City, where they arrived at two o'clock in the afternoon. Decker took lodgings at Augustine's Boarding House, one of several such establishments in town. The two men then bought two mules and a wagon and hauled dirt for the miners in the Coyote Diggings. They had no luck in the claims they filed for themselves, for the best sites had already been taken up before they arrived. Hauling paid expenses and nothing more, so Rogers and Decker dissolved their partnership and Decker decided to go into business, feeling that selling merchandise to miners was more lucrative than being on the other side of the counter.

Nevada City had its beginnings in the late summer of 1849 when the first settlers in the area—Captain John Pennington, Thomas Cross, and William McCaig—prospected in Gold Run and built a cabin there. A month later, Dr. A. B. Caldwell, who had previously kept a store in Beckville, four miles down the creek, erected a cabin on Nevada street, back of Main street, on the slope of Aristocracy Hill, and opened a store, from which he supplied goods to the miners who had begun to settle in the vicinity. The locality became known as Caldwell's Upper Store. During the same month a Mr. Stamps, with a family consisting of his wife, her sister, and several children, came to the locality and built a cabin on the forks of the ravine back of Coyote street. This was the first family to settle in the area.

About the time Caldwell's store opened, John Truesdale built a cabin on Broad street, and later on a few other cabins were built, and early in the winter canvas tents and brush shanties were erected in great numbers by the miners who were attracted by the reports of fabulous richness in the diggings along Deer Creek and Gold

Run. The place became known—beside the name previously given—as Deer Creek Dry Diggings. The number of miners who wintered there—driven from the rivers by high water—is not certain, but it was probably in the neighborhood of one thousand.

By March, 1850, the collection of tents, brush shanties and a very few board houses began to assume the appearance of a town. The people recognized that a government was necessary, and as the new courts had not yet commenced to function in that area, the election of an Alcalde, a judicial officer under Mexican law, was determined upon. At this election some 250 votes were cast and Mr. Stamps was elected Alcalde. A better and more stable name was wanted for the growing town, and a meeting of the leading citizens was called at the store of Truex & Blackman, for the purpose of selecting one that would suit all parties and be a credit to the place. Among the names suggested were: Sierra, Aurora, Nevada, Deer Creek and Gold Run. The name selected was suggested by O. P. Blackman, and the little town was christened Nevada.

By the summer of 1850, a number of streets had been mapped out, and business buildings sprang up along Main and Commercial streets. Among the commercial enterprises, there were two hotels, several stores, a reading room, express office, and blacksmith shop. In August, 1850, the *Placer Times* of Sacramento reported numerous jobs were available: . . . "drug stores, hotels, livery stables and all other concommitant pursuits of a veritable city, are represented upon 'posters' of every size and style. Those are sure signs of business and of the good sense of those who are engaged in its various branches. The population of Nevada City is estimated at about 2,000, but there are supposed to be four times that number within a circuit of four miles."

As winter approached, the merchants began to lay in enormous stocks of goods. The previous winter had been so severe that transportation had been impossible, and goods had been extremely high priced. The population to be supplied being now eight or ten times as great as the previous winter and the season being represented to be as severe, the merchants made their calculations accordingly. The reverse of their anticipations was the result. Little rain fell that winter, no water could be had to work the diggings, hundreds of miners abandoned the place in disgust, and prices of goods sank, merchants failed and closed their doors, and Nevada City seemed to be in the last stages of the mining camp of mushroom growth.

But the mournful predictions of the croakers, and the obituaries in the newspapers—such as appeared in the San Francisco *Alta California* for December 22, 1850—failed to end the career of Nevada City. The year 1851 opened with no less than 250 buildings in the town, and scores of tents and cabins spread all over the surrounding hills for a radius of two miles. Mining operations became active again and business revived.

Decker had built a store on Broad street in association with George C. Addison, an owner of John Fall & Company, wholesale merchants of Marysville. In spite of the throngs of miners in the town he discovered he had commenced business at the end of a boom, and not at the beginning. Had Decker the patience to stick it out during the lean winter months, he would have later profited, for with the discovery that same year of fresh gold deposits on Deer Creek the town again came to life. Decker realized this himself, for in his diary entry of May 1, 1851, he wrote: "Nevada City is pretty lively—I went there at the wrong time and left the wrong time." He auctioned off his stock of goods and left April 1, 1851, bound for Marysville, which was rapidly growing into the largest city in the Upper Sacramento Valley, and the central supply point for the Northern Mines.

II

In the spring of 1851, John Fall & Co. of Marysville bought out the store of Addison and Stambaugh at Park's Bar on the Yuba River, and Fall sent Decker to take inventory of the stock. Park's Bar was a busy mining community some fifteen miles above Marysville on the Yuba and the road to Timbuctoo. In 1852, it became one of Marysville's liveliest competitors. At Mr. Fall's suggestion, Decker took over the store and remained at Park's Bar until December, 1852, when, having a great urge to see his family in Ohio, he sold out the store and prepared to return east. "Having sold out my store of goods in December," Decker wrote in his Journal under date of January 27, 1853, "with a view of closing up business for the purpose of leaving for the Atlantic States, I have been busily engaged by day & by night in accomplishing my purpose, and accordingly today at two o'clock bid farewell to many excellent friends on Park's Bar."

Preparatory to his departure, Decker took up lodgings at the Fremont House in Marysville, where he waded in the muddy streets settling up business matters. He gave a farewell supper to his friends, among whom were Dr. Colton, Mr. Price, and his old friend from the days of '49, Vantine, of the A. A. Vantine Company of Marysville, and George Woodward. He then "loaned out, exchanged and packed" the funds he had earned, and took the river steamer *Bragdon* for Sacramento, stopping there overnight and continuing on the next day to San Francisco. On February 1, 1853, he sailed through the Golden Gate on the *Pacific,* a ship of the Vanderbilt Line, bound for Nicaragua with some 450 steerage and second class passengers. Those going first class numbered about 150.

Three steamers left San Francisco on the morning of February 1, 1853, the *Cortez, Pacific,* and *Tennessee.* The *Tennessee,* on March 6, 1853, was to run aground a few miles north of the Golden Gate in a thick fog. Due to the calmness of the sea no lives were lost, but a sudden storm broke the ship in two before it could be towed to deep water.

On board the *Pacific* that February morning in 1853, Decker was watching the coastline disappear as they put out to sea. Among the first-class passengers were Michael Nye and his wife, the former Harriet Pike, a widow who had come to California with the Donner Party. Nye had been one of the owners of the Cordua Ranch and his many business interests caused him to make frequent trips to the east. William Foster, another friend of Decker's, had settled on the Yuba in 1842, and in 1848 had moved his business to San Francisco. He and his wife were making the trip in order to settle permanently in the east. Also on board the *Pacific* were a group of orphaned children being returned to the States. Their parents had met death in one way or another in California. Decker mentions that the first-class passengers took turns seeing that the children came to no harm.

The *Pacific* arrived in Acapulco on February 8, and the passengers were taken ashore "on the backs of native, all for 50 cts apiece." Dinner was eaten in a Chinese restaurant, the menu offering "Chicken, eggs, spare ribs, yams, oysters, tomatoes, etc." One of Decker's concerns on this trip was that he was carrying with him one hundred pounds of gold dust, which had to be packed across the Isthmus of Nicaragua. Arriving at San Juan del Sur the passengers exchanged their transit tickets for orders for mules, "each taking his turn like they do in the post office in California." Passengers and baggage traveled over the Isthmus on muleback, Decker's gold packed along with his other possessions. There were no mishaps.

Decker sailed into Havana on Thursday, February 24, and proceeded to the eastern seaboard of the Atlantic States. The remainder of the trip was uneventful. Decker arrived in Columbus early in March. He did not record his stay there but one must assume there was much conversation over his California adventures with his family during his three months visit. On May 26, 1853, he left to return to California, when he resumed his Diary with

these words: "It is hard to part from those we hold dear."
He traveled eastward via Buffalo and Niagara Falls. In
New York he put up at the Astor House where, he commented, "the elite of the city and foreigners domicile."
He left New York on June 4, retracing the route he had
taken east. It took twenty-eight days from New York
to San Francisco. At San Juan del Sur, on the Pacific
side, he boarded the *Brother Jonathan* for the last leg of
his journey. At Virgin Bay he was robbed of a bag containing his valuables. Such happenings were not uncommon, and he was fortunate he had not lost his hundred
pounds of gold dust on his way east.

The *Brother Jonathan* was commanded by Captain
Baldwin, who Decker found a "scientific gentlemanly
officer, but does not keep the ship cleanly in any respect."
The trip was swift and uneventful and on July 1, 1853,
Decker came down the gangplank at San Francisco five
months to the day since he had set sail for the east on
the *Pacific.* He took a room at the *Niantic* Hotel on the
northwest corner of Clay and Sansome streets, and was
soon reunited with his old friend and trail companion of
1849, John Walton. On Sunday, July 3, Decker attended the Baptist church with Dr. Skinner, and John Marsh
and his wife, who were visiting the city from their home
on the Rancho Los Meganos in the San Joaquin Valley.
Marsh, the Harvard graduate and California pioneer of
1836, was the lord of countless acres, cattle and sheep,
and was married to a New England school teacher who
had come to California for her health. The 4th of July,
always a day of great celebration in early San Francisco,
began with a parade of the military, including the Sutter
Rifles from Sacramento. The parade was reviewed by
General Sutter himself, and Decker thought he made a
striking appearance in his uniform.

Three days later Decker took passage on the river
steamer *New World* for Sacramento in company with
the delegates to the Whig Convention. After his trip to
the east, Decker seems to have welcomed every aspect

and vista of his adopted State, and even the dry "oat hills and scenery around the Bay looks quite natural and inviting." He described Sacramento as a bit dull, but remarked on its growth and the fact that it bore little resemblance to the town of 1849—"when I was lodged under a tree where now are good buildings." Lola Montez was playing in Sacramento and Decker remarked that she was "serenaded at the Orleans last night with Gongs, Bells, Tin Pans a/c on acct. of dissatisfaction at the concert."

Once back in Marysville he was warmly received by his friends and business associates. Decker soon turned his attention to commercial interests and began casting about for suitable prospects. An opportunity soon presented itself when in partnership with his old friend Levi Hite they bought out the grocery of Packard and Woodruff. In the Marysville *Daily Evening Herald* of August 15, 1853, there appeared the first advertisement for the firm of P. Decker and L. Hite, successors to Packard and Woodruff, located on First street, below the Plaza. Here they invited their friends and the general public to inspect their "heavy and well assorted stock of foods." The training Decker had received in his brothers' firm in Columbus, Ohio, now stood him in good stead, and the firm of Decker and Hite prospered even though the competition was keen. By the end of 1853 there were at least thirty general stores in Marysville, and the number increased as the traffic to the mines of the Yuba and Feather Rivers became heavier. In May of 1854 the name of Charles Lambert was added to the firm and it became Decker and Company with sales totaling over half a million dollars per year. By 1858, Marysville was said to rank third in California in population and wealth. Success stories were many during the generally booming economy of the 1850's. However, there were equally times of recession and some panic, and stories of fortunes lost. It took a man of business acumen to retain his early fortune when the economy of the State began shifting em-

phasis from mining to agriculture. Decker managed his
interests with considerable success. He sensed when it
was time to turn from one type of enterprise to another.

One of Decker's activities during his early business
career in Marysville was to aid in protecting the river
trade that had rapidly increased when such transportation
became the life line to the mines. He was one of the
founders and directors of the Citizens' Steam Navigation Company that ran steamers between Marysville and
Sacramento. This company was purchased by the California Steam Navigation Company in 1855.

As early as the year 1850 river traffic on the Sacramento and Feather Rivers had been steadily increasing
and keen competition had brought great pressure to bear
upon the operators of river boats. By 1854, matters had
developed to a point where the only outcome would be
financial disaster unless some measures were taken to
combine competition under joint management. A group
of owners and captains formed the California Steam Navigation Company with Richard Chenery as president, and
F. F. Lowe as the agent in Marysville. Lowe was later
to become the ninth Governor of California.

Decker's business and personal integrity were held in
esteem by the community, and in 1856 he was offered the
nomination for Mayor of Marysville. This he declined.
His friend and business partner, Levi Hite, was elected
in his place. Probably one reason for Decker's refusal
to run was that he was considering another trip east to
Ohio. At about that same time he liquidated his interests
in the firm of Decker, Hite, and Lambert. It must have
been evident to Decker that the profitable years of merchandising were drawing to a close—especially merchandising that catered to a mining economy. Meanwhile, he
remained active in civic affairs. He took a particular
interest in forming the Marysville Library Association,
and later, in 1858, he was instrumental in transforming
that Association into the Marysville Free Public Library.

On July 5, 1856, Decker left Marysville for his second

trip east to Ohio and returned via Panama in March, 1857. Upon his return to Marysville, Decker formed a partnership with John H. Jewett. This was to prove a profitable association, for Jewett was an astute business man and Decker had great respect for his judgment. Jewett had come to California in 1849 with the Knickerbocker Company on the steamer *Panama*. It was his intention to go into business with goods he had brought with him from New York. From Sacramento he went to Yuba City, driving a pack-train loaded with his goods. Finding Yuba City not to his liking, Jewett swam his mules across the Feather River and settled in Marysville, February 10, 1850, where he went into the grocery and freighting business.

In 1857, Decker and Jewett were to travel extensively in Oregon—and later that year Decker in Southern California—to make a survey of business opportunities. It is more than likely that on these trips Decker made investments which subsequently strengthened his financial position. Decker recorded his impressions of Oregon and Southern California and these will be touched upon later.

Decker did not keep a record of his activities for the remaining months of 1857, but it would appear he spent the time profitably by consolidating his position financially, politically, and even romantically. Sometime toward the end of the year Decker and Jewett bought an interest in the banking house of Brummagin and Company, the new firm going under the name of Decker and Jewett.

In the spring of 1858, Decker was elected Mayor of Marysville. On August 4, 1858, he married Jennie Merritt Scott, in Benicia. The ceremony took place in the home of the Honorable John Curry, a prominent California lawyer, and later, in 1866, Chief Justice of the California Supreme Court. Judge Curry's wife, Cornelia, was the daughter of Ebenezer Scott of New York State, and while it seems impossible to establish the exact relationship, Mrs. Curry was evidently Jennie's sister. The

Rev. Sylvester Woodbridge, founder of the Presbyterian Church in Benicia, performed the ceremony.

Decker and his wife became prominent in the social life of Marysville. Four children were born to the couple, but only one, a daughter Alice, lived to maturity. She married Elliot McAllister, who became in later years an officer of the Decker and Jewett Bank.

Apart from his two trips to Ohio in 1853 and 1856, Decker traveled extensively in California, and in 1857 through Oregon Territory. His impressions during these trips are recorded in his miscellaneous Journals and Notes. Trips to several mining camps in the 1850's were usually prompted by business matters, but his descriptions of the camps, the people, and the events are written in his usual observant style and provide interesting insights in terms of regional history. His trip to Oregon and Northern California in 1857 is of special interest. It was recorded in a small notebook and its closely written pages contain an amazing amount of information on that territory.

The first entry is dated in Portland, May 29, 1857, where Decker and Jewett spent the day at the Metropolis Hotel. There they met the Territorial Governor, George L. Curry, who had traveled overland to Oregon in 1846, and whom Decker described as "a sensible, practical man who puts on no airs." In his talks with business men in Portland, Decker found them anxious for Statehood, but considered it might prove to their advantage to remain a Territory a few years longer on the speculation that more government appropriations would be forthcoming under a Territorial status rather than under Statehood. He also found considerable sentiment in support of slavery, but felt in the final analysis Oregon would not make a decision in favor of the South.

The trip to Oregon had been made by steamer, but Decker and Jewett returned to California overland, visiting enroute the towns of Salem, Roseburg, and Jacksonville. There is not sufficient space in this Introduction to dwell on his descriptions of the towns, the people, the

potentials and opportunities represented by each; all are
of considerable interest to the economic and regional history of the Oregon area, but should be construed as a
subject outside the scope of this work.

Sixteen miles out from Portland, they crossed the Willamette River by the Boone Ferry and three miles beyond
it came to a store or hotel kept by some Germans. The
old gentleman proprietor gave Decker a very unfavorable
account of Oregon—"of six months rain, impassable roads,
and attributes all the success of Oregon to California, the
'Mother of the Pacific'." In Salem on June 4, they
searched for the capitol building and found it a rather
unpretentious frame house in the bushes off the levee.
In the Willamette Valley the people struck Decker as
comfortably well off—"indeed a large portion quite so"
—for many had made money in the California mines in
1849-1850.

In their journey southward they saw many places
where men had been killed in the Indian uprisings in the
early 1850's: "On Woolf Creek saw the place where a
man was killed by Indians and his cattle and team shot,
their bones lying by the wayside. Nearly all the homes
and improvements along this road were not long since
(during the war) destroyed, burnt up, and the stockades
through here show how the races have been contending
for mastery amongst these mountain wilds. Again we
hear of great numbers—members of many families having been killed and wounded—and but little better are
many of the whites. Horse stealing, murder & robbing
are indeed too common. This seems almost out of reach
of news or civilization — have to go hundreds of miles
either north or south through the mountains to get to any
place."

In Jacksonville, situated in the southwest corner of
the Rogue River Valley, Decker met a man he had known
in Fremont in 1849. From this man Decker was told
that John J. Rogers, his companion on the South Yuba
and in Nevada City, had been killed by Indians. In hear-

ing this news, Decker was moved to write: "Thus have passed away and are scattered over the world my companions of '49." Decker might have saved his regrets, for Rogers had not been killed, but lived beyond Decker's span of life and in later years recalled their mining days together on the South Yuba in an article for the Nevada City *Miner's Transcript,* after Decker's death, in 1888.

Decker and Jewett crossed the Siskiyou Mountains on the stage from Anderson. He described the journey as "rather pleasant ... at or near Coles, just this side of the mountains is the line between Oregon & Cal — which we crossed at 42 degrees and are again in the state of our adoption. Yreka broke upon us all at once ... indeed it looks quite a pretty city and has some life. Was sorry to see so prominent and near the road just before we enter town the gallows a permanent sort of fixture apparently but quite too public." To his delight, Decker had gained five pounds during his trip to Oregon, but Jewett had gained nothing upon which Decker commented: "Fleas and bugs have bled him more freely ... and he has missed his tea oftener, and I drink water— that's the difference."

They left Yreka on June 15 and traveled to the head of Scott's Valley. On this route they passed through Fort Jones, at that time composed of several log houses, residences of officers, and garrisoned by some 80 men. The Fort had been established in 1852 by the First U. S. Dragoons, under command of Major Edward H. Fitzgerald. It had been occupied in 1853 by Captain Bradley Ripley Allen commanding Company E, 4th U. S. Infantry. This company had marched all the way from Fort Vancouver on the Columbia River, nearly four hundred miles distant. On the Scott River, Decker observed some mining activity and remarked that the dust would bring 16.25 to 16.50 but did not assay well. Forty miles from Yreka they reached Callahan's, near the junction of the east and south forks of the Scott River, and the last stopping place on the stage line southward. From there the trip was made on mules over Scott Mountain to French Gulch and Trinity Center.

Arriving at Trinity Center, Decker described it as "a little wooden mining town of half a dozen houses . . . Yes, in '49 I was on this river under different circumstances . . . never shall I forget my sad stay on this river in those days of trial." He was, of course, alluding to his trip and subsequent hardships in the Trinity mines in the fall of 1849, all of which is fully covered in his Diary. Decker and Jewett traveled next to Shasta and followed the Sacramento River down to Bidwell's Rancho. Decker was impressed with the Rancho and they spent some time there—"Has some 9 leagues of good land with the best improvements I have seen in all Cal. A fine mill—a gardner's house, a douby Indian quarters, a stock house of two stories and an excellent barn with fine corrells, yards, gardens & walks all beautifully shaded with cottonwood and locust trees—the garden of some 10 acres has every variety of vegetables growing luxuriantly—Peach trees, the largest and most thrifty I have ever seen—only 4 years old and loaded down with fruit . . . Major Bidwell seems to be the ruling spirit. Has two brothers, keeps 40 or 50 Indians at work whom he treats well." Their trip ended in Marysville in late June of 1857.

That fall, in October, Decker was again off on another trip, this time in company with John Brummagin, whose Marysville banking house Decker and Jewett were to acquire interests in that winter. Decker and Brummagin left San Francisco on October 3 aboard the steamer *Senator* bound for Los Angeles. This was Decker's first trip to Southern California, at that time still a pastoral and essentially agrarian part of California. The *Senator* arrived in the roadstead of Santa Barbara the following day, and Decker visited the adobe Mission, found it in a fine state of preservation, and took a side trip into the Santa Ynez Valley where he was curiously struck with an enormous grapevine that encompassed an arbor 50 x 60 feet and was said to produce one ton of grapes a year.

Passengers were taken ashore at San Pedro in small boats. Transportation to Los Angeles was via stagecoach drawn by four California horses. Decker was immediately struck with the "tardy movement of everything here ...so unlike our portion of California." Decker described Los Angeles as "decidedly Spanish"—the most prosperous town in all of Southern California, and its trade in cattle with the northern mines had earned it the name of "Queen of the Cow Counties." He found an atmosphere of leisure in the wide streets, and the long rows of one story adobe buildings with flat roofs, the warm sunshine and the somnambulistic pace of activity. "Half of the population here," Decker wrote, "are mostly Spanish. This was a considerable town when Gen. Stockton landed at San Pedro with his men to fight the Mexicans and deceived them as to his forces." Decker was referring to the story that Stockton had horses driven back and forth over the dusty hills of the Rancho San Pedro in order to raise such a cloud of dust that would suggest to the Mexicans a far larger force converging upon Los Angeles than was, in truth, the case.

One of the highlights of Decker's visit to Los Angeles was his visit to the vineyard and orchard of Louis Sainsevain, which he described as "the largest vineyard in California, 50 acres of vineyard makes 80,000 gallons of wine, 2000 a day." Sainsevain was from Bordeaux, France, as was his uncle and partner in the winery, Jean Louis Vignes, and together they made wines under the label of Sainsevain and Company. At the time of Decker's visit in 1857, the winery was turning out the first California champagne, and shipping it to San Francisco.

Decker was also a guest at Lake Vineyard, the home of Don Benito Wilson, situated two miles from the Mission San Gabriel. Don Benito Wilson had come to California in 1841 with the Workman-Rowland Party from New Mexico. He was the first Mayor of Los Angeles, and a leading citizen of Southern California. General George Patton, of World War II fame, was a direct descendant of Wilson. The orchard at the ranch was probably one of the most prolific in Southern California. Decker noted that it contained virtually all the trees in the catalogue of fruits — oranges, lemons, limes, olives, figs, English walnuts, pomegranites, pears, peaches, apricots, plums, and French prunes.

Decker concluded his notes on Los Angeles on October 11, and returned to Marysville, where he resumed his business activities with John Jewett. Brummagin remained with them for a time in the banking house, but retired the following year, when Decker and Jewett assumed controlling interest.

In 1865, Decker and his family moved to San Francisco, although he continued to retain his business interests in Marysville. He established a residence at 47 South Park, that elegant residential district just off Third street, between Bryant and Brannan, that had been planned by the Englishman, George Gordon, who laid out South Park after London's Berkeley Square. Here the Decker family had as their neighbors the cream of San Francisco society.

During the remaining years of his life Decker continued to achieve financial success and a respected place in the community. Later Decker and his family took a trip to Europe. His last trip was taken in 1871, when he made a short journey to Yreka to inspect certain lands in the vicinity of the eastern slopes of Mt. Shasta, in Butte Creek Valley, where it is evident he owned certain lands.

Two years before his death, Decker moved to the Palace Hotel. He was in failing health, and died there October 8, 1888. On the occasion of his death, Decker was eulogized in the California press. The following obituary appeared in the Marysville *Daily Appeal*, October 9, 1888:

A telegram received by Mr. Bingham yesterday announced the death of Peter Decker, at the Palace Hotel in San Francisco, at 9:40 A.M. The fatal termination of Mr. Decker's illness had been anticipated. His ailment was of the stomach, but the precise

nature of it the *Appeal* has not been able to learn. The remains
will be buried in San Francisco, where the funeral services will
take place tomorrow afternoon at 2 o'clock, at Grace church.

Mr. Decker, who was one of the most wealthy and prominent
citizens of Marysville, was himself the architect of his fortune.
He was born upon a farm in West Hanover, Dauphin, Pennsylvania, and came of revolutionary stock. His birthday was Nov.
9th, 1822, so that he was in his sixty-sixth year at the time of his
death. He attended school near his birthplace until he was sixteen,
when he moved with his family to Columbus, Ohio, where he had
elder brothers engaged in business. At Columbus he attended
Covert's Academy, one of his instructors being Lorenzo Sawyer,
who has since become Judge of the United States Circuit Court
in California. After leaving the Academy, Mr. Decker applied
himself to work in the general merchandise establishment of his
brothers, where the outbreak of the California excitement found
him. He helped to organize a company of thirty men to come
across the plains, and in April of 1849 the long journey began.
It was not until August of that year that they arrived at Sacramento, and a little later the company disbanded at Coloma. The
Trinity River region then became a subject of glowing tales, and
about the close of August Mr. Decker and his two associates
started for that destination. The illness of the latter, however,
broke up the plan of operations, and the party retraced their steps
through what was then a wilderness. After resting at Sacramento,
the subject of this sketch went to Fremont, at the mouth of the
Feather River, and in March of the following year, having formed
a mining partnership with Mr. Rodgers, repaired to what is now
known as Nevada City, then Caldwell's trading post. After mining
for sometime with fair success at Irishman's Bar, on the South
Yuba, Mr. Decker joined a party of prospectors for the exploration of the Gold Lake region, which proved to be disappointing.
In September of '50 the mining partnership was dissolved and
Mr. Decker went to Nevada City where he formed a partnership
with Capt. G. C. Addison, who was at that time a member of the
firm of John C. Fall & Co., Marysville. Results not proving entirely satisfactory, Mr. Decker closed up his business in Nevada
City in March, 1851, and removed to this place. In the following
April he opened a store at Park's Bar, where he did a prosperous
business. He sold out in December, 1852, and made a journey to
the East. On his return he bought out the wholesale grocery
business of Packard & Woodruff in Marysville, and took for partners Levi Hite and Charles Lambert, the firm doing business under
the name of Decker & Co. They had a thriving trade, the value
of their transactions in one year exceeding half a million dollars.

In 1857 Mr. Decker sold his interest to his associates, and on January 1, 1859, entered into banking with Jacob Brumagin, John H. Jewett and John A. Paxton as associates.

Mr. Decker never engaged actively in politics, always declining to be a candidate for any political office. In 1858, however, he consented to serve a term as Mayor, and was elected. He took an active interest in the formation of the Marysville Library Association, and during his term of office as Mayor he brought about its establishment as a free institution under the support of the city. He was always keenly alive to everything relative to the general welfare of Marysville. In politics he was a strong Republican.

In 1858 Mr. Decker was married at Benicia to Miss Jennie Merritt Scott, who survives him. They had four children, only one of whom, Miss Alice, is living.

Success in accumulation of wealth makes many men arrogant and pretentious, but it had no such effect upon Mr. Decker. He was always considerate, unassuming and modest in his manner and conversation. Holding positive opinions on many subjects, he was yet deferential to the views of others. His mental capacity was superior, and he had a faculty for clear statement that enabled him to make his ideas thoroughly understood. As a conversationalist he was interesting to an unusual degree, close observation, experience and study giving him familiarity with a wide range of topics. His habitual expression was so grave and serious that none but those who knew him realized what a fund of humor he had, or how greatly he enjoyed a joke. Scrupulously exact in all his dealings, his integrity was one of his most marked characteristics. His word was as good as his bond among all those who had business transactions with him. In disposition he was kind and obliging, and, while careful in the use of money, he was charitable, giving with discretion and without ostentation. No man commanded more respect or led a more exemplary life.

Peter Decker was a member of the Society of California Pioneers, organized in 1850, which as its name implies, selected its members and still does, from the pioneers of 1849 and their descendants. In an obituary written by the Pioneer Society at the time of his death, the following excerpt seems a fitting final tribute to the man:

> In a word, he was a good and valuable citizen, a sincere friend, a genial companion and a kind and indulgent husband and father. What we have said of him is not a eulogy but a plain and truthful statement of his character and career.

EMIGRANT TRAIN, GOLD HUNTERS 1849

Bound for the Land of Sun Down

HAVING SIX WEEKS AGO concluded to make a trip to California I have during that time been busily engaged in making necessary preparations for the journey & placing my business affairs in a condition for a contemplated absence of 18 mo, or 2 years and this (April 4, 49) is the day set apart for taking a long leave of home & friends, yes, many & *dear* friends & a home which I have enjoyed eleven years. To break off these ties of association with a Father, Brother & Sisters is too much for cool regret. I have lost control of my feelings and the heart speaks language of tenderness in tears. The journey of thousands of miles before me I have studied

and make the tour for the sake of the tour. Golden
dreams of gain induce many to go this season of which
I have availed myself to associate in a company for safety
and protection in order that I may enjoy the gratification of a trip which I long since desired to make. Our
company consists of 30 men under the title of "The
Columbus California Industrial Association." Our men
with 10 light wagons & 40 mules left on Monday for
Cin. Well the farewell word is spoken. I have left the
embrace of friends in tears. Coach is ready with heavy
feelings. I mount it for the danger & difficulties before
me are numerous which I enter upon with hopes & fears.
Had in charge Miss Mary —— of Dayton O & found
it difficult to be sociable while reviewing all the incidents
of my past life & the history of events of our family in
connection with my anticipations of the future. But her
voluability of words did something towards restoring me
from being "the knight of the woeful countenance."
Having left C. at 6½ o'clock P.M. with a crowded coach
(12 passengers) we reached Springfield at 2 o'clock ac-
quiring one passenger, now 5 bound for California from
different parts of Ohio. After a rainy day the evening
was blustering but moderate which during the night
changed into a cold wind from the N.W. the moon strug-
gling through the clouds occasionally. Left my friend
Miss M. at S. & took the cars in company with my friend
J. Walton[1] President of the Association who arrived in
S. on the mail. Also my friend J. R. Scroggs with sundry
other acquaintances. Our trip to Cin. was pleasant.

APRIL 5

A beautiful day, arrived in Cin. at 10 Oclk & found
the teams had arrived a few minutes before us & were
already on board the Steamer [J.] Hancock. Walton
and I put up at the Pearl St House kept by Mine Host
John Noble famous as a landlord. Purchased a few articles of clothing necessary for the trip. Went to the wharf
& found our wagon taken apart, boxes strewn round —
men, women & children working, looking on & enjoying

the bedlam and confusion which the wharf exhibited on acct of the display of 4 or 5 California Companies with their fixtures about being shipped, by 9 o'clock all on board — 3 companies & other passengers bound for St Louis & Independence Mo. Reached the boat at 9 o'clock & found it jammed, officers no control of passengers — each looking for his own baggage & confusion worse confounded. Came too late to get a stateroom or berth, the whole floor was covered with mattresses & one blanket to each for a bed, some 400 passengers some playing the violin, some dancing, some firing pistols, some singing others walking and some uttering their misgivings as to the comfort of the mass bed spread, 150 ft long & 15 wide. 10 o'clock found all the blankets in use — gathered up two stray sheets which McColm[2] & I agreed were table cloths a few hours before & laid me down in my scanty bed amid noise of every namable as well as unamable kind, in an hour I was in "Morpheus embrace." (I had slept nothing the night before.) A little after twelve o'clock woke up & found our craft animated by an application of steam — a few snorts & puffs and we were off on our way to El Dorado. Was anxious to see North Bend but passed it last night.

APRIL 6

Servants snatched the beds from under us to make room to set the table. Had tolerable breakfast—by dint of management found myself at first table some waited for the fourth which brot breakfast nearly to dinner. Our large steamer moves along as a thing of life "a castle on the deep." The scenery has freshness, variety & beauty I did not expect to find along the Ohio. Vegetation is fast appearing & in the vicinity of Cin. seems 10 days more advanced than at Columbus, Kentucky & Indiana both those villages and villas along the river on their respective banks quite inviting in appearance. Was informed this morning that a Steamer from the south arrived in Cin about the time we left that had several deaths on it from Cholera[3] which makes some of our pas-

sengers feel uneasy. But withal this day has been a joyous
time on our craft. I feel perfectly at home. Touched a
few hours at Louisville passed through the city, is less
of a business place than Cin. & looks smoky, but rather
a pretty scene surrounding & a fine location. Passed
through the market which was held at 4 o'clock P.M.
having a market on different days at different times of
the day. Articles for sale look cleanly saw vegetables
and bocas of flowers in abundance. Prices[4] some lower
than in Columbus. Passed through the canal 2 miles long
around the falls at Louisville, took 3 hours having broken
a wheel in passing. Called on & saw James Porter[5] the
great Kentucky Giant who is 2 ft taller than I, being
7 ft 8 in. & proportioned. I could only reach to his chin
with my hands — he is rather feeble. The afternoon was
extremely warm for temperature in my room 76 degrees.
The evening cool and pleasant beautifully clear & moon
& stars shone brilliantly. By invitation I room with Mr.
Denig & Dr. Boyle[6] two in a berth is close sleeping.
Left canal at twilight this evening.

APRIL 7TH

Arose refreshed — raining this morning, cleared off at
10 o'clock temperature again as yesterday 76 in my room.
As we advanced down the river vegetation shows more
advancement, the woods green the banks of the river less
broken and hilly — the country on either side improved
and cultivated. Although the crowd on board makes it
unpleasant yet nothing afforded me more enjoyment than
the varied scenery on either bank with farms, villas &
villages — the graceful bend of the majestic Ohio. Had
a meeting of the Board of Directors of our company &
appointed J. Walton a com, to wait on & advise with 3
of our number concerning their vulgarity & a too free
use of *ardent*. Hope it may do some good. Passed a
steamer this morning from St Louis, the *Lamartine* with
several cases of Cholera aboard. We have pretty good
order on board considering the large crew, fiddling, dancing, card playing & gaming generally being considered

a matter of course employment for a majority of the
folks traveling on the river — Steam boats are wicked
places. Feeling a feverish thirst Dr. Boyle put his hand
to the powder flask and gave me ½ of a rifle charge &
its effect was cooling — it is difficult to keep the bowels
regular in using river water when unused to it. Four
tables are set one after the other & hard is the scrambling
precedence. Our officers are pretty good fellows, especially the Captain, W. Houk & the steward he has a soul
and has it with him. Sundry pocket hdkfs &c have been
missed but now found on board. Rogues "follow the
river" for a living. Have carried some $1200 as Secretary
of our Co. I felt uneasy with it. Lay it and one of Allen's[7] revolvers together under my pillow every night.
Spent the afternoon on the hurricane deck a fine breeze
refreshed the outer man & the scenery was perfectly delightful to the mind. Near Evansville Ia. is an island
so enchanting that I almost became a convert to the doctrine of a sufficiency & capability of external objects for
enjoyment — This Island has like the banks of the river
here a sandy bank of an easy slope ——is the shape of
an egg & covered with small willow trees & sundry growth
making a grove unsurpassed. My thoughts of home &
friends frequently come up & with them mingled a melancholy pleasure, melancholy because of my absence from
the family circle which to me is a loss of pleasure which
cannot be supplied here among strangers or even ac-
quiantances.

We are passing around the great bend which is 20 miles
around a neck of land at which distance the river again
came very nearly together. Passed the mouth of the
Wabash the clear water of which seemed for some distance to preserve its identity—both to mix with the muddy
water of the Ohio. Stopped an hour to take in wood &
coal at the mouth of Trade Creek. Coal cost 7 cts a bushel
& wood 1.78 per cord. One Northern passenger in the
true Yankee style asked the coal dealer innumerable
questions which were answered with a degree of fore-

bearance & patience seldom seen on the river. Noticed several guide lights on shore which the Pilot seemed to keep in view in coursing. Passed Cave Rock an interesting place on the Illinois side of the river. Huge rocks strewn around in profusion. Enjoyed the beautiful moonlight eve on the hurricane deck in company with Breyfogle[8] & Dr. Boyle who discoursed natural philosophy seemingly more for the sake of description than to arrive at true conclusions each trying to see how far he could disagree with the other & appear consistent — being frequently appealed to to settle or decide points at issue I found myself as often interrupted in contemplating over the scene of home, the incidents of our journey thus far & the probability of the future. The moon sailed athwart the sky in all her wonted loveliness the broad bosom of the river was without a ripple on its mirror like surface. On our right hand was beautifully duplicated the bank with all its trees invested like fairy groves playing off antics among fairy tribes for the amusement of passers by.

APRIL 8, SUNDAY

It being by previous arrangement made the duty of our mess no. 2 to attend the mules I rose before break of day to assist, found some 50 passengers & hardy men women & children laying around on pig iron barrels, boxes, bundles of hay & on the floor which was not occupied by horses & mules of which there were 100. It was by the steam made hot as I could bear & smelt badly, poor wretches how can they escape cholera. The heat makes animals stand uneasy, how very dry our 40 mules, drank some 80 buckets of water this morning, felt after I got through as though I had gone through a regular course with a Steam Doctor, came up took 15 drops Dr. Zoril's cure all medicine & felt well took a hearty breakfast. Appetite very good since I got on the river. In my stateroom changed clothes read in the Bible (presented me by my dear Father) meditated a while, went on hurricane deck. Entered the Mississippi at its junction with the Ohio which forms a large space at the con-

fluence Cairo on the right & Ohio City on the left are
deserted villages resting on stilts would be the best location for a City in the west so far as trade &c is concerned
but there is no plan to build on the banks of the river
are for some distance almost on a level with the river.[9]
Although the Ohio was muddy the Mississippi is much
more so & differs much in appearance, looks more slug-
gish of irregular width the banks covered with Cotton
Wood which looks beautiful, some Islands as in the
Ohio covered with the same timber look picturesque.
Three of our men unwell this afternoon. Banks of river
higher & some hills & farms on the banks of Missouri &
Illinois. Struck a sandbar & had to back out from it.
Had but little observance of the Sabbath, some fired rifles
& pistols. Played various games & others did better.
Steamer *Missouri* passed us, is the largest on the Western Waters 300 ft long. She laid up on shore to bury a
man who died of cholera, so we are right in the midst
of it but I feel but little uneasiness, take care of myself.
Dr. Boyle gave asafedita as a preventitive & it smells
enough to keep off cholera & everybody else. McColm
of our company being about "half seas over" felt like
showing his smartness & in attempting to show Price
how to dip water lost his balance and fell overboard &
was rescued by the men in yawl with difficulty after having floated or swam quite a distance.[10] I was present when
he fell & snatched for him but did not quite reach the leg
of which Price had hold & when the rapidity of the current took him off I feared to be rescued no more & for
the moment my feelings were awful — but providence
permitted it in mercy to pass off with a warning. This
evening passed grand tower rock on the left of the river
encircled with water & rising (cone like) 60 or 70 ft high
with a few bushes and small trees on top seemingly growing out of the crevices of the rock. On the right of the
river is a romantic cliff rising singularly called the *Devil's
Bake Oven,* and by us the Devil's Tea Table. Passed
many & beautiful islands today & cliffs or perpindicular

bluffs on our left rising some 100 to 200 ft in places cut
into arched forms by stratta of soft stone & slate crumbling away as the water drips over them. The river is
more regular in width & more interesting on shore as we
ascend, used my spy glass to advantage on the river in
looking at scenery. Saw several loons & a lot of swans
white as snow. The Captain tells me that McColm is
the second he has rescued from overboard although many
have been lost — the rapidity of the current along the
boat & the danger of the wheel is the cause, he says
McColm had a thousand chances against him, being an
old sailor & good swimmer saved him. 9 o'clock found
the cabin strewn all over with beds & a hundred or more
lying down in great confusion cutting up more funny
antics than my gravity could bear, so I like all the rest
enjoyed it & had hearty laughs, a few crusty old fellows
growled & threatened to punish the officers for not keeping passengers from taking the liberty of enjoying themselves.

APRIL 9

Banks on the right low & covered with Cotton Wood
& I guess some oaks, then sandy banks low & covered
some with a delicate looking brush appear lower than the
river. On our left is broken & hilly — occasionally high
& beautiful bluffs, large trees cast their shadows into the
placid stream, occasionally meanderings & frequent bends
with fairy like Islands making lovers of the beautiful
delighted — then as you float on the endless maze before
you ever varying leave an indelible impression on the
mind — Some of these exquisite Islands covered with
trees of the most delicate foliage would afford lovely
situations for a retired residence. Within 5 miles of St
Louis on the Missouri side is a fine situation for residences. Two mansions of much beauty & good taste are
located here. The bluff or banks are from 70 to 100 ft
high. Two shot towers are built up against the bluff and
the foundation of one remains, which fell down some years
ago crushing one or two men & wagons & teams. With

my glass viewed the City and wharf looking forest like
with steam boat pipes 40 or 50 of which lay here & were
receiving & discharging cargoes consisting of every variety of goods, chattles, produce &c an immense quantity
of which is here shipped. The City as viewed from a
distance with glass looks well, landed here at 2 o'clock.
Held a meeting of our company in the cabin to arrange
business matters. The ladies thought it a novel legislative
assemblage for they peeped out of their cabin frequently.
Met Sells & Armstrong[11] as old friends, was glad to see
them.

Visited Travellers Rest Lodge No. 1 and felt myself
at home among my brother Odd Fellows. Their Hall
is a very fine one, their building is 5 stories high and
large is owned by the order brings good interest on in-
vestment. 6 Lodges meet in this hall. Have also a reading room. 9 in the city, one of which is German. Went
in Company with Bros. Sells & Walton & Boyle to the
Planters Hotel, a large fine Hotel.

APRIL 10

Laid in St Louis, found all articles cheaper than at
Cincinatti and any quantity. Never saw a wharf so
crowded with boats, drays, good, produce &c. 50 S Boats
are preparing to leave here tomorrow. The wharf as well
as the streets in the lower part of the City much too
narrow. Wharf two miles long, streets are mostly muddy
& lower part of the City filthy, entirely too much so for
Cholera times — which prevails here now to a limited
extent. Was in the Rotunda a fine building with yard
around. Court room in it and a large circular room in
amphitheatre form capable of holding probably 2000
persons — built to hold public meetings of all descriptions in. Saw the wall which formed part of the old fort
while in possession of the French & shows marks of the
assault by Indians. On Chestnut Street took an omnibus
(many of which run here) went out two miles & returned
for a dime. The upper part of the City is pleasant many
fine dwellings. The ladies tread the streets freely and

ride horseback — they generally dress very richly—more so than any place I have been in and some are handsome. All possess an air of dignity & selfpossession peculiar to the Slave State—arising perhaps from conscious superiority to those who attend to all the menial affairs for them. Many mounds at St Louis.[12]

APRIL 11

Took an omnibus (with Breyfogle[13] & Denig) out Franklin Avenue to Camp Spring. Some fine situations & buildings here. In the suburbs rather broken but being built up. Out of the City fine rolling land tastefully cultivated in places fine groves. Among the narrow streets and wharfs frequently see wagons & drays jammed together for a square so that they all have to come to a halt & then may be heard awful oaths & threats from drivers & dray men, each swearing for himself & letting his neighbor do the same. There are a number of fine Churches here.

Left St Louis at 3 o'clock in going out noticed a very large shot tower to our left in the suburbs of the City which answers also to conduct telegraph wires across the river, above St Louis some distance is a lovely landscape, a mansion surrounded with grove & fenced in by a circular fence. On the river bank are buildings & a ship of respectable size bound for California, freight & crew engaged for trip. Some rather pretty land along the river. Current strong, water muddy, banks low in places. 17 miles above St Louis entered the Missouri at its widest where the river is two miles wide. The Mississippi looks clear the Missouri very muddy. As we entered the Missouri the sun set in the west in a gorgeous field of fire.

APRIL 12

Dr Boyle & myself aroused by Dewitt[14] to see Breyfogle instantly. Had bowel complaint & thought it was Cholera, is better this morning. Dr Boyle also called up to see Crist[15] who was sick. Took my first breakfast on the turbulent Missouri the longest tributary stream on the globe. Its uncommon length turbidness & impetuous character & the singular country through which it passes gives it grandeur if not sublimity. Rising in the Rocky Mountains it passes through every variety of scenery & country in wending its way thousands of miles to the Mississippi and to the Gulf of Mexico. The banks here are generally several feet high & of sand crumbling. Bottom of boat grated on several sand banks. I wear a scar on my forehead (organ of casualty) from the dropping down last night while sleeping—of a board or the bottom of the berth over me. Had on board a box containing a corpse & landed it & young man who had it in charge on the bank of the river where the family of the deceased were who mourned & cried together, and Oh my feelings! I was carried back to the scene when the loss of a mother wrung my feelings as theirs seem to be now. This afternoon bank of river broken on the left before got to mouth of Osage River, beautiful bluffs and hills rise from 50 to 400 ft at places perpindicular and betimes high hills pressing over each other & fine dale between. Mouth of Osage River is finest & most picturesque scenery on the trip then far on the left are several bluffs with jagged rocks 3 to 400 ft high with a few dwarf pines among the crevices in front courses the clear waters of the Osage, a stream navigable for some distance. On the right and in the distance rise beautifully undulating hills & bluffs. Having turned up the main stream of the Missouri beautiful Island rises in the river like a fairy land covered with delicate foliage. From our hurricane deck this whole scenery is seen at one view. Touched & took passengers at a village picturesquely located among high hills, were told the boat just in advance of us had on board 7 or 8 cases of Cholera. A rush was made for Boiler Deck which was afire near the boiler, but was soon extinguished. Passed this evening at twilight two fairy like Islands rising paralel & dividing the river into three streams of equal width which look like streets of a city & remind me of Venice in her glory. These Islands are like most of the Islands & low banks along this & the Mississippi, covered with cottonwood of small size straight & delicate as willow. Commenced to rain, night dark — laid up.

APRIL 13

Slept with J. Walton. McCommon[16] in upper berth taken ill as if by an attack of Cholera — is better this morning. Passed Jefferson City the Capitol of Mo. located on hill. Penetentiary in view. A fine State House[17] near the river on a high hill stands in bold relief—built of lime stone, two stones high on the side a semi-circle assent to the door supported by 5 Ionic columns. House looks well. Had another alarm of fire — the thought of fire on a boat is awful. The sparks fall into the hay on deck so we are much exposed. Run on sand bank but got off easily. Passed Boonville a village scattered over hills on our left, takes its name from the daring pioneer who flourished in this State of Kentucky in a very early day. Here trees look bleak & vegitation seems nearly a month later than on the Mississippi. Our course on the Missouri being north of west, passed Glasgow a village on the right bank. We are so far west that large towns are no more found. Banks of the river begin to look more like Eastern rivers banks of moderate height — in places bluffs, land fit for tilling, in spots rolling & hilly. Stream seems more muddy as we ascend. One man had difficulty with an officer on boiler deck on acct of taking (without leave) the pump & hose to water mules after many oaths (in which boatmen are accomplished) he granted the privilege. Officers are bothered by passengers, no one should use a tool or fixture without leave as they frequently need them & are thus nonplussed.

APRIL 14

Sleeping on boat soon becomes a habit, I now lay down in evening & in a few minutes the motion of boat rocks to sleep, like a child lulled to slumber in a cradle. Weather cold, N.W. wind temperature 38. Had cold wind yesterday struck several sand banks but got off without much trouble, as large boats as this seldom go up this high, sand banks continually change in bed of this river baffling all knowledge of pilots. One pilot gets $50 per day from St Louis to St Joseph & back perhaps 10 days or two weeks labor. No very interesting scenery on river today in places level with sand banks but mostly broken banks. Cold wind, gloomy sky — prospect of having to lay at St Joseph am sorry to say that a few wish themselves home again. Cards, checker, chess & domino playing is done on a large scale.

APRIL 15

Sabbath morning landed at Independence early. The town, however is 3 miles back from the river, on left side.[18] Went out after breakfast passed over high hill where large rocks overhang & scenery below picturesque. Good farms over rolling land lay along road. Town has from 1000 to 2000 inhabitants has a beautiful location on a gentle rise, fine green lawns in suburbs. In center is a square with pretty good Court House, use a hard blue limestone good for building use. Although stores generally closed doors were open some & goods could be bought. Some of our folk remarked that the Sabbath had not got so far West, it seemed, although two or 3 churches are here & some folks going to them. This village is pretty. Saw here a Mexican an Indian, a crowd of all sorts of people, some Indian ponies & many mules. A lady riding are of the latter in company with a gentleman perhaps on their way to church. The number encamped about & within 10 miles of this place waiting for groups to grow on prairies to enable them to start for California is various & estimated from 3 to 4000 this being early many more will leave from here. Also a government train of perhaps 1000. Was told Capt. Bryant[19] author of "What I saw in California" is in town but did not see him. Saw Col. Russel[20] who goes out as Captain of a company. He is a large robust looking man. Returning to boat found on board a Santa Fe trader who also sells goods at Independence trying to have us stop here treated liberally & got pretty high. Had two or three friends with him & among them got up a quarrel

with our steward (a good peacable fellow). Geo Chadwick run out of his room & took steward's part, the difficulty threatened once to end in a general row which one
of the Santa Fe men drew a knife of large size to mow
his way in the crowd which was taken from him he put
out a number of blows given him, bled freely & left. In
this way was spent forenoon of Sabbath. After dinner
Allen & Bodly[21] of Delaware (who graduated in Delaware College) and I with another young man got into
there room (they being both professors & Methodists).
We talked on religious subjects, each had his Bible & we
read a while in Testament & asked & answered questions
in regard to what we read. We 3 in this way had a good
Sabbath afternoon. Passed at twilight mouth of Kansas
River water clear & runs in against the current of the
Missouri, on our left is Indian Territory.

APRIL 16

Last night ran on Sand Bar worked some time to get
off in doing which got under branches of trees on bank
that took both chimneys midway up making a great
crash. Many on board were alarmed. I being in the embrace of "Morpheus" heard it not. Passed Fort Leavenworth[22] on left bank at day break. Many soldiers out
watering horses, it is a pretty place did not rise early
enough to see Major Sanderson[23] who is here expecting
soon to leave with a train for California or Oregon.
Weston on right bank is a considerable village located
with hills around. Vegetation & foliage was backward as
we advance up the Missouri. Landed at St Joseph on
the south of town a beautiful level camping ground a mile
or two up & down the river & to a mile wide. Surrounded
as is the town with peculiar unnatural looking ridges &
hills — like drifted snow banks. Encampments scattered
all around perhaps 4 or 5000 for California.[24] Met Morgans company like old companions. Led out horses of
Delaware company, were very playfull. Led out mules
of our company & were frantic with wild delight as it
seemed & were unmanageable, got loose, rushed around,

Walton kicked badly at side of head bled profusely, also
kicked on abdomen. Dr Boyle dressed wound.[25] A. Pake[26]
offered fenced lot put mules in, asked 25 cts a head per
week. I jewed him down to 10 cts put them in & set a
guard over them as it was reported six horses had this
evening been stolen, at 8 o'clock rained & blew. Breyfogle
& McColm sick and could get no house for them to stay
in — perhaps for fear of Cholera. Arrived early to take
things from boat, weather very cold & high wind got
chilled through. Took last good hearty breakfast on boat
— did it ample justice, cost 50 cts. Some folks eat nothing till evening. Price[27] & I went to town for eatables
could find no butter, cheese at retail 15 cts & wholesale 10
bot a large Western Reserve cheese at $9\frac{1}{2}$ pr lb. Eggs
10, bread hardly to be had. Engaged 50 loaves to be
done at 4 o'clock, went at the time & found baker had
set clock back to 2 o'clock & got bread at 8 o'clock. Ham
5 to 6 sides & shoulder, 3 & 4 large stores here & doing
well. Just myself on way to camp a mile from town
with a dozen loaves of bread, found camp, very tired,
all in bed on wagons except guard. Took off boots &
overcoat, laid down & slept for first time on wagon, the
night remarkably cold & windy, was cold all night. Had
ham, eggs & cheese for supper also sea bread (in absence
of any other) & coffee. Although cold had fun & novel
times for first supper in camp.

APRIL 18

Cold and dreary yesterday, vegitation a month later
than at mouth of Ohio, McColm very sick serviced wagons
&c preparatory to puting in readiness for a long journey.
Breyfogle gone to country to recruit health (not being
able to get into any house)[28] Walton out again. Boat
here on upward passage had 21 cases Cholera, 7 deaths
a few cases in town also smallpox. A good many articles
& preparations yet to be made although we thought ourselves in readiness.

APRIL 19

Nothing peculiar occured today, had a cold hard nights

rest. Stood guard for first time last night from 9 to 12
o'clock & felt reluctant to wake up McCommon to succeed me on guard duty & why guard mules &c here in a
civilized country? Reason, some good & many desperate
fellows are here natives and emigrants who are not particular as to the manner in which they obtain mules &
other valuables. St Joseph has 1500 to 2000 inhabitants
is all bustle & business now & a variety of business done.
Seemingly considerably to farmers around. A lot of
ground purchased 5 years ago (when the town was laid
out) with hemp or a yoke of oxen, now a building in one
room of which last year was sold $75000 worth of goods.
Stores keep all sorts of goods here. A store here is selling
$900 in a day now. I have been unwell today. Head
& bones ache. Not having used meat of any kind (except
fowl & fish) for 10 years I commenced eating it a few
days ago. Camp life does not agree with many at first.
Being continually exposed to sun, heat & cold of day &
night has its unfavorable effect.

APRIL 20

Felt quite unwell today, very much as if fever & ague
was about to make me its victim. Visited McColm at a
house we procured for him, he is slowly mending. Was
suddenly taken ill as if fainting, laid down a while & improved. Got in tent & washed all over with warm water
& put on clean flannel & feel better. The annoyances of
camp life are not a few, makes most of men fretful, some
swear that did not before. Articles of furniture liable
to be mixed up among the messes which are returned to
one after a sharp repartee of words. The real dispositions
& talents of our folks already much developed some few
favorably & some unfavorably.

APRIL 21

Our President or Captain blew the horn at break of
day our omen to rise all hands soon out some cooking
others feeding horses & mules, left our first camp of 4
miles from east side of River to a ground 5 miles (by
upper ferry) on west side of river. Teams left as they

got ready, I am with one drove by Dungan,[29] on north side of St Joseph passed through a place where road is cut through sand bank 30 ft deep, width of wagon & going down hill after passing this cut the mules became unmanageable running down this long rough hill at full speed, nearly at bottom upset breaking tongue, wheel box, bows, &c. Had heavy load on, & mules being rested were hard to manage, no lock chains on & green driver. My advice was to take off the leaders, two being easier to manage than four. Our mules was doubled up under the wreck of the wagon, but mules none hurt. Left two Waltons, Price & Krumm[30] & took Waltons Poney went to ferry 3 miles distant for Dewitt a wagon maker missed the road, got lost in woods. Woodchoppers directed me to follow the sun till I got on right road. Sent Dewitt, stayed at ferry where all the rest of our teams were to go over. Every one enquired particulars about running off scrape all criticised some blamed Dungan &c &c. For $10.00 had our things ferried over took from 10 o'clock till midnight, was hardest day we have had so far. Loading of Dungan's & Walton's wagon brot to ferry with ox team, D— & I pitched tent on west side of river looked for rain put all things in, Dungan, I & Walton stayed here all night. I started for camp at dusk leading mule our 9 wagons safely in, supper ready, bread & ham. Ate very hearty supper, it seemed delicious, drank a quart water of an excellent spring near by. Grass is out some, mules were all picketed out & have to be brot in & tied within "camp fire range" so as to be seen by watch. Assisted in bringing in mules in rain.

APRIL 22

SABBATH DAY. Had a good rest last night & feel well. Our camp ground No. 2 is on a bottom on the river, well timbered, rich soil. This bottom enclosed by a pretty high range of hills, back of our camp, found some other California Company encamped near by us. This is Indian Territory & is the first land I have trod out of the States of the Union. Some of our company & others

are firing rifles & pistols frequently making this seques-
tered spot resound with anti christian profanity of the
holy sabbath. One of our Delaware friends encamped ½
mile above here says he saw a ½ dozen deer in a drove
a few days ago near by here. Pretty civilized Indians
are to be seen in this country. Went to camp of Delaware Company in afternoon. How pleasant to meet
friends at a distance, went in company with my young
Methodist friends of that company [Jedediah] Allen &
[Moses] Bodley on the hills31 back of our camp one mile
where is a scenery the like of which I never beheld before
from a high eminence before us lay a ridge of beautiful
hills divided by dells & ravines curiously formed & spring
of crystal pure water in each, at the foot of the hills lay
a wooded bottom rich soil level as a board a mile wide
on either side & back of us as far as the eye can scan is
rolling prairie with occasional clumps of stunted oaks.
In the distance rolls the Missouri, a steamer descending.
St Joseph is in this view & bluffs beyond it. Enough to
fill with delight lover of nature & its beauties. Amid this
fairy like scene us 3 sat down & each read in Bible &
Testament commented & conversed on spiritual matters.
A sweet time this was.

APRIL 23

MONDAY. As usual since we camped here had a fine
serenade by the feathery songsters in their sweetest lays
from 4 o'clock to 8. A variety of birds take part & make
the trees bending over on wagons (beds) vocal, the Whip-
oorwill among the rest having come down from the hills
above us. Weather beautiful, pleasant now to sleep on
wagons. Had meeting of Co. resolved to sell some vinegar, saddles &c & put goods in sacks to lessen load. Each
somewhat independent, some growling, especially those
who expected this to be a jolly trip — they are fast being
convinced of their error. Having anticipated nothing
more than what we have seen so far I am quite satisfied
as yet. Report says the various tribes of Indians through
chiefs are holding a council the object being to head &

cut off emigrants. I fear it not but many do. Run bullets
today. Painted wagon & [J. C.] Lunn & [J. P.] Stone[32]
brot into camp two large black snakes they are pretty
plenty, also rattlesnakes. Had tires of some wagons reset.
I fear they are too light for our load, being light two
horse wagons. 4 mules to each & perhaps load of 1400
might have got mules or oxen cheaper here than in Ohio
& other things for outfit, especially provisions.

APRIL 24

TUESDAY: Awakened by caroling birds. Went to St
Joseph got letter for self & others of company. All very
glad to hear from home. Mine from brother Charles
awakened affections which alone are felt to the fullest
by one separated far from a circle of dear members of
a family. Town full of strangers. Business men reaping
a harvest. P. office crowded from morning till night.
Encampments in all directions. Found Major Hunter[33]
& Co. all well &c. A number cases of Cholera in town
& proving fatal, many. Was in company with Barcus[34]
& took dinner. Pittsburg Co divided after a quarrel 300
men too many. Hard to keep together.

APRIL 25

WEDNESDAY: Repacked bread & gear out of boxes
into sacks to lighten load. Are preparing to start for
Big Blue river 80 or 100 miles distant. Have our flag[35]
out & gives animation to camp scenery wrote a letter to
Br. David.

APRIL 26

THURSDAY: It is a bad plan to lay in camp more
than two days, men become restless, forgetful, lazy. This
trip has already developed who are *men* in our company.
Weather fine and dry. Never saw but two ladies in St
Joseph & they had no attractions for me.

APRIL 27

FRIDAY: Three wagons sent out 20 miles for corn, returned loaded. Got it at 20 cts & sells in town at 40 cts.
Took a little of Dr. Zoril's medicine to purify blood &
did me good. Weather pleasant & dry.

APRIL 28

SATURDAY: Aroused by blowing of horn, our meal of
bread coffee & ham being over all hands went to shelling
corn to be taken along to last two weeks on journey
grass being short. McCommon & Dr. Boyle are our cooks,
one from each wagon of Mess No. 2, two men being left
to attend to each team. A. B. Crist & myself attend to
ours. Bryden[36] shot at a prairie wolf being too far off
missed. Dr Boyle shot a gopher, see Lieut. Albert's account of gophers, and partly dissected it. It was collor
of a mouse & size of common sized rat. They are plenty
here & throw up the ground in fine hillocks. Encamp-
ment increasing around us. Mules without number
around our camp. Price & I visited the grave of an
Indian on a hill of bluffs. A pole 15 ft high with white
flannel flag & red cross in center marking the place, beside it is a pealed wooden pillar six inches in diameter
two ft high with hieroglyphics, 6 headless trunks painted
on rudely, also 12 long straight marks & six short marks.
The grave is up as usual, an upright at each end supporting a ridge pole against which from each end lean
rudely split sticks or clap boards 3 ft high & ground
thrown up against it ½ way up. At the head is an oyster
tin box with some preserved crabapple preserved with
wild honey. Around the grave for ten ft it is clean &
tramped hard. Sympathy touched my feeling on behold-
ing this memorial of respect for the dead. At 3 o'clock
P.M. left camp & broke axel of Ruggs[37] wagon. This
is a discouraging circumstance & augers ill for the future on this trip. Left one mess behind to repair. Passed
the bluffs & continued upon the boundless prairies, rolling or hilly in every variety of shapes. This scene of
undulating with only here & there a clump of stunted
trees, verdant with its new carpet of grass, present scenery romantic grand & fairy like. As the rays of the setting sun kissed the hills the scenery was grand. Went 4
miles & camped at twilight on a ground beside a ravine
with water of crystal purity — ground selected by Cap-

tain & myself found on ground encamped a German
family,[38] man & wife & three interesting little girls bound
for California. He had been in country some years, was
from Baden in Germany. With Price in afternoon met
company from Louisville, Captain Huey & son had their
wives with them who wore masks to protect from sun.

Sabbath 29 — Cool morning, windy sun rose beautifully over the undulating prairie. Walton & I at 9 o'clock
took ride in advance on road 8 miles to Mosquito Creek
on return took new road on trail runing nearly paralel
with old. Soon found it leading a wrong way & started
straight across to old trail, missed it & lost ourselves.
Followed for miles a stream we thought passed over old
trail. Were mistaken & followed it to within sight of
Mo. River & where men encamped told way back to
Mosquito Creek & found we had gone some 8 miles out
of right road. Returned after a hard ride of from 25
to 30 miles hungry & dry & sore. In passing along little
stream crossed several ugly ravines some dry & others
with water in. Made horses jump as best they could.
On this trip saw much of country & its truly beautiful
in places. Wind blows tremendously on these prairies,
was unhatted twice in ride today. Pleasant evening. Was
4 o'clock when Walton & I got to camp from our stray-
ing trip. An Indian came to camp with many beads on
& comfortably clad with pack on back. He looked filthy
& George Chadwick[39] gave him whiskey which he accepted gladly.

30. Monday morning very cold east wind. Called up
at 4 o'clock washed where wind almost swept me away
& ate breakfast in face of wind. Watering, feeding, har-
nessing & hitching up mules (that are very unruly)
Made me feel for my country, my hands are very sore
also nose & lips, but "bashful lover never won fair lady."
Left camp at 6 o'clock went a mile when front axel of
my wagon broke down. Unharnessed & picketed out
mules. Set Krumm, Dewitt & Moores[40] to work & they
put in axel tree (which had been prepared as a duplicate)

had it finished by 12 o'clock. Necessity is truly the
mother of invention. These men had only draw knife,
saw, file, chisels & wrench. These few hours we unloaded
laid by & climbed a high prairie ridge with wind blowing
in force. Went 5 or 6 miles & came into camp on Mosquito
Creek an hour before dark. Passed fine prairie scenery
rolling beautifully as hills could. My turn to watch from
9 to 12 o'clock & for first time heard Prairie Wolves.[41]
Several howled in different directions, one came among
the mules & several broke loose, mules much frightened
by these noises & hear them approach at a distance. The
blaze of the prairie on fire presented a splendid appearance, the fire runs as blown by wind often presenting
grotesque & curious shapes & figures as it runs over hills
& valleys.

MAY 1ST: Aroused at 4 o'clock. Cold & windy left
camp at 6 o'clock & made good speed and had an hours
work in preparing for crossing Wolf Creek, 4 or 5 miles
distant. The scenery is varied & fine as could fairy land
be. We passed what is called "The Station"[42] a farm
well fenced & owned by the First Presbyterian Church.
This is a Mission. Ten or twelve persons live here. It
is the prettiest place I have seen. A church & school house
& several houses. Saw fine wheat. Back of the farm is a
fine ravine well timbered. Passed an Indian village of
4 or 5 miserable rush thatched huts was up & saw a few
filthy looking "natives" 3 or 4 intelligent looking Indians
at Wolf Creek distance about 25 miles. Stopped about
4 o'clock.

WEDNESDAY 2 — After Walton & I had rode round
some miles for a camping place & found a place with
wood ½ mile off, bad water & the boys in evening found
across a hill a spring of cold crystal pure water with
grass near by. We all went & drank freely & moved
mules to grass there. I watched from 12 to 3 o'clock. 4
watched mules and 1 the camp. I heard only one or two
wolves howl — they howl piteously. Distance some 25
miles. Men tired & as a consequence dissatisfied & "rily,"

they know hardly what for. Had last night first shower of rain since we landed at St. Jo.

THURSDAY 3RD — Cool, windy. My & other horses run off some two miles we overtook them & caught them by assistance of Walton mounted them bare backed & gallopped toward our train with "prairie freedom." Had table board resting on Elk horns to breakfast from. These Elk horns are plenty along the trail some are very large 5 ft long & of great thickness & weight. Many write their names on these horns & trees, make post offices of them to leave messages for friends behind. Passed the grave of some one who perhaps died here of an emigrating party. As I looked upon this lonely grave where nothing marks it but a large pile of ground I thought of the friends who mourn & would cherish the last resting place of him who died in a distant land among strangers perhaps. The almost constantly blowing wind of these prairies sing a doleful requiem over this grave.

Have each day passed a train of ox teams & they in turn passed us while stopping. One of these trains remarked "You can travel faster than we for you pass us every day." Met a Mr. McCoy[43] who formerly lived near Columbus & knew many of my acquaintances. He lately lived in St. Jo. Has been in Santa Fee & is going to California. Prairie still rolling & beautiful beyond description. Every variety of shapes are those hills green with rather a fine & good grass looking something like "civilized grass." Wattered at a lot of holes in the ground or rather little standing pools or lakes in ravines, these little lakelets are met with pretty frequently. The water is tolerably good this season of the year. It seems to spring in some. Wood is seldom seen except betimes in a ravine or along little streams which are very rare. Distance alone limits the view of gently rolling prairies green with the "carpet of nature" often presenting panoramic views enchanting as could be fairy land. Although hardly a level spot is seen yet the rises or hills are so

gentle that we have only locked the wheels once today.
At once come in sight of a stream, the Nimahaw [Nemaha
River]44 fringed with timber. Timber grows along this
stream immediately on its banks, trees rather stunted,
Oaks generally. Near the stream on a high hill are peculiar stones & pebbles mixed with Iron. These stones are
generally hollow or in center filled with a light porus
yellowish substance. This is the Nimahaw from appearances of rubbish drifted on brush this stream rises from
30 to 35 ft. Banks high, let wagons down by ropes, took
off leaders. Hand pulled out, stream low. Encamped
on bank at 3 o'clock. Distance 16 miles. Camp on level
bottom scenery pretty.

FRIDAY 4TH. My rest or rather want of rest last night
made me feel aching in every bone & in back in particular. 3 men to each wagon & a tent to every two
wagons. Tents are troublesome to pitch so we sleep
mostly 3 in wagon. Our bed is small 3 men covered it
& since we changed boxes for sacks it is difficult to make
the bed level. I can sleep as well on a board with a
blanket round me but an uneven bed is uncomfortable.
Last night we had rain nearly constantly, it commenced
before sun set preceded by peals of thunder & flashes
of lightning, the latter often very bright making all
around appear as illuminated, & continued in night. Had
trouble in bringing in & watering two mules & my horse
and had by order of Captain to stake them near the
wagon in doing which I got wet. Rain poured down in
torrents stood on footboard in front of wagon to undress.
Wet clothes hard to undress, boots made me much trouble
to get off. Rain spattering on cover & around me put
me the sooner to sleep. Our wagon covers shed rain well.
They are made of Osnaburg with one coat of linseed oil
and bees wax mixed by boiling, gives them color of light
sand. Wagon covers are frequently taken off in traveling on account of the almost constant high wind which
sweeps over the prairie like over the ocean meeting with
no obstructions by nature or art. Raining, cold, and

windy this morning found harness, saddle cooking apa-
ratus, halters & picket ropes extremely muddy. Mules
& horse shivering in the cold wind. Cooks (McCommon
& Boyle) had breakfast ready at 6 o'clock (fried bacon
very fat & plenty of it & sea biscuit & coffee) Stood out
in rain & took breakfast with good relish. As usual jokes
passed freely to keep up spirits. Nothing tends to check
ones resolution as such a morning. Fisk[45] anxious to go
on. President put question of starting to members, decided negatively by small majority. On acct of too much
independent action & sparring, on motion the President
was authorized to give orders in all things necessary to
be done according to his judgement. It is hoped it will
do well. All hands went to woods on banks of Nimahaw
& fetched logs & made large camp fire. Along this stream
are wild rose bushes plumb hazel, gooseberry & straw-
berries &c, also blue flowers. Passed through prairies
yesterday that seemed much as if cultivated in places
are large spaces of old grass looking like fields of grain
near harvest time along side & stretching far off as eye
can scan are fields of grass of beautiful green, occasionally are large spaces lately burned over which at a great
distance appear like mahogany wood, varied in curious
forms by the different colors of the ground. We are
now in the territory of the Otto[46] Indians. Took walk
with Cain[47] and Crist to a stream emptying into the
Nimahaw and as large. Has high banks from 30 to 50
ft. Dark rich soil on bank is from 4 to 5 ft deep. This
stream is narrow & deep & appears betimes to get very
high. Met in woods & bushes along this stream 4 deserted
Indian huts. These huts are put up by bending over &
driving into the ground little trees fastened together
with withs & bark, some are square & others circular.
Covered with grass, bark & rushes. Had no arms & felt
no uneasiness although 2 miles from camp in wilderness
where Indians frequent. Saw deer tracks. Water deep
at confluence of two streams. Crist & Cain returned &
fished. Cain caught a cat fish weighing perhaps 8 lbs &

Boyle in evening caught large turtle. Waded through water 1 ft deep to bring in mules.

SATURDAY 5 — Was on last watch last night out of 5 messes, one watch of each mess the whole night, making 5 watches at a time. To make it easy 3 watch from each mess, one from 9 o'clock to 12, another to 3 o'clock & a third to daylight. So each watches every other night & takes in succession 1st, 2nd, & 3rd watches. A little foggy this morning. Filled water casks & canteens on acct of being informed that there was no water for next 23 miles. Saw ravines with clumps of trees & passed two little streams in forenoon. Let water out of casks at first these little streams have high banks making difficulty in passing. Prairies more hilly than formerly. Fisk & Prices horse ran off from camp had trouble to catch it so that Fisk was loading his rifle to shoot the pony. Made an arrangement to day to travel in company with 17 persons from Illinois who have 5 wagons.48 We travel together for mutual protection. Were today seldom out of sight of valleys or rivers, with trees making the scenery more picturesque. Betimes the prairies appears like the oceans rolling waves, green & the rises or undulations of every conceivable variety of shapes. When out of sight of wooded ravines it is easy to imagine oneself out of sight of land. Wooded ravines universally have water & some not wooded have standing pools or ponds, some deep. This water is passably good at present. I will call this prairie "Uncle Sam's" Pasture Field. Farms will no doubt be opened out here before another generation passes away. The soil is generally very rich — in places like Sciata Bottoms. It only wants ploughing & ditched in place of fenced. Timber in ravines is generally rather stunted — some is tall. Oaks I saw had limbs within 2 ft of ground & very stunted. Stones are rare only found along ravines & on ridges are little stones or pebbles of every kind, have seen but little interesting to the geologist. Came to a ravine where ox team 7 yoke were stalled, had to unload, oxen very stubborn. All on hand cutting

brush & threw ground on & passed without much difficulty. Our mules know nothing of flanking. Encamped
on this little stream in company with our new associates
& formed the first coral of our wagons. Picketed and
let run out from stopping time (4 o'clock) to 8 o'clock
then brought all within coral & set guards from 8 o'clock
to daylight 5 at a time, stationed out side of camp &
mules & each guard to walk back & forth in his allotted
space. Guards now changed every hour. My turn came
from 9 to 10 o'clock, night chilly, muddy & rainy. All
rains commenced after night so far. E. E. Canfield[49] is
& has been sick for a week or more our accomodations
poor. A man among those we gained been sick for ten
days, had, I believe, Measles & is discouraged. Offered
me liberal pay to procure a bird for soup, but none seen
today. Prairie hens are scarce, Snipes we have shot a
few of, Black birds are in great numbers on the prairies
& along wooded ravines everything is musical with their
noise & that of other birds. Distance perhaps 20 miles.

SUNDAY 6: The second Sabbath for me on the prairies.
Captain decided to travel today. Price & I made objec-
tions & others disliked it but we had lost Friday & another
day to be lost was too much for some of our company.
No church bell reverberates its solemn tones of invitation
to worship & no restraint of fellow men surrounds us
& without either the sabbath is too violated, although the
almost solemn stillness of a prairie seems like a celebration of the Holy Sabbath. Passed over several ravines
with steep banks. Roads heavy after rain, scenery fine.
For last two days we stopped ½ hour at noon & it is
the best plan so at noon 15 minutes time is taken for
making up my minutes on my knees sitting mostly on
ground. Approaching Big Blue[50] [Kansas] is hilly,
scenery pretty, some pretty high ridges of peculiar stones
or rocks piled in places perpindicular & they appear
rounded like sponge & crumble, are formed of small
separate stones of flinty & porous kinds, also shell in
some. Big Blue deep half way up side of a horse, un-

loaded wagons, put poles over top of wagon boxes & goods on them, some wagons raised their boxes by blocks under. I took across on my horse "Bob" 9 or 10 sacks of bread. Current is strong & some mules had to be led by man wading in. Got all our things over dry & safe in two hours except a few lbs of coffee lost among mud by sack opening. Also a powder horn floated off. Encamped on south bank of stream among high old grass & bushes. Repacked things on wagons, set sentinels as usual. Camp of 30 wagons above us had 18 mules stolen by Indians. This camp also has case of small pox. A team from St Joseph is taking back some of those afflicted & had the kindness to offer to take letters for our folks at 25 cts apiece. None sent. One of wagons of our companions stalled & had to unload, sunk deep in ravine & mules bauky, distance perhaps 20 miles, had artichokes for supper and felt unwell after.

MONDAY 7. Fine morning left camp at 7 o'clock after our mess partaking of turtle soup made of turtle & rice, the latter not done and scortched, first turtle I ate, meat good & tender. Walked in advance of train some 5 miles. Nooned a little beyond a ravine a few miles in advance of Independence[51] & St Joseph trail. A little before striking Independence trail got on high ground & saw most beautiful & picturesque prairie scenery I ever beheld. The grand panorama is only bounded by the horizon —the undulating scenery with an occasional wood-fringed ravine extends in every direction, inspiring the mind with awe. Saw at a great distance a train of several wagons. Horses & pack mules coming on Independence road. Dan & Bryden crossed to Independence road thinking it ours, lost 3 miles by it & were notified of error by Captain. It is 200 miles from here to Independence. Encamped at 5 o'clock on right side of trail on a gentle rise with good "Buffalo Grass," little wood & poor water. We get up in morning at break of day start at from 6 to 7 o'clock stop at 11 to noon & start at ½ past 12. Stop in evening at from 4 to 6 o'clock as camping ground found.

TUESDAY 8: Spent hour as sentinel pleasantly the ground beautifully inclining, pleasant breeze, stars shone finely & the moon sailed athwart the silver canopy in splendor, making the scene fairy like — in morning heard many prairie hens making peculiar cooing noise, one of company shot one. Heard Woolfs howl while on guard our men shot Snipes & Plovers along trail. They & black birds seem less timid than in the states. Here is a peculiar bird of the black bird species & associates with the many flocks on the prairie. Its neck, breast & lower part of wings are of beautiful yellow & other part black. A blue & yellow flower shows on Prairie, grass is good in places but generally backward. Have as yet fed some corn. Passed number ravines with steep banks, road otherwise good worn & plain as roads in the states. Passed ravine or little stream & let wagons down with ropes & found arriving other cards on trees, one from Delaware company, they had passed here the 2nd at 4 p.m. Cards & writing to friends or companies behind are often seen along road, again written on bones or Elk horns. Friday pleasant & warm, sky clear as any Italian can be. Sun rose beautifully, & moon appeared same time bright, going up a gradual rise for a mile I looked back & around & the scenery was truly sublime. The distance I looked back on seemed to be 50 to 100 miles undulating & bound only by the horizon. Passed a little stream around which was wooded ravines & broken picturesque country. Passed lot of ox teams two of which were bound for Oregon, having their families the men had been out before, several intelligent ladies were in this train. We have passed quite a number of ox teams & emigrating parties, some ox teams now go from 15 to 20 miles in cool weather, "catching up" oxen to hitch is a scene of noise & confusion & takes but little less time to harness & hitch mules, although mules are very annoying & troublesome animals. Am told a man was shot accidentally on the trail from Independence and buried by the side of the road. On the road I am told boxes, furniture, trunks &c &c are strewn along being left to lighten loads. That road is worse than the St Joseph trail. Encamped ¼ mile from little stream at 5 o'clock where wood & grass was scarce & there being dissatisfaction as to the ground & several "riley" &c. I will call it *Camp Contention*. Distance 25 miles.

WEDNESDAY, 9: Left camp early 5 o'clock. Stopped at 10 & went a mile from trail to a water hole with mules having met no water to day before. Some of our men dissatisfied & talk of "disunion &c." Much occurs on way to stir men's baser passions & little to influence favorably the better feelings. Having expected this I am not disappointed much. While I write (10 o'clock a.m.) two deer are streaking over the prairies at a distance of ¾ of a mile — some of our men followed but got no shot at them, these are the first we have seen. Buffalo[52] occasionally roam here but none have we seen. Made an addition to cooking provender by soaking in cold water & frying in fat sea biscuit. It is good as a change. Bacon with fat 4 inches thick I can eat raw or fried. There are no bounds to my appetite & I have gained in weight probably 12 lbs since I left home. Passed a little stream that gets high betimes & along stream is sand several feet deep along whole stream. I will call it Sand Creek. Passed several steep banked ravines & another sandy stream around which wheels cut in a foot deep. Water tastes a little sulphur like. Camped ¾ mile from last stream on a bottom on right of road with excellent grass — all hands pleased with Captain's selection. An Elk horn 5 or 6 ft long & weighing 16 to 20 lbs had many names on of travellers from N.Y. & other states. 3 of us set on it at table. Went to stream after dark for water, alone with no weapons. Sun sets on prairie is more beautiful than other places & this evening was the most sublime sunset I ever beheld, a large cloud seemed to partially hide it & in places openings blazed like streamers of liquid gold. The cloud was bordered around its whole mountain like edge with a spangled light as if silvered.

Over all ran a highly arched flood of rays. Had storm & some rain tonight. I had a frightful dream which made me scream & rise in my bed until McCommon waked me.

THURSDAY 10: Beautiful morning & warm day. The sun rose with but little less splendor than it set last night. The prairies are adorned with a great variety of flowers this morning, all different from any I have seen before. They look cheering & give sweet scent & are some of the most delicate tints of purple, blue, pink yellow &c. Saw a clump of Prickly Pair or cactus with leaves like hands growing low on ground. Met a man going to California afoot all alone carrying what makes a little world within itself here on the prairie, meat, bread, &c &c. He expects to get supplies at each fort. This man a few might ask & obtain privilege to sleep under one of our wagons, a rainy night & guards kept him from leaving until morning. "Little Blue"[53] on our left pass up it for miles, willow brush & cottonwood on banks stream 20 to 30 ft wide & deep. Men fishing caught cat fish, large ones. This is a beautiful stream quite refreshing to the prairie traveller. Here on the plains the trees of delicate foliage on its banks winding around seem like an army marching through ravines. Trail is along its banks for 50 miles. Water is clean & tolerably good. Passed 15 wagons at 11 o'clock where we nooned, & they together mules & oxen mixing up in confusion. Two of their men a few days ago being away from camp some miles horseback were pursued by 12 Indians to short distance within their train. Indians are lurking round to cut off stragglers & steal mules but came not to camp.[54] I have several times lately grazed my horse back or in advance of our train alone perhaps two or three miles off which was imprudent. In afternoon one of Canfield's mules gave out—our mules are too young, only three years & two of them only two years. This is discouraging. Camped near Blue for night at 5 o'clock. Moores caught a salmon trout of 12 lbs. Distance 18 miles.

FRIDAY 11: Rose as usual at 5½ o'clock, picketed out mules by pickets 6 inches & ropes 30 ft. The soil is so deep that pickets easy go in to top. Along the Blue there are places looking rather sterile & broken between road & river saw a mound 40 ft high rode to top of it & had a fine view of the stream, bluffs & surrounding country with trains winding their slow way over the plains bound for the land of "sun down." A flood seems once to have made vast ravines & hollows, fine cool bracing air or wind today, have had delightful weather for travelling since left St Jo. From the Nimahaw have often seen Artemesia or Wild Sage, wild rose bushes in abundance are not yet in bloom, every variety of flower along here, horses tramping among them emits fine scent. I saw 5 deer crossing the trail ½ mile ahead. Fisk with my horse "Bob" & the Captain rode after them but no success. They run fast & there is danger of ones losing himself by following far. The Captain saw 9 in another lot in another direction. We are looking out for Buffalo & Antelope now. On prairie see singular phenomena in rising from a vast area without trees today the horizon all around presented the peculiar appearance of being nearby — the country being around below hid, the horizon was marked high where clouds floated in creamy undulations, looking like a vast sea with ripples which we were approaching closer until we reached the ascent where the delusion was evident, such & other phenomena as to the horizon sky &c are often curious matter of speculation for travellers on the prairie. Appearances often remind one of being at sea. "Nooned" at 11 a.m. on the Little "Blue" where any quantity of little flies & mosquitos & other insects bite one. Our folks have killed a number of Rattlesnakes of moderate size since we left St Jo. Snipes, Plover & black birds are here & on the whole route in flocks as well as mocking birds & a variety of others. Saw at distance a flock of Antelope this afternoon the first we saw. Camped on the Blue at 5 o'clock. Grass, water & fuel good. Wolves howled, musquitos pretty plenty.

SATURDAY 12. Fine cool day, pretty brisk wind. Left camp at usual time. An Antelope run along Blue & passed me within 70 yds. Had no rifle. Wild garlic is in bloom & answers us well for onions. Left valley of Blue entering on high land the shout was given, "Buffalo ahead" perhaps two miles. All hands but drivers ran for them until near enough to see that they were a lot of Indian Warriors horseback. One man returned speedily to protect wagons. I drove our team & saw the Indians divide, those horseback 36 in number rushed toward 3 wagons opposite them & ½ mile ahead of the other wagons, the chief at their head raising sword while approaching the wagons. Then wagons at once turned back to the others, by this time our men all returned, the wagons had hurriedly drove up in coral form for defence, mules unhitched & tied to wheels & all arms ready & men drawn up in "battle array" & with the enemy (36 in number) advancing on us all hands expected a fight, they approached one deep & changed in order to two deep when the Captain rode out & they seeing our strength stretched out arms, shook hands cordially (how deceitful). The large body on foot I expected were approaching us on the rear through a ravine behind us.[55] They had Rifles, Arrows, a few swords, scabbards, shields &c &c. Some looked intelligent, majority were large athletic men well clad in Robes, Blankets, Skins & much in the way of ornaments, fantastic & Savage in appearance. Horses generally good but poor, some stolen from Emigrants being large. Our men traded "knickknacks" for Mocassins quite ornamental, admired little glasses much. Gave them tobacco, displayed our arms & got rid of them, & called this the "Buffalo Fight." I felt cool & collected & our men generally. They called themselves Chians.[56] Moved now more in military style, armed. Scenery on highlands good. Before night saw fine scenery, looking round can see undulating panoramic view for miles, in advance are seen the bluffs of the

Platte. On the left bound along several Antelopes. Ahead we see for miles, on our right is a little lake (perhaps dry at times) the ripples appear like silver crested. Over this landscape the beams of the declining sun cast her beams with rare beauty. Camped on barren ground without wood or water. Took raw bacon, hard bread, & divided little water in canteen for supper in cold wind, brot all mules & horses within coral which filled it, twenty wagons in all, on acct of Indians, another small train added to ours. This camp called "Frys Nest" being bad & he advising to camp.

SUNDAY 13 — Left camp at 5 o'clock descended on bottom of Platte or Nebraskie opposite Grand Island, bottom perfectly level & in width from 5 to 6 miles, closed by undulating bluffs of moderate height. Plain stretches out verdant & beautiful beyond description toward the bluffs, two or three antelope graze & bound off when one approaches within 400 to 500 yds, as the sun rises beautifully birds hold a jubilee. Came on Platte unexpectedly — it being a distance on this side of the regular line of timber which seemed to be the river course & which was the limit to the bottom on the right miles ahead, rode up to river 50 yds wide, pretty rapid current & water muddy. River high within two feet of bank which is height of bottom. Camped on river, cooked little breakfast at 9 o'clock with fine brush & "buffalo chips" which make a hot fire. Had little family or mess quarrel about cooking. McCommon wished to cook no more, Fisk being dissatisfied. Boyle fetched sack of "B. chips" & made good breakfast for us hungry fellows & all difficulties again amicably settled by making chief cook assistant, and assistant chief cook. Sod on prairie matted together by ages springs under wheels of wagons. Strange looking hillocks of from 2 to 60 ft high on edge of table land perhaps washed around by freshets, soil sandy, bottom in places black soil. From camp when sun shines the river a certain distance above & below looks like a column of smoke. Are informed by a man of a forward train that the Indians who attempted to attack us yesterday are of the Sioux Nation, 150 in all & are at war with the Pawnees. 4 Pawnees & four Sioux Indians had a fight & Sioux brot a scalp & hand into camp of a forward company with great exultation. The Sioux are bloody fellows & would if they dared attack us yesterday. Stood sentinel from 9 to 10 o'clock, heavens hung with black clouds making it dark as pitch except when the lightening illuminated. Lightening on the prairie is much grander than East, along the horizon it was betimes all illuminated with serpentine streaks piercing the clouds making it blinding to the eyes while taking advantage of it to look all around for Indians. Rained several hours during the night.

MONDAY 14 — Cold & chilly wind unpleasant to handle & hitch mules. Left camp at 6 o'clock. Fort Childs [now Fort Kearny][57] came in sight unexpectedly at 9 o'clock. Houses to us are a novelty & reminds one of civilization. Fort consists of 6 or 8 buildings for officers, dwellings & quarters built of sod, one story high. Some with windows others kind of grated holes. Roof of ground or sod others of brush & grass. On one of former is a garden, vegetables growing as if on "Tera Firma." Several spots of several acres each for cultivation are enclosed with a mud fence 3 to 4 ft high & ditched around. These improvements are nearly all made lately — temporarily lot of timber shingles &c are preparing to build more permanently. A horsepower saw is at work. This Fort or mud town is now a miserable looking place externally. The houses are comfortable, thick walls, warm in winter & cool in summer. Roofs hard to make water proof. Ceiling of muslin, some ground floors & a few board. Captains & commissary officers comfortable & Brevet Captain Walker now in command is as all the officers & men here accommodating & gentlemanly. Had a wheel of a wagon repaired at blacksmith shop. Called at House of a Mormon family[58] in company with Canfield & took supper & a good sized supper it was, seemed strange to eat at a

table. Had Liver, Ham, Coffee, Milk, Molasses, good
light bread, biscuit, pickles & butter &c &c all cleanly &
nice & bought of old lady a large gingerbread for 30 cts
as a rarity on the way. This Mormon family lost their
stock last year on way to "the brethren" at Salt Lake
& stopped here & expect to go on next year, are making
something of emigrants &c, get provisions of the Commissary here. A daughter of this family who attended
at table is well dressed, tidy & lady like & withal pretty.
Our camp a mile from Fort. Wrote letter to Father
which he will perhaps get in a month. Bought Beans &
Corn meal of emigrants overloaded & whisky at $1.50
per gallon at house of Mormon family who get it of
Commissary. Good 100 pr ct higher than at Columbus
retail. Buffalo robes bought of Indians for pint or quart
of whisky or a hdkf sell at $3 and 3.50. Money made
trading here. Fort 300 miles from Independence. Officers have fine lot of Grey hounds. Have fun after wolves.
Where we camp Buffalos without number last winter
shot 8 or 10 [a] day. Colored interpreter for station
raised among the Indians thinks we will hardly see Buffalo because of many emigrants in advance. Gave items
about Indian character. Otoes jealous of their women,
other tribes do not have as many wives as can support.
Soldiers took from Indians who approached us (150 in
number) a boy of Pawnee parents. He is at the Fort.
The Cheyennes killed his parents & sister. Also have
a scalp of Pawnee. This war is to distinguish some one
of the Cheyennes for Chief. Much mischief done in name
of Pawnees. Indians say white men plenty of grass on
prairies this year. Winters here very cold & always windy.
Snow much as 3 ft. Blows so they cant tell when it quits
snowing. Summer nights cool.

TUESDAY 15 — Chilly morning arose as usual at 3½
o'clock. Picketed mules, took breakfast, harnessed & left
camp at 5 o'clock. Travelled all day on level bottom
with Platte on right & bluffs on left hand. Beautiful
bottom from 2 to 5 miles wide. In places ground is white

with salt. Dr Boyle found a human skull by way side of pretty good development & not long dead. Saw two wolves prairie hens & quite a number of antelope. On opposite side of river is a bottom as on this & higher ridge of bluffs. The river above Grand Island from one to two miles wide, a pretty sheet of water & although high — nearly bank full shows no driftwood, some distance above counted at a view 21 Islands some jutting up beautifully & covered with Willows &c, sand bars show also. The water like in the Missouri eddies & boils,— effect of sandy bed washed into hole & hillocks or bars water much like Missouri only not quite so muddy. Dewitt plays fiddle in evening at times & enlivens by it the camp. Camped at 5 o'clock, good grass. In little stream by camp caught little fish — are very abundant. Made a good breakfast. Distance 28 miles.

WEDNESDAY 16 — Cold & rainy day, disagreeable to start & camping worse. Met traders with 4 wagons, ox teams loaded like hay loads with Buffalo robes & furs. Asked $3.50 & $4 for them. Met lot men with horses from Salt Lake traveling 50 miles a day. Give encouraging news from the "Gold Digings." Passed a village of "Prairie Dogs." Stopped for the day at 10 o'clock while rain fell in torrents. Was wet & chilly. Elected general officers, J Walton Capt., Havecroft 1st Lieutenant & Black 2nd. Dr. Hardy Wagon Master. Crossed a slough nearly knee deep to bring in mules. Distance 10 miles.

THURSDAY, 17 — Rainy. Aroused at 3 o'clock started at 4½. Found a skull by the way side. Were again deceived by mistaking a lot of oxen for Buffalos. Rode to Bluffs, got wet, looks like one mile off, it is 2½. Bluffs range along regularly by rolling & washed into ravines in places. River from here looks high above the level of the plain & looks like a streak of silver jetted with Islands. Grass fine along the Platte & wild Peas & Beans abundant grow on low bushes. Garlic in bloom & in places abundant. Nooned at 10 o'clock. Roads muddy.

Rode with Dr. Boyle to bluffs, distance very deceiving on level bottom, 4 or 5 miles to bluff. Here Captain & others tried to surround Antelopes. We saw perhaps 12 Antelopes & 2 Wolves, couldn't get near, ascended bluffs through ravine as far as could ride then dismounted & walked to top. The most desolate scenery amid bluffs I ever beheld, hills still high behind the rather barren bluffs. At the head of a ravine a few little trees, and among grass of ravine wild Peas or Beans in bloom is only relief for eyes, from top a splendid view, bluffs perhaps from 100 to 200 ft high. Bottom of 5 miles wide & any length stretching at foot of bluffs. River jetted with foliaged Islands & bottom & bluffs oposite makes a grand & extended view. Dificulty getting wood to cook. Distance 25 miles.

FRIDAY 18. Aroused at 3½ o'clock. Feel sore, not sleep enough. Cold & windy & gloomy, started at 6 o'clock. Road on acct rains bad. Picked up piece of human skull, saw fine plant growing out very thick leaves of locust shape color of geranium. I call it "Queen of the Prairies." Several other delicate plants very pretty, in places large cactus in abundance grows in ravines, leaves large. Passed a lot of traders from Fort Laramie with 4 or 5 wagon loads robes & furs. Had lost a horse here. Had Buffalo meat of which we bot a small lot, was very sweet & good. They got Buffalo across bluffs which they say are many. Some of our mules lazy. A party of six crossed bluffs for Buffalo, Capt. Walton saw some, McCommon & Price lot of Mountain Antelope — large brown. Fine scenery, dells with grass & variety of evergreen trees. Camped at 5 o'clock, wood, water & grass plenty by going into hollow. Doubled guard & had blustering dark night. Distance 18 miles.

SATURDAY 19. Rainy, laid by until noon. One of Illinois boys shot a wolf at bluffs, quite a curiosity, pretty large and looked ferocious. We lighten by burning boxes &c & packing in sacks. All trains lighten loads, some sell provisions & many sorry for having so much. Bluffs end here abruptly & only rolling hills in place of them. Indian hut here. Stones in occasional banks are white or light gray & brittle. Several large trains look like childrens toy wagons strung on bottoms when looking from bluffs. Distance deceiving on prairies. Camped by a little stream winding beautifully through bottom with good grass & wood. Price & I gathered "Buffalo chips" & had a good supper. Tea, Buffalo meat, bacon fried bread & flitters [fritters] made by stirring flour, water & saleratus. We sit around stove surrounded with chips to dry & while yet cooking eat & although we have two cooks we all have a hand in & many are the jokes cracked at each others expense. High cool wind afternoon. I remonstrated with Capt. against traveling on Sabbath but to no purpose. No Sabbath observed on the plains.

SUNDAY 20. Wind blew incessantly last night & today, it rocked my bed (the wagon) like a cradle & nearly blows one away to-day. At 6½ o'clock left camp & observed several other trains on their march, while the bell tolls our friends in a distant land to the temple of worship. We have here no evidence but inward feelings that this is the first day of the week. Nooned on a ridge where wind blows high as this writing shows. Met Mr Stevens formerly of Columbus. Flowers plenty on prairie, yellow & blue mostly. Lights & shades passes over bluffs beautifully when the sun rises & sets & clouds float. Camped at 4½ o'clock on swail. Antelopes near by. Distance 17 miles.

MONDAY 21. Rainy last night went to bed with pants wet of hunting mules. Had a miserable uneven bed. Aroused at 3 o'clock to watch. Weather cold & windy, overcoat comfortable. Illinois company dissatisfied with regulations give notice they would leave us to which we don't dissent. At noon they drove on & thus parted peacably. Passed a mound & bank of very pure sand near the river several acres in extent. The river is sparsely timbered with cotton wood & willows & in places looks picturesque. Saw lots of Buffalos across the river 2 or 3

miles distant. Have now been camping over a month &
all look hard. Our friends would not know us, some let
their beards grow & others only whiskers. All are indifferent about appearances. I threw out my clothes box
& find it inconvenient to put articles in sacks. Prairie
life has many annoyances. Men often mad & here one
can learn human nature in all its aspects. Camped at 5
o'clock on the Platte, a pleasant night, saw herds of
Buffalo opposite. Lunn & Stiles crossed on foot to
"catch em."

TUESDAY 22. Chilling morning Lunn & Stiles59 out
yet & fear they are lost or in Indians hands. Sent 5 men
to hunt them. All returned by 10 o'clock with a Deer
Denig shot, dispute as to its being Deer or Antelope.
Meat sweet & excellent, boys got no Buffalo but put
balls in several. Two men looked for that were lost from
a company & found again. Very warm afternoon. Boys
shot Badger & Prairie dog. Saw drove of Antelopes,
Deer, Wolves & Buffalo today. Spots white with Potash
or Alkalini. Water here turtles of all kinds. Camped
on Platte, place selected by Price & I. Dug 3 ft & got
good water, can be had along Platte by going 2 to 4 ft
deep. Found white & yellow mica in soil. Water comes
in quicksand. Soil pretty deep on bottom.

WEDNESDAY 23. Windy, cold, rainy, all day, killed a
skunk. Reached upper ford of Platte where Indians annoyed us by begging. Indian girl gave me a bead worked
necklace. Some intelligent, two girls, pretty. Old chief
had certificate of Van Buren. Unloaded, put rope work
over top of beds & load on it, put 6 & 8 mules in wagon,
crossed in rain & chilling wind, bed of river uneven &
quicksand, hired guide paid him in sugar, coffee &c,
wanted "whisky." River high, ¾ mile wide, got all safe
over. Horse of other company sunk in river. 7 lodges
of Indians by five poles crossed at top covered with
Buffalo hide. Smoke of little fire out at top was in
several women making bead work & mockasons, white
husband.60 Camped on bank of river, annoyed by In-

dians, fine Indian rider & horse, spurred him with heels.

THURSDAY 24 — Cold, windy, rainy. Left camp at 7 o'clock. Price & I remained to get our lame mule left on opposite of River. Guide promised to send an Indian for it for pay of quart of brandy. Stood while in rain & then told Indian had returned without mule. Guide said he had sent another & cursed the first one & was no doubt in league with him. Waited until 10 o'clock in lodge with Indians for mule but none came. Indians dripping wet with robe on came in & took breakfast in little pan, nude before us. Missourian promised to bring along mule, left & rode 5 miles in torrent of cold rain without arms among those Sioux Indians whom, and the whites with them, in the mule & other matters we found perfidious. Tried to trade Rings for Lariat & took Silk Hdkf from neck for which he traded but finding torn refused. Laid on Wagons afternoon & chilly cold rain brot discouragement having no wood for fire. Made a soak of hard bread in water & alcohol for supper.

FRIDAY 25 — Thermometer 36 deg. & disagreeably windy. Left camp at 6 o'clock, clear, windy & cold all day, walked most of time in overcoat. Had palpitation of heart. Called this Woolf Camp, Wolves being in sight nearly constantly. A Buffalo with wolves after him came in sight, wolves scampered off & Buffalo crossed trail a few hundred yds before us. Shot at him without effect, beautifully rolling prairie, on elevation looked into ash hollow,[61] quite a desolate scenery as if volcano had heaved the masses of huge rocks & hills & ledges around, let wagons down along steep hills into the hollow a dismal place 3 miles long, one to 300 yds wide walled by high cliffs & irregular, hollow wooded with stunted ash &c. Wild cherry, peas, grapes and goose berries plenty. Camped at bottom of N. fork of Platte 4 to 500 yds wide, high & bold perpindicular bluffs. Surrounded an antelope & nearly hit him with a stone. Held election of officers, was reelected Sec'y. Dissatisfaction in camp, disolution seriously talked of & my troubles great about it.[62] Old grey bearded man going on foot to California from Maine. Report of firing gun on prairie & at bluffs here peculiar.

SATURDAY 26. Fine cool & windy today. Left camp at 6 o'clock road over sandy bottom cuts in 6 to 12 inches deep. Passed over a swail the turf of which rests on quick sand. Passed ravine with banks of drifted sand pure as can be 4 ft thick. Passed castle bluff[63] a beautiful bluff 250 ft high. I & Stone & Boyle crawled to top, a giddy height. View sublime, back high hills & ridges in front extended bottom of ½ to one mile wide. River jetted with Islands, some covered with fine Cedar. View very extensive, Bluffs shelved with white & red rock in places hanging far out & washed into peculiar fantastic shapes. Afternoon ascended hay stack shaped hill on bluffs of cone shape of sand cement washed clean, names cut on top, but defaced, extended & beautiful view of hills, ledges, rocks, bottom, river, Prairie &c. Lizards in abundance, abound further last 100 miles. They are some 4 inches long & an ugly white. Water of Platte sandy & bad & other water alkalini like weak lye. A plant of the species of "old man" [sage] abounds. Roads heavy & sandy, sand banks for miles which in places produce good grass. Wolves howl near camp. Canfield's team "fagged."

SUNDAY 27 — Beautiful cool morning, warm & windy day, sandy heavy road. After leaving camp at 6 o'clock, Walton met Capt. Goodhue one of the "Bohoys" of long hair & chaving, been to Salt Lake & is a "Mountain Man."[64] He had California mules & mustangs, (wild horses) caught them with lariet. Walton bought one for $50. Were brot from Salt Lake in fall, eat no corn & most starved in Missouri. Old "Farnissy" Davis found in only tree for last 40 miles 2 corpses wrapped in Buffalo robes, one of a child & other larger person. Nooned on Platte, "no Sabbath on the plains" is again the word. Capt. took sense of company & a majority for travelling. I always oppose Sabbath breaking. Bluffs on left with many scattered Cedar trees looks picturesque & we at times easily imagine it a town. Cedar wood from Ash Hollow burns well & is light. Distance probably 20 miles. Took circumference of major wheels counted revolutions in an hour & are going 2½ miles an hour. Camped on fine prairie ground with excellent grass. Water like salt, dug 4 ft and got good water.

MONDAY 28 — Enjoyed watch last night, sky clear & stars light moon ½ full shone bright. Ground a little undulating, camp all in good humor (a rare case). Black & other birds, frogs & toads &c keep up lively music. This morning as beautiful as ever golden beams of sun rested on. Went to sand bluffs, a space of some 50 acres of pure sand as ever was drifted in beautiful shapes like snow, some 4 ft high. Road in places sandy but mostly good. Crystal clear & cold stream across road & fine cold spring. Stopped at a lake of 2 or 3 acres large to water. It looked like lye & road in places white. For miles today white & yellow flowers nearly covered the prairie. At 10 o'clock saw Chimney Rock[65] 25 miles off like a speck of cloud in the horizon. At noon stop 8 miles from Court House[66] or Church, its dome & Chimney Rock in sight. Day very clear, an "Italian sky." The moon shone bright in day time. Bluffs on other side of river like huge embankment 100 to 150 ft high are in view for miles making our nooning place a grand panorama. Left camp at noon on foot with Shade[67] & Krumm & Walton, McCommon & Price horseback, for the Church or Court House over rough barren prairies, hills & vallies, found it a very hard walk. It seemed to recede in the distance until I almost despaired reaching it, finally reached it a huge mass of conglomerate or soft sand stone standing out in bold relief lonely & singular looking with an almost perfect dome. Ascended it some 50 ft & had the folly like others to enscribe my name on it with knife on this perishable rock or sand pile. By its side 50 yds off stands a column or tower of same material with deep hard beded ravine separating it from the Church. Good view from the Church. On return rode "Bob," & saw the first Sage Rabit I had seen,68 looked like a young antelope. Fremont describes it. Grass hoppers in great numbers, some rudely leaping against ones face. Musquitos & gnats in swarms tormented me. "Old Man" Sage, Cactus &c in abundance, a large leaved white flower covers the ground in places, also a little yellow & blue flower, after walking & riding some 18 miles to satisfy curiosity got to camp for night little before twilight, tired, hungry & dry. On these extensive plains distance deceiving. Distance 25 miles road good.

TUESDAY 29 — From camp Chimney Rock appeared 4 miles off, drove 5 miles & started for & found it some 4 miles distant, approached it on level plain & Rock surrounded with deep, ravines, going into one my horse fell, jumped off & led him. Some hundreds of yds off are dreary bluffs & hills of great height with clumps of cedar looking at a distance like little dark spots. Chimney Rock stands alone with a base covering several acres, receding all around to a cone 150 ft high on which sits a sandy column of rock 100 ft higher & will soon crumble. I ascended about 150 ft by a winding steep path, many names cut in rock, inscribed mine, fired one of my holster pistols & echoed greatly. Scenery unlimited in extent, west are huge piles or bluffs 4 standing separate & appear like ruins of ancient buildings. One has a dome similar to Capitol in Washington. A variety of flowers at base of rock, returned to nooning place at 11½ o'clock. West of C. Rock looks like ruins of ancient city & fortifications, vast domed castles and turretted fortifications. One like Capitol at Washington, at a distance domes of peculiar regularity. Bluffs here high, rugged & bold, covered with stunted cedars. View beautiful, grass hoppers & gnats in swarms, the latter annoying. Wild onions abundant in white bloom. River jetted with Islands all along, counted 60 at one view, current rapid & regular, water muddy but best found here. Cedar trees stumps & limbs & other rubbish laying on plains in places high,

seemingly washed here by a great flood. Afternoon very
warm ½ hour changed to chilliness with overcoat. Walton & Fisk looked out camp, wind blowed in hurricane
style & rain soon drenched us, put mules out into place
1 foot deep under water, thunder rolled with peculiar
noise around bluffs. Lightening flashed, rain in torrents,
wagons wet inside. Went into wet bed with boots &c on,
slept pretty well as water dripped over me. Watched in
cold rain. Distance 25 miles.

WEDNESDAY 30 — Rainy, cold & muddy, call this
"Camp Disagreeable" — let out mules. To bed slept till
9 o'clock had breakfast out in rain same as supper last
night. In tent with 6 or 8 of our merry with fiddle &
music enjoyed ½ an hour, to bed till 12 o'clock. Clear
in the west all day left camp, raining, at a few miles
distance no rain, looked back & still rain at camp, road
heavy, teams bogging. Camped at 4 o'clock at Scotts
bluffs[69] in valley, bluffs ranging on three sides, splendid
panoramic view, lights & shades of clouds & setting sun
add to beauty of bluffs in places like buildings with chimney, others domes & spires in centre, some small others
large dotted with cedar & pines. Went a mile to a ravine
for water, plenty pure & cedar wood (dry) on plain.
Had flitters, tea, bacon &c for supper. Had 2 men all
night on way to Fort Laramie (44 miles distant).

THURSDAY 31 — Clear cool morning & cool windy day.
Left "Camp Beautiful" at 6 o'clock, ascended a few miles
up the valley between ranges of bluffs on either side.
Passed blacksmith shop[70] even it looks sociable in this
wilderness, from tip of bluff as crossed in a depression,
is most splendid view imaginable. 150 miles distant I
saw distinctly Laramie Peak & could distinguish the snow
on its top & sides, looks like a huge blue mound. In this
view we see rising one above the other into wilderness
distance ranges of bluffs, valleys, hills, &c in every variety
of shape & form. This view the most extensive I ever
beheld. Walter Fisk & George came from B.shop to
"nooning" place met man there who had been robbed of

horse &c by the Crow Indians. Could not bring Laramie
Peak much nearer by spy glass. Warm afternoon,
crossed bad swail & took boatman over with horses.
Camped by ponds of water like lye. Dug for water &
hole caved in, being thick soda — found no water. Took
basin warm water went to ravine & washed thoroughly
& felt well over it (put alcohol in), among swarms of
musquitos with which we are all marked. My ears raw
with their feasting. Difficulty about picketing mules,
complaints against Captain without cause. Men hard to
please, Captain thinks could not be all pleased were the
Good Being to direct affairs. Distance 19 miles.

FRIDAY, JUNE 1ST. The golden beams of the sun kissed
the undulating plains & lighted a clear & beautiful sky.
The heavy drops of dew hung like pearls on the "wild
oats." The day quite warm. Herded the mules ½ mile
from camp, marched over sand banks on our right for
miles, bluffs of pure drifted sand like snow 10 to 30 ft
high. Saw plainly the snow on "Laramie Peak," a bluish
white cloud hangs over it. Other peaks in view today of
blue color not so far off. Antelope, Wolves, Geese, Ducks
&c plenty. "Nooned" on a clear little stream, on bottom,
in places, covered with a beautiful white flower with yellow heart which I will call "The Queen of the Prairies."
Dr Boyle & I crossed over barren prairie full of Prickly
Pear running along on the ground. Also little bulbs and
very fine large round one like a pint cup. Beans & Peas
plenty. Scared up a Sage Rabbit & found a Mare that
had had a colt & was poor, perhaps turned out by some
train. Rugg[71] took her along. Broken country in places
dry, sandy & desolate looking, bluffs in spots. Camped
where wild oats was abundant. Mules prefer it to any
grass, is now shooting has small grain & long head. Cactus
of several varieties in abundance. Distance 22 miles.

SATURDAY 2ND. Cool fine morning. Panther crossed
the trail some 400 yds ahead, got no shot at him. Ate
an orange I have brought from the states, & it was quite
a luxury. Dr Boyle found a Rocky Mountain Sheep horn

16 inches long & 4 to 6 inches through at butt & very heavy. Passed over sandy roads. Descended into valley or ravine washed into desolate looking ridges & rocky high banks with stunted pines & cedars growing as if out of rocks. Very curiously colored stones & pebbles. This place is desolation itself. Came before we expected in sight of Fort Laramie[72] & though not all satisfied as to its being Laramie. We hailed it with joy as a pleasant sight to see a human habitation on right is a Fort being prepared for U.S. troops. Nooned & wrote to Charles & Amos, mail to go out in 10 days, paid 20 cts a letter. Some wagons passed Laramie River close by Fort on ferry. We crossed a mile below at Ford by raising load on wagon. River 200 yds wide, pretty deep & current very rapid. Water clear — stopped & examined the Fort, looks rather hard built of sundried brick or sod. No trade to be made for mules & horses, men answered one gruffly, parties registered the date of passage here on wall in great numbers. I did the same. Were informed that Laramie Peak, one which snow shows so plainly, was 60 miles distant. Lot of emigrants here, one laying on bed, of shot, received two, (one passed through hat) of Men he had outfitted for their services on road, they would not work & after the affray passed on with his team (this is life on the plains). Fort situated pleasantly immediately around, but surrounded at some distance by desolate hills. Saw Indian graves near the Fort. Wagon & blacksmith shop at the Fort. Emigrants had left lots of provisions to lighten loads without receiving anything for them. Wagons left here by parties that packed. Some wagons & provisions destroyed to not let men at Fort have them. Passed some 3 or 4 miles over broken & hilly country & camped, saw parts of wagon &c deserted by wayside. $1.00 for 4 drinks at Fort.

SUNDAY 3. Cold wind but clear day. A Yankee with buck pants following ox train said he was from every place but this & trying to get away from this as fast as possible. Dutchman from Santa Fee had pack with

two ponies having absolved from his comrades swore much
& had plenty of bragadocia, was going through himself.[73]
Passed through broken country & ravines from one to
two feet of sand & pebbles on which the hot sun shone
& the reflection most blinding. Watered at warm springs
gushing out at foot of desolate hills. Water clear as
crystal & nearly milk warm. Spring boils up constantly
eddying quick sand. Descended a wildly romantic &
desolate ravine walled in for a mile or more with rugged
bluffs & hills, thinly wooded with Pine & Cedar some
of which are beautiful, 2 stunted pines grow out of crevice of a large rock. Ascended cobble hill a steep long &
rocky place, & nooned on top — a beautiful panorama
sort of plain of table land surrounded with bluffs & hills
at a distance. Passed part of wagon, trunks, stove &c
left by parties in advance. Sun very hot in afternoon
making the now distant view of the snow on Laramie
Peak seem a phenomena. Passed along of & crossed
Bitter Creek several times. This & dry beds of streams
& ravines present evidence of great floods at times by
large Cedar trees & drift wood. Barren country mostly
in high sandy places growing wild oats, other places wild
flax, mustard & sage of the latter is enough on Bitter
Creek to make tea for the whole universal Yankee Nation.
Passed Porters Rock (a large sand rock surrounded by
verdure) Camped on first grass on B.[itter] Creek, a
meadow looking place where is "cold spring" covering
nearly 1/5 acre land is several feet deep clear as crystal
& cold as ice. Dutchman with pack ponies came up and
on application was allowed to put his plunder on Chadwick's wagon. He to work as other hand & give use of
his ponies to work &c. Two men with a "Spike team"
drove up & camped with us, were in search of a friend
a day ahead.

MONDAY 4 — Clear & cool all day & windy. Road over
desolate broken country & through sandy ravines, nooned
at foot of steep hill. From top is first real mountain scenery on road. Can see quite distance round, a panoramic

view on all sides chains of high mountain ridges at great
distance & immediately around hilly rocky prairie, a few
very large stones, conglomerate &c. Scenery all around
covered thinly with Pines & Cedars. Descended hill of
several miles in places steep, road over steep hills. Sold
one of our wagons & set of harness for $50.00 & put load
on other 9 wagons turned 4 mules out for extras. Camped
on rather barren hill by little stream. Trouble & agitation
about dividing load of wagon sold & the use to be made
of extra mules. Cold wind while I stood guard, heard a
number of wolves howl as if holding concert. DeWitt
& Breyfogle fired at 3 or 4 Indians while on watch who
were at distance approaching the mules.

TUESDAY 5 — Cool & pleasant day. Left camp after
throwing away some 60 lbs load & dividing the load of
wagon sold. Pass camps daily where furniture, goods &c
are thrown away. Lot of Buffalo (9 or 10) came nearly
to train, 2 calves in lot, they run keeping calves in center
& the old bull in the rear at time looking back to the
source of danger as if he was sentinel. The boys chased
some Buffalo, some horses, & killed one of the calves (it
showed fight) was some 6 weeks old, as a choice piece.
Cut off its head & brought to nooning place on Duponte
River,[74] a poor camp where another company had killed
3 buffalos last night of which we took a lot. Two lank
wolves came to within 100 yds of road & lazily trotted
into ravine. Road is hard & good as a Pike, but very hilly.
Very extensive & sublime views on road at places are valleys or ravines hundreds of feet deep occasionally wooded.
Trees look small on acct of depth, peaks on left. Peaks
some miles on our left rear their heads into the clouds.
Clouds float beautifully along the sides, among them is
Laramie Peak the highest & has banks of snow which the
sun shines at times very hot. After nooning went 4 miles,
last mile I rode through a tremenduous thunder storm of
rain & hail, horse went sideways. Peals of thunder reverberated among the high hills as one sharp clap succeeded another. My team (drove by Crist) was halting

at a freshet stream with steep banks 6 inches deep which now in an hour was 4 ft. Road here is red as brick dusty, huge hills in all directions some of black rock & stones piled as if artificial. Distance 18 miles.

WEDNESDAY 6 — Being rainy evening & stopped early yesterday & had Buffalo Veal & two Prairie Hens, there was general good living for the evening. Cain brought me a plate of excellent Pot Pie which luxury reminded me of civilization. The Buffalo Veal & Prairie Fowl was good, the former much like common veal but sweeter (the hump very thick) the latter tender but a little wild taste. Am sorry that Fisk deals out weakened alcohol at times & last night several were corned & oh how funny they were. Roads heavy & over pretty steep hills, Sage scents the air, it has large old stalks. Road & hillsides & ravines quite red, variety of stones but most of iron color & heavy, also a red soft sparkling sand conglomerate. A peak or conical mound 100 ft high very rocky rises from an irregular plain & several smaller nearby appear like a volcanic production. Am rather unwell of palpitation of the heart which is discouraging. Passed a board at the head of a grave inscribed "Child who died July 10/47 aged 1 year 11 mo & 7 days, Oliver W." Mountain ridges on left of road bare of vegitation & smooth ridges of rock even with surface running regularly over such undulation. Crossed Laprele[75] River a fine stream. A thunder shower came up at 4 o'clock, rained & hailed, afterwards a pleasant evening & rainy late. Scenery varied. Passed over high prairie ridges where cold wind blowed. Camped on crystal clear & cold little stream sparsely timbered. After supper veal & rice soup went in company with Crist, Fisk & Price to shoot deer. Saw one, shot at him at too great distance we being stationed at different points, chased him from "pillar to post." He ran & snorted & came within 100 yds of us — stood & looked at Price at a distance & I had not another load for my rifle which was provoking indeed. Rain came as a cloud over the mountains & give up chase. Average distance about 18 miles.

THURSDAY 7 — Called at 3 o'clock & help herding mules in a pasture spot ¼ miles off, dew very heavy as the sun rose in a golden horizon & shone on the distant mountain peaks, the view was romantic & over the hills near by at 2 different places came deer as it were to enjoy the cool morning for cold it was, if not colder. On the cotton trees in the ravine where we had built a fire the birds sing their morning songs. Returned to camp at 5 o'clock, day pleasant & cool. Road very solid & good except several steep hills broken hilly country. Crossed the Box Elder Creek & Fourchibore Creek.[76] Struck the N. fork of the Platte again & hailed it like an old acquaintance. It is some clearer & smaller than below. Nooned on Deer Creek[77] in a fairy like grove of cotton woods, even trees look sociable on this houseless road. Before got on Platte are fields of sage, scenting the air. Saw wild Sun Flower of small size, country rather barren except along streams. These little mountain streams are pure & crystal & cold. Some good times on road & often disagreeable on acct ill humor &c. Take it as it comes is my motto. Feel very well again. Moores on bred mare & Cain on little mule fine cuts for a comic almanac. Can stop mule only by letting it go against a wagon. A mule train of folks with us run off on acct of a dog. Mules will run off if ever so much tired out. Had thunder shower, wind, rain & hail at 2 o'clock, always have to turn wagon or mules back against rain. Curious lone rock on left of road some 20 to 30 ft high as if cement were poured down. Snow on mountains on left. Are told that 300 wagons are within a days march of us, often see parts of wagons & furniture left at camps. Lunn & Krumm shot a Badger while swiming the Platte, saw a lot of antelope opposite. Dr. Boyle bringing it along some one throwed it away which raised his *Irish,* cooking therefore done in general. Dr Boyle went & got badger, partly dissected it. This camp on Platte therefore called Camp Badger. Distance 21 miles.

FRIDAY 8 — As usual here the morning cold, road heavy, crossed 2 sloughs with high steep banks, traveled

along the Platte on left the high mountain ridges were
this morning beautifully enveloped in clouds. Snow in
banks & ridges on mountains constantly in sight. The
ground is literally covered with grass hoppers of peculiar
kind of all colors. Indians make pie of them or sweet
meats. Toads with prickly backs & horns are here too.78
Moores found a geological curiosity, a clam shell of salt
water species petrified into a solid stone. Fine row of
Pines & Cedars on left of road like a hedge or fence. Came
to ferry of N. F. of Platte79 kept by a mormon, charges
$3.00 per wagon, several trails here to cross, also B.smith
shop here. A stone at the head of a grave seemingly
opened by wolves, the inscription pretty defaced. Stream
high, 10 ft deep, 250 yds wide & rapid current. A young
man found a living young Eagle which fell out of a nest
was [with] large black tremenduous claws. A company
from Ohio dissolved — cause, too many Doctors & Lawyers. A majority of companies on road have dissolved.
Had snow here the 30th of May. A fellow from Pennsylvania in camp near *corned* swore & talked awful was
getting a pistol to shoot a man which being snatched
from him was in the act of pouring powder on fire, tu-
mult at blast quelled. 260 wagons ahead of us. Ferried
over 40 wagons today & will probably [be] 50 tomorrow.
Distance 14 miles.

SATURDAY 9. At day break aroused. Swam mules &
horses & Ferried wagons over River by 7½ o'clock. "The
Latter Day Saints" did swear at the ferry, although
clever fellows. One exhibited California gold & says it is
there plentifully. Got Breyfogle mule which had strayed.
Beautiful variety of Blue & Purple, White & Yellow
flowers on north side of Platte, for the last few days see
much of a low stunted kind of thorny green bushes like
cedar, would be pretty for garden. Nooned on river early
to recruit mules. Large trains coming up & crossing the
river about 100 wagons ready to cross. On Platte picked
peas that lay around the bushes on vines in thick clusters
plentifully, are the size of hickory nuts. Barcus cooked

some & eaten with vinegar are palatable. Crossed long
sand hill with heavy road, after leaving Platte[80] passed
over undulations & ascended long hill with curious rocks
on the left that are in general in a row, some round as
bullet others worn by the elements into curious shapes
rise 15 ft high, in one place piled along like a mill dam.
One large rock but a shell is hollow opening at one end
and 3 oblong windows divided by 2 pillars like uprights.
Some of these rocks are rent, one rent I noticed is filled
by rock coursing downwards. In a crevice grows cactus.
Dust blown in road in places white like snow with Alkali.
Here is a very extensive & beautiful view of bluffs, hills,
ravines & mountains rising one above the other until the
view is lost in the vast space the eye discovers on either
hand. The sun very hot & snow plenty in sight, very
cool wind in the evening. By oversight did not fill water
casks at Platte, good water being 3 miles off. We &
animals got extremely dry, found a little hollow in the
ground dug by wolves 3 ft deep, 2 inches water in & one
inch grass hoppers, drank & filled canteen & went to
spring called poisonous (when black sediment stirred up).
Tried to keep mules from it but some drank & we used
it for cooking & drinking — a kind of yielding to necessity. Sherman[81] & Boyle sang Carryer Dove & The
Soldiers Return reminding one forcibly of "Auld Lang
Syne." Distance about 19 miles. Found Shade wrapped
in Blanket on ground, asleep.

SUNDAY 10 — Fine cool morning left camp at 6 o'clock
road hard & smooth but in places hilly. Road & Water
has Alkali or Potash & is dangerous for use. Nooned at
a spring on left of road. Ascended 2 hills of several miles
length, passed willow springs reached prospect hill where
is a splendid view of the surrounding bluffs & high mountain ridges for many miles, back of us & on the right is
for miles a continued scenery of bluffs divided by ravines
looking like watered silk. Some days travel back of us
is in view. In the west rise mountain peaks in grand profusion of which are the Sweet Water ridges some covered

with snow & ice, snow in places looks like a steamboat's
puffed steam. This is a great elevation & very pleasant
view. Crossed an ugly slough. Camped on a fine little
creek. Dewitt played the fiddle, & a few songs were
sung unsuited to the Sabbath day.

MONDAY 11. Had cold watch last night, air very chilly,
roads level all day & very sandy, dry bed of pond white
as snow with seemingly pure saleritus from $1/4$ to 2 inches
thick, sand & water all seem filled with alkali. The water
is in appearance & taste like weak lye. The sand hurts
ones eyes. Passed very rocky ridges of mountains &
through a kind of valley walled in on either side by high
ridges of rock with pines growing out between the crevices snow in sight & air very cool. Reached that great
curiosity, *"Independence Rock"*[82] indeed a curiosity in
its way 600 yds long & 20 yds wide & some 100 ft high
of solid grey granite—primitive rock rising from the level
plain, fine grass & pretty flowers grow at the foot in abundance. Many names inscribed on it of which I saw that
of my friend M. N. Wambaugh[83] of California. Had the
vanity to put my name on it also C. M. Fisk. A couple
was married on the top once in a time. At its base runs
the beautiful Sweet Water. I ascended the rock & had
fine view from top. Wind almost blew a person off. Appears very high from top. After nooning here passed up
the valley to "Devil's Gate"[84] ($5\frac{1}{2}$ miles) & camped.
The Devils Gate is a narrow gorge through a mountain
through which the Sweet Water rushes, the perpindicular
walls on either side 400 ft high. The walls are of immense
& somewhat regularly piled up rocks of granite, length
of gorge some 400 yds. This scenery is grand & almost
overpowering to the mind at first view. Could not pass
through gorge, & passed with much labor over mountain
hard by the precipice. Here are immense rocks in profusion, on top are pools or lakelets with water & saw
cactus near top, Pine & Cedars grow out of crevices of
rocks, to relieve the eye from the scenery of desolation.
Plucked a few flowers here. The sound of a pistol fired

in the gorge sounded almost deafening & reverberated for some moments. Large rocks in stream through gorge. Distance 21 miles.

TUESDAY 12. Left camp in this pleasant vale walled in on three sides by high rocks or mountain ridges of rock at 6 o'clock. Sound of a pistol or rifle echoes along the mountain through the Devil's Gate which is near by camp. Rained when we started, quite chilly, abundance of snow on high mountain ridges on our left some miles off, snowed on one high ridge, stopped on acct of rain after going 3 miles (near the Sweet Water). The mountains have all seem to be solid rock of grey color & pines growing out of crevices. Some of the boys found large clumps of saleratus. A young man of the Howard company[85] drowned in attempting to swim across the North Fork of the Platte on a mules back — had no rain on the road passed this afternoon. Rains have been in streaks. Captain & I rode some 10 miles ahead for camp ground & found a good one on Sweet Water near mountain bluffs with regular domes of rock, to the south are ridges with snow banks which at sunset were curiously illuminated by the rays of the setting sun. Captain & I passed a little stream where sage bushes are 5 to 6 ft high & stem 4 to 5 inches in diameter. Sage answers pretty well for fire — burn very quick & makes hot fire but one gets tired of seeing & smelling it so abundant is it. While Captain & I struck the Sweet Water 6 Indians came over bluffs horseback but returned, this is the Crow country, arms all reloaded for the watch tonight. Cold & damp, wind blowing & the sky looks gloomy with winterish looking clouds, appearing like a day in January in Ohio. A cloud enveloped a high peak on our left beautifully after the rain which stopped at 10 o'clock. Saw a small herd of Buffalo at a distance. Ground white in places with alkali which makes it & the grass on it crusty & in places the grass withers. Distance perhaps 15 miles. Captain shot an English Whistler, large as a pullet with a bill 8 inches long.

WEDNESDAY 13. Aroused to watch at 2 o'clock & I found it windy & cold. The snowy peaks, the rocky bluffs, the lowering sky & wind added to the desolate winterish scene. Had coat, overcoat & pair of blankets on & was chilly. Got out my thermometer & found the temperature 32 degrees, not as cold as I expected. Had two men from an advance train on return for ponie. Stay all night with us. They took meals with us, had cheese, quite a luxury on the plains. Passed mountain ranges of solid rock looking bare & running irregularly in different directions. The road very sandy & heavy, wheels sink in 4 to 10 inches. Large sand banks of purest kind supporting sage in abundance with a prickly or thorny green bush I believe called Greese Wood. Also tall grass sparsely, with various kinds of flowers. One of a mossy kind beautiful. Nooned on road on sandy valley, wolves howled at a distance. Krumm shot a young antelope large as a lamb 4 weeks old. Two men & wife of one with ox team & one Pony came to camp asking permission to travel with us—granted, they left another train on acct of rude fellows. How strange! Our whole camp is quieter, obscene & improper language not heard just because a woman is in camp — seemingly intelligent, the couple not long married. This is the refining influence of woman, without society men almost become desperados, *men care not for men.* This lady is very cheerful & adds much to our camp. His name is Hurd[86] was once worth $75000 inheritance, lost in firm of speculators all but $7000. Bot land in Wisconsin for $3000. Bot Pork for $4000, sold it for $6000 & lost it, creditors for improvement of land pushed, sold land paid debts & balance fitted out with for California. This was fortunes wheel. Left Rattle Snake mountains on our right struck Mormon route again some 10 miles off. After nooning Breyfogle & I in advance ascended a sandy hill from which is a sublime & romantic view for miles before us is stretched out the verdantly undulating valley of the Sweet Water walled in on the right by ridges of bluffs of granite rock. On the left by a high range of mountains, & in the far distant 60 miles off is the range of Wind River mountains raising in giddy heights peak above peak till their snowy whiteness mingles with the hazy clouds & requires close observation to distinguish these romantic snowy heights from the clouds. Through the valley on our right the Sweet Water threads its winding way and as we view the ice clad heights before us the sun pours his heat down on our sandy road with a heat the reflection of which nearly blinds the eye. Filled casks at Sweet Water and camped on a bottom without grass & appearance of much alkali after traveling through bottomless sandy roads 25 miles ½ of which I walked & found myself the worse for wear. Had after going to bed pain on my breast. Tried to herd mules on hills — got very dark gave it up, drove to camp. Commenced raining, were in danger of losing mules, was 10 o'clock before we got to bed. Barcus & others sleeping on ground nearly run over while catching mules.

THURSDAY 14. Aroused to herd mules at 3 o'clock, had a little "passage of words" with Shade. D---(quite common on the plains).[87] Found ice like window glass on Barcus & Chadwicks bed, on the oil cloth where water stood. Temperature 30 deg. The sun rose in golden splendor over the hills came the Antelope. The Wind River mountains covered (save in small spots) with snow banks, glistened in the sun. Started on our winding way, Walton & I started to hunt nooning place. Passed beautiful hilly scenery on which the sun shone in splendor. Mistook a range of rocks at a distance for a train. Saw 10 to 12 Antelope, several Elk gamboling near an isolated rock on our right & 2 mountain goats. Waved a red hdkf at one Antelope & he stopped gazing at it, but had only holster pistols. Prairie squirrels played antics & scampered to their holes without number. They are grey & red (quite fancy) have no ear above the skin and look pert & cuning. Ascending a high hill the peaks of the mountains rise in their white drapery before us in splen-

dor. Peculiar mounds & large hills are numerous here
on the Sweet Water. Stopped & nooned, a cloud having
arisen & a shower of rain fell. Called the company together & divided brandy. The Iron City Rangers[88] camp
here having traveled nearly together for weeks. Roads
good but hilly, camped on fine little bottom on S.[weet]
Water, beautiful flowers here. Breyfogle saw place of
Indian burnt offerings or sacrifices made of wild animals.
Dewitt played the fiddle & some good songs sung. 2
mules sick. Dr. Boyle cured them, had drunk too much
Alkali Water.

FRIDAY 15. Up at 3 o'clock. Left camp at 5, morning
moderate but cold wind, after ascending several steep
hills with very rocky spots. Road good but hilly, are
ascending the South Pass some 30 miles off. Snow banks
& ridges in abundance. Canfield & I "balled" each other
on a snow bank 3 ft deep & gave the Captain some snow
balls. Curious rocky riffles or rows of rocks running
lengthwise over ridges of hills, sticking out bristling
toward the West, one to 2 ft high & on level of ground.
3 pretty lakes of an acre each on a high ridge. The wind
drives little waves on sandy & in plain rocky beach like
a little ocean or lake cross a steep banked crystal clear
branch of S. Water with banks of snow on side 10 ft
deep. Another branch of stream we nooned on with no
grass. Met a Mexican family from St Louis, formerly
from San Antonio, with an old poor grey horse packed
for California, all alone, very dark skinned, left a train
he traveled with. Met at stream a white trader dressed
in fantastic fringed buckskin clothes who had come from
Fort Bridger & a few miles in advance had companions
with mules & horses to sell & trade & had days ago traded
with the Delaware Company.[89] Wind blows hard & clouds
of dust nearly blind one. Ascending the South Pass[90]
the height is too great for one to breathe easily & free.
I feel it considerably today very much. Scenery hilly but
not mountainous except at the "Wind River Mountains"
on our right. Reached the Sweet Water crossed it &

camped on bottom, found several traders with skins, robes, horses & mules trading with Emigrants, they are a sharp set of traders, Mr. [Louis] Vasquez & [James] Bridger[91] are interested in Forts Bridger & Laramie — these men have habits like Indians, long hair, skin clothing, quick perception & active motions. Rather intelligent men. Old man of 3 score been 17 years here they have a peculiar brogue, and remarkable fact is they do not swear. Not all talk Indian language, have 3 or 4 lodges here saw several filthy looking children & squaws. Bacon worth $10.00, offered good Robe for 1 gal whisky. Asked $4 to $5 for Robes got liquor at Mormon Settlement. Had conversation with Mrs. Hurd, is quite sociable intelligent & ladylike. With D.[ayton] Rugg & Canfield visited lodges could make no trade. Cold day.

SATURDAY 16. Herded mules opposite side of River, morning cold & windy. Fisk, Barcus, Breyfogle, & Mc-Colm sick, mostly on acct of altitude or great heights there being want of outward pressure. I feel effects of it mostly on lungs.[92] One can hardly walk & converse at the same time. Hurd traded oxen & wagon for other wagon harness & horses expects to catch up & travel with us. Passed the South Pass at 10½ o'clock a.m. The *back bone* of North America & nooned at the Pacific Spring.[93] I stood or rather stopped my horses on the highest place or culminating point, & gave a farewell to the East & thought of the associations that cluster around the words "sweet home." Here the waters divide from into the Atlantic & Pacific. Altitude 7490 ft got on top curious stones of a volcanic character as monuments. The road is very good & hard ascents & descents rather good to. On either side of road are pretty high ridges on the left we see beautiful patches of groves of cedar & pines the only trees in sight & they appear small. Hurd with his Horse Team came up as we were standing and went with us. I desire his company for the influence of his lady on the conduct of some of our men. She is seemingly affected by the altitude. Passed a number of graves with the last few days, mostly children. Graves along road mostly of 1847 of Mormon Emigrants. Generally a board or stone at the head with either initials or names on. Pacific Springs I hailed as the first water emptying into the Pacific (on our route). Springs are in a quagmire bottom, 2 springs, one pretty large, water boils out of the bottom in several bubbles bearing up sand. The other has one large hole boiling up in centre & is smaller. Lunn & Crist went to one of the garden spots of miniature trees on side of hill for Elk & came up with train some hours after with Elk meat of one large as a mule, meat sweet & good. They went up they said 3 miles & found those little spots forests one of them 20 acres & trees large, distance very deceiving here. Passed many snow banks. Noon pretty warm, springs 1 mile from top. Messrs. Rugg gave to Captain to cut beautifully sugar ornamented Pound Cake (which was well preserved) and kindly insisted "everybody" partake which we all did & it was the best I ever ate. It was baked by Messrs. Ruggs sister Mrs Phelps of Blendon. Little perhaps did she think it would be eaten 2400 miles from home & gratify 30 men as it did. We are now in Oregon Territory. Have been in the Territory of the Snake Indians[94] for some time. Went 8 miles without descending much over good road except one ravine & camped on road side on high land with good grass, grass on upland is preferable to bottom grass, had filled water casks & found plenty good sage fuel. One Sage Tree 6 inches in diameter & 7 or 8 ft high. Wind River mountains in full view rearing their snowy peaks thousands of ft above the plain. Am tired of seeing snow in mid-summer. Dayton Rugg after antelope with red hdkf, stared at him, our folks thought him very near to it had not shot at it. I got out the "Star Spangled banner" & planted it on the South Pass, a breeze waved it, our folks met around it & passed a cheerful evening, fiddling, singing, & dancing on a sheet of zink. Distance 21 miles.

SUNDAY 17. Cool, made Sage fire, herding mules. The

sun rose in splendor over the heights. Would like to enjoy Sabbath privileges today. Passed over fine road, & descend but little. Curious hills & mounds on either side. At junction of the Oregon and California roads[95] quite a Postoffice, news on boards & cards to friends behind. Messages are often left at these News Offices. Took Oregon road reach Little Sandy, a fine stream. "Nooned" filled casks for 35 miles dry road. Passed this morning brakish (salt) little stream not good, Alkali in places along road, many flowers finest mass of several kinds with flowers & a small pear shaped cactus. Altitude has affected us much. Fisk & Breyfogle still sick. Reach unexpectedly the *Big* Sandy[96] 8 miles from the Little one passed yesterday which we thought was the Big Sandy. The bottom of the Big Sandy very uneven and had heavy getting through. Camped on bottom. Road very good. Distance 20 miles.

MONDAY 18. Aroused at 3 o'clock & left camp at 4½ o'clock. On our 35 mile desert[97] without water. Had a little *mess, misunderstanding* as to cooking but all passed off with the occasion. Ascending hill out of bottom Mr Hurd stalled & had trouble with his balky horses. His Lady who is unwell got out & walked up she had my sympathies for her situation. After passing over pretty upland with singular lone rock on right, 50 ft high[98]— we descended on the desert here for some miles perfectly level & barren & appears like the bed of a lake or pond. We again ascend some where Rue, Sage & grass grow in most places — the road excellent except one mirey slough with Alkali. A small shower of rain came & laid the dust in part which blew today in clouds before the rain. Saw a few Cactus plants, Red flower like hollyhock, peculiar pebbles & horn toads. The Captain sick today. Altitude affects us yet, have not descended much yet. Mountains on our right & front covered with snow deep & as clouds shading & the sun lighting the tops alternately it looks romantic. Nooned 18 miles on road. Dr. Boyle & I boiled gruel of corn meal which was good.

Afternoon passed several long & very steep hills considerably stoney, steepest hills were descending, good grass & wild oats in places, ground barren desolate prospects in places, hard days march in place of being 35 is 40 or 45 miles from Big Sandy to Green River. Hailed the River with joy at twilight, saw it from hill several miles distant like a silver thread in the bottom some 200 ft below, silvery cloud specked sunset being a reflection from snow peaks a range of which seems to surround us. Cold dreary, & wind blows very hard. View from high bluffs that wall in the river bottom, a grand & very extensive view of desolate barreness. See road some hundred ft below in bottom which we reach by a long winding descent, the steepest thus far, reached river after dangerous drive in night at 10 o'clock fatigued & cold. Dr Boyle made supper watched mules in cold after a drive of 45 miles over hills without wood or water.

TUESDAY 19. Ferrying the river being the only work for the day. I got up some after the sun which glanced in golden beams over the romantic scenery with a sky clear as any Italian & cold breeze as with us in November. Ice froze on the river where water had no current. Having had anxiety as to the fate of the fatigued mules which were in a small triangular bottom I looked for & was glad to see them still grazing. What added to my anxiety was the known fatigue & therefore unfitness of our men to watch well & here many hundreds of miles from settlements mules are our only safety & hope of deliverance among the things temporal or in our power. Drove down stream (or bottom) some 2 or 3 miles to Ferry99 & waited for other wagons. The bluffs on the river some 200 ft high & washed very curiously in semi-circular shapes on sides (in places) & very symmetrical domes in places on tops. These bluffs approached to from "Cache" or gorge through which the river flows below the Ferry one mile. Bold deep & rapid stream 300 yds wide. A wagon lost on yesterday at this Ferry. $2.00 per wagon, an imposition. Feel well today after fatigues of yesterday. Washed

on bank of river in cold wind in tepid water & feel fine
after it. Mrs Hurd grateful for a copy of "Godeys
Lady Book" I gave her. Kentucky Company came up
with 3 or 4 slaves old darky made cute replies to taunting
questions from some of the boys. Swam stock across &
had wagons all ferried over (by assisting), by twilight.
Found 8 or 10 Wigwams in fine grove of scattered trees
which fringe the bottom of the river with 5 or 6 white
Traders all French & Snake Indians. Old benevolent
looking Chief tried to trade for double barreled gun, got
necklace of his companions. Went to lodge after night
& saw "Indians traps" much in demand from emigrants.
Saw fancy beadworked crooper [crouper] worth $15.00.
Lariets hardly to be had, some cost $20/ The squaws con-
sulted in sale of croopers & lariets. Always sit down around
the fire after entering lodge without ceremony, usually on
Robe or Skins. Squaws generally at work &c dressing
Skins. The men sit & look on open & free countenance
arwquired [acquired] to trade with them they know
something of human nature. The Snakes here are rather
cleanly & dress comfortably in skins — are good looking
Indians. The traders of the Forts all connected, trading
2 lb powder & one box caps for a skin hunting shirt.
Distance 3 miles.

WEDNESDAY 20. Left camp at 4½ o'clock before
breakfast. Men in wigwams to trade. After train was
some miles off Stone & Chadwick returned to look for
2 lost mules. So Price, Chadwick & Stone & myself took
a hearty breakfast with folks of wagons that have touched
with us, (from Missouri) & were also waiting to get a
strayed horse. Rode around in search of mules & until
11 o'clock when we found them & returned to train &
caught up at 2 o'clock. Our boys traded for 3 horses.
The Snakes have fine horses & the traders are doing well
with the emigrants. Saw the prettyest iron gray colt (3
years old) I ever saw price $80 — here as all along &
at St Joseph huge wooden stirrups are in use. Saw Indian
boy shooting Prairie Squirrels &c with great skill with

bow & arrows. Saw in Wigwam Prairie Mice & Squirrels preparing to eat. Traded this morning a little Alcohol, rings, gun caps & trinkets for Buck Pants, 4 skins, Lariet & Whip. Liquor, Ammunition, Blankets (red) heavy boots & shirts, Flour, Corn, Bacon, 12½ cts. coffee, 25 cts & sugar 25 cts are good articles of Trade. Was offered $3.00 for qt Alcohol. Snakes fear being called drunkards. The women cheerful, carry infants on backs against board. For some miles from river after leaving bottom pass over high continued ridges of dreary looking bluffs or barren ridges, then descend to bottom of small stream & follow it for a few miles, then over high ridges when at 4 o'clock we arrived at a beautiful grove of Tamerack trees where we camped for night. This grove has several springs in ravines running down the mountain side. The water falls over cascade beneath the fine trees & is cold. Fine view of grove at a distance. The road generally hilly but hard except a few ravines & chuck holes crossing little streams. Wolves howled much tonight & scared mules had trouble to keep from "stampede." 4 or 5 of our men unwell mostly of altitude felt while walking a strange dizziness of same cause, also affected in lungs. A few miles on bluffs on a high point is the grave of some one (name forgotten) and was buried in 1847. Alkalin in places, saw an abundance of snow in every direction. Distance 22 miles.

THURSDAY 21. The golden beams of the sun kissed the icy ridges on the heights & a clear sky. Price hard to wake up (Chadwick). Left camp at 6½ o'clock, ascended a steep & long hill & descended two very long & steepest hills on route so far. Stony broke. Sand bound & cracked axel tree crossing deep muddy little stream & stopped to noon at 10¼ o'clock & had all repaired to start at usual time. Wood[100] jumped off of falling mule while rising from a slough & even before "hoved" off of a mule, was fun for those present. From top of hill this morning is extensive scenery of highest ridges on every hand & snow in huge banks. From top of other hill see down some 300 ft into a beautiful valley with little stream walled in on either side with beautiful high ranges with snow on tops, the one side throwing shadows of hills over the valley grotesquely. Saw ice here froze last night ¼ inch thick. Roads very hilly but solid in places, stoney & a few bad sloughs. Curious riffles of rough stones or rock along highest ridges. Afternoon passed several bad sloughs & very steep hills. One hill descending steepest thus far. Crossed stream, fork of Green River, through bottom swollen by thawing snows & we had to raise load in wagon bed on ropes, roads generally good otherwise. Snow all along walked over a bank perhaps 10 ft deep. On a peculiar ridge with a perpindicular front walled high & caves in I found lot of oyster shells. On our left passed a mountain ridge with nearly bare rock rising in a ridge like Mahogany work. Fisk[101] talks of not going much further with train seems discouraged & unwell. Distance 24 miles.

FRIDAY 22. Left camp at 6½ o'clock white frost, clear morning, left bottom of stream, fork of Green River & ascended steep hill. Captain, Breyfogle & I rode ahead. Passed a fairy like grove of cotton wood of most delicate foliage, lighted on a snow bank & for fun snow balled each other. Musquitoes in swarms bled us freely, they cover us & the horses closely & are very annoying. Looking through a deep hollow with picturesque hills on either side & beyond—is a sublime & grand scenery, from this high place we see the road traveled a day back & hills with fine groves of Cedars. Pines, Tamerack & Cotton Wood on depressions on this side for a great distance with a clear sky. Nooned at a romantically beautiful grove of several acres of Cotton Wood & finely tapering Tamerack trees, looks quite sociable cool & pleasant with in places small banks of snow, road winds narrowly through this grove, grove set on fire & burned like tar, and from top of hill begins a descent of a mile perhaps 1000 ft winding through a narrow gorge with high hills on either side & here we met in one place a descent of

30 or 40 ft over a rocky precipice. Unhitched & let wagons down with ropes ascended & descended sundry steep hills. Ruggs horse threw him & run off. Chadwick, D. Rugg & Barcus went ahead for him, this evening. Nooned on a little stream on a bottom. I will call Musquito Bottom. Mule of our team "Rough & Ready" taken sick with the Alkali Chokes like several mules did before & was almost instantly restored as were the others by Dr. Breyfogle giving Tartaric Acid. Saw here wild flax in bloom. Distance 20 miles.

SATURDAY 23. Left camp at 6 o'clock, soon struck the beautiful but alkali bottom of Thomas Fork[102] 40 ft wide which like all mountain streams now is swollen on account of snow. Has an almost irresistible current & run 6 inches over the front of our wagon box, held wagon from topling over by holding on with rope on bank & got over safely. Dr Boyle traded pistol shot &c for a pony with an Indian who with several more filthy & that one over here also a droll looking "pocket edition" of an Indian boy some 4 years old dressed in skins like the rest. Nooned on opposite bank where Rugg & others came without horse having slept out & had no breakfast. Rugg saw Indians picking lice from them, are very filthy. Passed up a beautiful & romantic bottom to Smith Fork,[103] 30 ft wide, ford dificult. Again unpacked & put load on top of box. Camped on opposite bank where all around is lovely save the musquitos which are here all day in swarms. Barcus says, "they sing a little & then present their *bill*." Yes, and take pay in the scarlet. Ascending this level green bottom of a mile & less wide on the right is a mountain ridge 500 ft high dotted with groves which look like trees in miniature & banks of rocks pointed & shaped in Gothic forms, on the left is a finely sloping ridge of bluffs. Here as for some days past the best of grass in abundance. Distance 20 miles.

SUNDAY 24. The golden beams of a brilliant sun lighting an Italian sky kissed the distant peaks & threw a charm over this fairy like scenery. Wild flax in bloom.

Ascended the bluffs & soon found ourselves ascending a very long steep hill under a scorching sun from the top of which is a pleasant view of hills, dales & winding streams for many miles & the snowy peaks glisten in the sunlight & heat. After passing over several steep hills struck the bottom of Bear River on the banks of which we nooned. Several Indian lodges here with a few white men. Looked at lot of horses, had one would not give for $500. Other horses cheap, good one for $30. Cows are kept here as also at ferry of Green River (good stock). Smith[104] a Kentuckian who lost a leg — a fat, high strung good liver makes $100 per day now. Dr Boyle sold him my & his company brandy, one quart for $8.00. Made a rapid drive on bottom through scorching sun & at 4 o'clock a storm, rain & hail stopped us. Got wet & having in a few minutes space got quite chilly felt uncomfortable. Camped hard by a small creek in good grass. Wild sun flowers plenty here. Had a feast of trout — large fine ones we traded with Smith for, they are caught in a mountain lake 16 miles distant, are spotted & very good. Distance probably 22 miles.

MONDAY 25. Disagreeable watch last night in wet grass. Left camp at 5 o'clock & made a rapid drive over good roads, met an Irish mountain man[105] of intelligence on his way to Smiths, will go to California in a few weeks —desires again to live in Civilized life. Talked highly of Soda Springs — drank himself full, says it is very healthy. Several Indians passed on horseback as they always travel here — seemed unsociable. Indians all know the word "whiskey" & "howdy dew." Musquitos a pest while I write, have to vail like a monk to keep them off. I feel quite unwell today, head & bones ache. Passed mostly over bottom roads with occasional sloughs. On left of road some distance before reaching Soda Springs is a very large spring of the coldest water some 200 yds from the road on the level ground just before reaching the mountain ridge. Passing some distance between two mountain ridges on the bottom of Bear River we reached

the celebrated "Soda Springs,"106 and camped near by
for the night. There are 4 or 5 of these springs, the first
is near a little creek on the left of the road, two or three
are near by a little natural knoll or mound pretty near
the river being the furtherest west, these spring up in a
large body of water like boiling & sink to all appearances in their own bed or pond. But *the* great curiosity
is the "Steam Boiler Spring"107 hard by the river to the
East of the last named, the river is now on a level with
the outlet (the river being high) this spring boils or
gushes up through a hole 2 ft in diameter & the spring
is 8 or 10 ft in diameter, making the whole boil like a
huge boiling kettle. On the right bank of this spring is
a hole or cave of some 2 ft in size which shows another
curiosity the water boiling up as in the other only more
fiercely. Putting ones head in this hole & breathing the
mist effects one similar to gas. Some of these springs
are impregnated with iron & the water is quite strong of
soda, seems healthy & good to the palate. These springs
are near a grove of Pines & Cedars. Bear River rolls its
rapid current by Rose bushes & the most delicate flowers
surround the spring & on either side of this bottom are
high & rugged ranges of mountains — making quite a
romantic spot. These springs would be worth millions
in the States. Here are Petrifactions and geological curiosities, evidences of Volcanic nature are plenty here. The
ground in many places sounds hollow in passing over it.
Before sunset the brightest fullest & most beautiful Rainbow spanned the heavens that was perhaps ever beheld.
It came down the mountain side to the valley like & give
in connections with the sun a rich brilliant shading to
the sky & mountain peaks & valleys. A shower of rain
came up at dark. Distance probably 22 miles.

TUESDAY 26. Left Soda Springs camp at 5½ o'clock.
Was very sick last night with the Mountain Fever had
pain in bones but especially in small of back. Could
neither sit nor stand. Took a cathartic of Dr. Boyle
(rhubarb) at 2 o'clock which in a few hours partially

relieved the conjestion in the back. Laid sick in wagon all day its jolting made my head pain much. Passed all day over bottom & prairie road with several bad sloughs. Passed peculiar dark knolls ridges & banks of black rocks showing volcanic action on every hand. Nooned on a rising, passed several squads of Indians, Shade traded for a pony (a shot gun). Passed this morning picturesque & bold ridges on our left thinly covered with pines. Pulled wagons through a mirey place with ropes. Camped near deep, still little stream on our left. Grass all along here good, mostly wild oats. Distance 22 miles.

WEDNESDAY 27. Left camp at 5½ o'clock, soon left bottom & ascended a long irregular & in places mirey hill running between & over high ridges & made picturesque by grove of cotton woods which for their variety is enjoyed well on this road. Before ascending hill passed a bad slough or mirey place. The sun beating down scorchingly. I yet unwell (though better this morning) felt heat much & rested several times with horse in groves & saw I. Clegg name on a little tree (June 23). Teams in rather bad condition worried down by hills & mirey road. Nooned in a rather barren place without water, & left camp at 1½ o'clock. The Lexington, Missouri Company[108] passed us, have good mules & many of them. Snow banks near road & sun very hot. Stopped & watered at a very cold spring that gushed out between two rocks on the hillside, being very dry drank freely. Camped at 5½ o'clock on upland, on left a high rugged ridge with a ravine through which runs down in cataracts the pure water of a spring at its head, on our right rises in rugged & bold grandeur a peak or knoll of some 40 or 50 ft high. I will in honor of our Captain call Mount Walton (although he says he is already *mounted* too much). Back of us an Indian lodge an old Indian[109] with two wives & 7 or 8 pocket editions came to camp with black mare he valued at $400 which Dewitt traded a rifle, caps & powder balls for. Several other notions were traded for by our boys (Saddle B. Robe &c) He had been to St

Louis, talks a little English. Eat very hearty but shared with his family, calls himself a Seneca Indian. Distance probably 17 miles.

THURSDAY 28. Fine & clear morning, Indians in camp early, great beggars — Old Indian goes with us to Fort Hall, says it is a trip of one corse of the sun (one days journey) had fun with him in trying to trade for a robe. Near camp passed through a very romantic gorge between high rugged ridges snow 80 ft high & firm near road, can look down 100 to 150 ft perpindicular & see the stream of a spring above rush through a narrow gorge of wildest character. Roads good. Nooned in sight of 3 large moundlike peaks on our right, the largest is very extensive. The view is extensive here. The snowy peaks in the distance on our right shine in the almost scorching sun which is only relieved to us by cool breezes. Indians where we noon look filthy, one old hard specimen the boys say is the man who struck "Billy Patterson." Saw fine Roses, Cactus & Tulips &c in bloom today of various & rich colors. Struck a sandy desert deep & very heavy. The sun scorching hot & no water till we struck a fine cold spring near a little stream two of which we crossed & camped by a very cold, clear, fine spring with a pebbly bottom. Musquitos in swarms, yes myriads, made a purgatory of this otherwise fine place for men & mules. Had lot of Indians to camp with us, seemed good natured. Distance 17 miles.

FRIDAY 29. Left Musquito camp at 6 o'clock. Passed Port Neuf River,110 forded with underbrush by raising load on bows. Crossed several mirey places with dificulty. Reached a fine grove & had first view of Fort Hall,111 a trading post belonging to the Hudson Bay Company, built similar to Fort Laramie but smaller & in better repair. Walls of unburnt brick, it stands at confluence of Port Neuf & Lewis Forks of the Columbia River. Stands on an extensive bottom. Fort looks white at a distance. Found Mr. Hurd & lady here who had left a few days ago to arrange his team better. Found a large lot of horses & fine cattle & calves here. Got milk at 5 cts a pint & the dairymans lady baked biscuit I got 4 for 20 cts were good for change. Sold box soap at 25 cts per lb. Had cheese at 25 cts per lb. Would not take bacon says it dont agree with them wild meat being better. Several white women here. A store of skin clothes, a few fancy & useful articles of goods. Fatty, lazy Indians & half breeds about acct here of dairy, family Mormons from N.Y. State. Traded two fagged mules for 2 working horses, difficult road ahead, they say will take 60 days more to go to Sutters, rather discouraging, "But go it Boots, Gold ahead." There is surely no Royal road to California & traveling it is labor indeed. Are waiting for provisions from Vancouver. Crossed one River & flat country & camped 5 miles west of the Fort on another river. Musquitos kept us from sleeping. I slept but an hour & have given my interest in the Gold mines to get rid of them. Distance 9 miles.

SATURDAY 30. Crossed the river a deep stream some 200 yds wide. Water ran over small mules. Crossed mirey place by drawing over by assistance of ropes & ascended very steep hill (all near to river) by doubling team. Passed all day over rather level fields of sage — an uninviting country. Also crossed several rather mirey places. I feel quite unwell today, laid on the jolting wagon. Nooned on a little fresh water stream where I am very sick for a spell. Sun shone with a scorching heat today. Camped for night near a natural basin where musquitos were as swarming as ever. Distance 18 miles.

SUNDAY JULY 1ST. Stone having broken axel tree our wagon was given him & our loads put on Fisks wagon leaving but one for our mess — this is inconvenient & unpleasant but comfort is not on this road. Being quite unwell laid on wagon again. Passed peculiar ridges of basaltic rocks showing volcanic action. Struck Lewis Fork & the American Falls,[112] a curiosity I missed seeing. Would have looked on it from my feverish bed with interest had I known the fact of us passing it. The boys say it is quite a curiosity & on a rocky arm or ridge into the river stood a lot of Indians looking at it. Here also near by are peculiar petrified Beaver dams. Had a warm day, struck the river (bold wide stream) at a bend where it passes round in rapids, & hills around make rather a romantic scenery. Camped on an Elevated bank of River where the wind blew most of the musquitos off—to our great comfort although quite annoying (in civilized country), roads pretty good but bad sloughs & hills. Distance 20 miles.

MONDAY 2. Had a fine shower of rain this morning giving freshness to the air. All day quite cool & I feel much improved in health. After giving D. Rugg all the plunder of his mess on his wagon & 6 mules & the other wagon used to lighten the balance, we left camp at 11 o'clock. Crossed a rapid little stream with very large rocks in bed & side. Captain announced Hurd had broken his harness so we sent a committee of horsemen (Price, Boyle, Barcus &c) to assist & bring his team up with the train. Passed wild wheat looks just like bearded wheat that is cultivated & is now in bloom. Animals like it much. Passed several bad sloughs which we cross by fastening rope to tongue & lot of men pull. Passed curious petrified rock I got a specimen of. Crossed a romantic mountain stream of curious falls with steep hills as banks. Crossed Raft River[113] & camped near it in a beautiful bottom of fine grass. Passed two graves today. Barcus & Wood tried to fight this morning. Distance 16 mi.

TUESDAY 3. Cool last night had a white icy frost this morning, almost froze my fingers. Passed all day up the valley of Raft River which in places is beautiful. Sage is still crowding everywhere & Greesewood. Passed luscious looking fields of wild wheat high as small mules. Roads generally level with exception of a few steep places & sloughs. Crossed a number of little streams as well as Raft River several times. As usual saw plenty of snow covered ridges today while the sun shone very hot. Washed where we nooned at Raft River & feel better. Camped on a rocky stoney ridge above Raft River. Distance 25 miles.

WEDNESDAY 4. Some of the boys made great noise & fired pistols &c at 3 o'clock in honor of the 4th, all the celebration we can have today, but all are talking how they have spent 4th of July heretofore & wondering what is going on in Columbus. Near our camp were banks of snow & the air fit for overcoat in which I walked an hour this morning with comfort. Raft River hemmed in on either side pretty closely here by high ridges. Left the river & passed through a kind of valley with high grass. Nooned in a very hot sun. I feel rather unwell. Roads pretty good but rough in places. Entered into the mountain ridge that divides the waters into the Pacific & the Great American Basin. We pass into these mountains through a gorge or ravine on either side of which are ridges several hundred ft high, very rocky in the gorge, the rockiest & most dificult road we have passed requiring great care with wagons. Here are rocks jutting out near the road of peculiar shapes from 5 to 100 ft high.[114] Some are hollow — this is a romantic spot, the rock of course is of granite. Passed into a basin of several miles extent & camped for the night. Distance 30 miles.

THURSDAY 5. Left camp at 5 o'clock & passed over a desolate lot of hills that were very steep. The sun very warm & I am weak & unwell. Nooned on bottom near a little stream & passed mostly over bottom & camped on a stream we called Goose Creek. At noon Breyfogle[115] of the Delaware Company came up in train back 4 or 5 miles. This was joy to us. Delaware Company came up after we had camped which was earlier than usual. We all glad to see our Delaware friends, has a rough gold coin[116] of Mormon make worth $10.00 & got in California. Feel quite at home among the Delaware folks. Had good rice soup of Mrs Hurds. Distance 20 miles.

FRIDAY 6. Left camp in company with Delaware friends[117] at 6 o'clock. Had generally rather rough roads especially after leaving the bottom & passing through a rocky gorge with peculiar high rocks on ridges, full of volcanic rock. Had many desolate looking hills covered with sage & greesewood & but little grass. Fisk broke our wagon tongue which we mended to answer at noon. There is for last several days travel evidence of volcanic action frequently, & in places prickly pears bloom which looks splendid. Some are red, some are orange like rich satin as well as other colors. Distance 25 miles, poor camp.

SATURDAY 7. Left the miserable sage bottom after hunting mules for miles around at 6 o'clock & passed through a bottom like a valley — good roads & for want of water drove until 12 o'clock & nooned on bottom in good grass & poor water, find my health improving. Roads for several days past dusty & wind blowed it in ones eyes & face & we look like powdered & find it often uncomfortable. Have been in sight of snowy mountains occasionally for several days. Drove all afternoon through a bottom or valley — these bottoms are like basins. Camped in a beautiful bottom in fine grass & feeling improved in health felt again at home in the mountains. Distance 25 miles.

SUNDAY 8. Waked by Price for picket guard. Left camp at 6 o'clock & passed over bottom until 9 o'clock when we entered into the high hills by ascending through a long ravine the descent of which again brought us into a Vale or basin where we nooned in good grass & a fine bottom with mountains near us in front covered with snow. It has been windy all day & the air quite comfortably cool made so by the snow ahead. Roads very dusty, clouds envelop the train & we all look dusty all over making some look quite ludicrous. The roads have been pretty good. Stopped at a little stream to water & found bunches of white Clover on its banks which here look like much at home. Passed patches of Wild Wheat and barley here looks like cultivated & in places are beautiful flowers among which is one similar to the Tiger flower, a species of Tulip. We are so used to traveling on Sunday that one hardly thinks of it unless reminded of it. I hope to get to a land of Sundays again before long. All seems to go pretty well in our train but we at times have squally times. Men develop their real dispositions on this trip. What were "clever fellows" at home are hard cases here where are but few restraints. The news we have from California by the Delaware boys & other sources is favorable & we begin to think of the future life in the "digins." Camped near a deep spring & mirey bottom opposite the snowy mountain that has been in view for a number of days. An object here at a distance of 10 miles appears but a mile off so clear & pure is the air. Had this evening the most splendid sunset ever beheld. A cloud lay along the horizon & as the sun passed down behind displayed its light through it in all colors of the Rainbow, & soon wavy streaks appeared along the horizon one like burnished gold ridges and peaked like a fine mountain scenery. Another silvery streak with similar openings at intervals in the clouds give an effect to the scenery not easily described. Distance 28 miles.

MONDAY 9. The sun kissed the hilltops which reflected their snowy whiteness on objects below giving a cast of winter & summer in the same scenery. Have a fine windy day, road passed along a bottom which begins to show a deep narrow stream which seems to head at the spring & pond of last nights camp. We call this *Marys or Humbolt River.*[118] Road very good but awful dusty it being several inches deept, blows constantly in our face in perfect clouds. On our right & left are mountains whose snowy sides & tops sparkle in the hot sun. This bottom so much like a meadow in Pennsylvania looks fine. Wild, or White & Red Clover is here. Passed this morning 4 head of dead oxen & nearby a notice on a scrap of paper warning Emigrants not to stop here on acct of a poisonous weed which kills cattle in two hours time. Alkali or Saleratus are plenty here. We are now in the great *American Basin,* crossed a large branch of the river. Camped on a fine meadow like bottom of Humboldt

River in excellent grass. Distance 20 miles.

TUESDAY 10. Having since the Delaware boys travel with us herded our mules our regulations are now for two of each company to herd. One sett to 12½ o'clock & the other until morning. It was my turn last evening — a delightful starlight night & all at 11 o'clock the moon in her 3rd quarter rose in splendor over the mountain ridge. In camp the boys sing "Old Ned," "Old Virginia Shore" & the "Carrier Dove" the latter is beautiful in sentiment. I thought keenly of other days & better — of the unbroken family circle I once enjoyed of a family now separated — of a fond Father — kind sisters & interested brothers at home on the other side of the great mountains. Yes, & many friends & acquaintances of the advantages of well organized & refined society, *all* these I bid farewell to but hope not permanently. Reflections like these soften the asperities of even a heart on the plains where selfishness reigns supreme.

Did my first washing (except socks) last evening and concluded the washerwoman earns all & more than she gets. Left camp at 5½ o'clock. As usual I walked 4 or 5 miles ahead in the start, had fine roads along the bottom of the river which looks meadowlike with mountain ridges on either side, that on the left snow covered. Here the sky appears near one & such a clear & at times beautifully blue canopy is seen no where else. The air is pure, no impurity seems in the atmosphere. It seldom if ever in the summer time rains, wind blows all day & universally from the west, the air is dry. Crossed a strong affluent of the river & passed over the table land or bluff to avoid mire which is in many places here. After going a mile from top of hill looked down into a little vale through which the River winds in a very crooked or serpentine manner, giving a singular appearance to the view. Passed whitened fields or patches of Saleratus. The road is very dusty & on that acct only is it disagreeable. Nooned on this little Vale through which the river winds its deep & rapid channel in graceful bends. Fisk, Crist & I got water, wood, &c & made fine dinner (for the plains) made tea, fried meat, & baked cake we make of flour & corn meal. The boys fished with hook & line but caught nothing. Crossed a ridge of hill again 2 miles & entered into a bottom of the river which we followed & camped on in the evening on a pleasant spot in good grass where we crossed two ridges of hills today the river runs through "Canons" or gorges narrow & emerges again with its rapid current into the bottoms, winding serpentine like all through. Roads good, weather dry, sky fair & clear except the clouds of dust we raise. On table land nothing grows but sage & greasewood. On the bottoms is generally good grass & willow bushes fringe the river. 25 miles.

WEDNESDAY 11. Cool morning had good nights sleep left camp at 6 o'clock. One day on the Humboldt River is an index for all the others, excepting the wind is from the Northeast today. Saw several antelope this morning. Passed currant bushes laden down with abundance of fruit of the usual size which is just beginning to ripen & as it ripens turns yellow, tastes good, the bushes are a little more straight, whiplike, than cultivated currants. Wild flax is in bloom an abundance of it looks quite like civilized flax. Wild wheat looking like tame wheat is in patches of acres. Barley growing in low bushes or bunches. Saw this morning steam rising on opposite side of river and rode up and found it a strong hot spring, it being on the opposite side of the river could not examine it but from the quantity of vaper or steam that rose from it must be boiling very hot, had good bottom road & nooned where the South Fork flowed in, before us is a hill to ascend & can hardly see the "Canon" through which the river passes between the hills. Dayton Rugg sick with the mountain fever. After nooning ascended a long & steep hill winding through ravine & had a yet longer descent. We were until twilight reaching the river bottom & drove on until 9 o'clock when we camped in indifferent grass. The hills were in places several hundred feet high

on either side of the road & of very peculiar shapes —
being as it were thrown about in huge masses looking
yellow & barren covered with a little yellow reddish stone
& sage bushes, a perfect wilderness looking desolate &
forbidding indeed. I rode & walked the curiously winding road alone most of the way & the deathlike stillness
seemed profound. In places high on the hills ridges or
juts of rock rise up as if by volcanic action. Walking
with Bradly of the Delaware Company & reaching a
high hill from which a scene of desolation indeed in the
shape of barren hills lay before us, he remarked aptly
that we had reached the "starving point." On the right
of the road bunch grass showed water, so McCommon,
Wood, Bradly, Barcus, Hinton, Plotner[119] & I set down
& took a drink of the just tolerable water to slake our
almost quenchless thirst caused by marching through the
hot sun & clouds of dust which insinuates itself into a
persons eyes, mouth &c. Clark who travels with our train
broke his wagon tongue coming into camp in the dark
& in crossing a rather difficult steep banked little stream.
Pulled out his wagon with ropes. Were all as well as
our stock much fatigued, dusty, hungry, made supper ate
heartily made beds in the wagon & by its side & went to
bed at 10½ o'clock. Distance 30 miles.

THURSDAY 12. Left camp this beautiful morning at 6
o'clock after having some trouble in getting all the stock
together. Soon ascended another hill & traveled all forenoon through desolate hills & dales & dusty roads.
Nooned at a spring on a small meadow spot among the
hills. The Delaware teams are lagging came to camp
an hour after we stopped. Horses (which they have)
will not do so well. Mules are best & should be from 5
to 8 years old. Fisk, Crist & I made good cakes for dinner. Our mess traded Seabread for 4 lbs Flour. We
being out of flour this was an acceptable trade made
with men who pack. Passed over hills until evening when
we struck the River & camped where there was poor
grass which created much dissatisfaction, some wishing to

cross the next hills. I call it *Camp dissatisfaction.* Barcus, Plotner & I took cut off down ravine, missed it & had to go through sage & rocks & up steep hill. Distance 20 miles.

FRIDAY 13. Left camp at 5 o'clock after hunting an hour for stock without breakfast to stop early or at first grass. Breyfogle's horse drowned by getting foot into lariet & falling into river. Marched over barren desolate sage hills until 9½ o'clock in a scorching sun & awful dusty road & camped in rather poor grass on a small river bottom. I was very much fatigued marching so long in the heat before breakfast. Had rather poor breakfast after stopping which we had to eat in the scorching sun & could find no cool place while we stopped here. My horse stumbled & fell over a bush & I lighted on my feet before him. On account of some horses of the Delaware company fagging we camped at 3½ o'clock on a pleasant bottom in good grass near the river. Distance 15 miles.

SATURDAY 14. Left camp at 5 o'clock Delaware folks left behind[120] expecting to overtake us this evening. They lightened loads, throwing out Dr. Millers medicines & burnt 2 kegs powder. Wood & I went ahead some six miles. The Wolves howled in numbers responding to each other from opposite directions among the hills. The birds add jubilee music among the willows that fringe the river, & the morning was fine & clear. Very warm today. Some of the folks talk excitedly about separating our company & have messes travel as they wish. The very men who so much opposed the "Ash Hollow" movement. Currants are in places abundant, three kinds, *black, red* and *yellow,* the latter sweetest. Nooned at 9½ o'clock in tolerable grass on the bottom which we followed today & have before us a desert of 25 miles to cross, are filling water kegs. I am now clothed in buckskin in real Indian style, coat & pants. Left at 2 o'clock & entered on desert of 12 miles instead of 25, part covered white with Saleratus & balance nothing but sage & greesewood, this desert

bottom or valley is several miles wide the widest we traveled since on South Fork of the Platte. I walked ahead
some miles & could see nothing of the train (a cloud of
dust being the signal of a trains approach). Laid down
by a sage bush to screen in part my head from a scorching
sun — here was a dreary scene, the road or trail several
inches deep with ashy hot dust, occasionally large sage
bushes & greesewood as far as the perfectly level desert
extended, the mountain ridges bare of timber looked
blue & seemed to reflect the almost insufferable heat, the
sky clear & crystal white clouds, volcanic stones on desert.
A profound stillness reigned here & the mind seemed to
be overpowered with the desert scene, when breeze came
up whirlwinds rose at several places. The train came up
had left Rocky Mountain horse behind refusing to go
further. The Delaware Co threw away a wagon & considerable luggage to relieve teams. Was suffocating dry
marching in the hot sun & dust & drank the riley tepid
river water to excess. Camped on the river in tolerable
grass. Hurd having led off & going too slow created dissatisfaction among our drivers & he wishing to lead to
keep his wife out of the dust. Will now leave our train.
Distance 22 miles.

SUNDAY 15. Left camp at 5 o'clock & passed down
the spacious valley of what the boys call *Humbug River,*
with but little grass & that dying off on acct of the dry
weather there being no rain this season here. Hurd stayed
behind seemed like his lady satisfied with us except the
driving (not being allowed to lead constantly). Broke
a wagon the boxes being loose & broken caught & twisted
off the spindle, put load on Waltons wagon, put 6 mules
in & in half an hour bid a good bye look to the broken
wagon left on the road with a little other plunder. This
hot dry road is hard on wagons. Kept the hubs watered.
Mules & horses eat no salt on trip except on first part of
the road. Did not think of this being Sunday until 9
o'clock, what heathens we are getting to be. Looked a
little cloudy & sky gloomy but got clear & warm, yes,

very hot. Nooned on the river in a very hot sun. The soil or ground here is peculiar being as it were scorched & gives under the foot like ash & in places one sinks in a foot & dust had a peculiar disagreeable smell like bars running hot. The river seems to be getting less the water tepid & the stream looks like a canal only rapid current & runs in short curves all along. Had this afternoon a few drops of rain after the reports of distant thunder. Lunn blown off his horse by a gust of whirl wind. Whirl winds are frequent here. Passed over a hot desert of some 12 miles camped near the river in a good patch of grass. Distance 28 miles.

MONDAY 16. Left camp at 5½ o'clock, the sky looked like rain occasionally very hot sun. Passed over a desert of some 6 or 7 miles struck river & nooned in the hottest sun I ever felt (at 12½ o'clock) Slept on the ground for the first time last night & found musquitos troublesome, road good, only very dusty & in places sandy. Many companies or fragments of companies have packed & are daily passing us. They say it is not comfortable as with wagon but more speedy though they average from 28 to 33 miles & we since Fort Hall have made some 26. Passed over a hot desert this afternoon & camped at 7 o'clock in big sage on table land on a mirey bottom of the river where Dr Boyle & I herded stock until 12½ o'clock among musquitos that were very industrious. Laid down in my out door bed & slept well until breakfast which we take at 4½ o'clock. A bed with the sky for a canopy & the room "large as all out doors." The twinkling stars shining on one give a poetical sleep.121 Distance 25 miles.

TUESDAY 17. Left camp at 5 o'clock & passed over alkali bottoms & very sandy upland, making road heavy & dusty to fill eyes, mouth & nostrils. On high bluffs or mountains are black porous stones that have been subjected to volcanic action. Marched today in the heat of a scorching sun & still in ravines near mountain tops not far off are banks of snow. In places the desert is white with Snail Shells. Nooned on the river in indifferent grass until 3 o'clock & started in a scorching sun over heavy roads sandy & dusty to quite a depth — desert country. Have information by packers that Captain Hunters Company[122] of Columbus is within forty miles of us. Packers pass us daily probably ¾th of the Emigrants will pack last part of trip. It was said today that from 1000 to 5000 wagons are on this road. I pity the hindmost trains & have no little trouble about our own & the probabilities ahead. Camped in a pleasant bottom. The river runs very winding in fact every point of the compass it runs to. Slept as I now do under the twinkling stars & not far from camp the Wolves howl generally from opposite directions. Some of the boys have seen several flocks of Antelopes. Lizards are abundant are from 6 to 12 inches long very beautifully colored. Delaware company back. Distance 25 miles.

WEDNESDAY 18. Left camp at 5 o'clock, struck the river & entered soon on the desert of very heavy roads, deep sand & dust being as most roads on this river very tedious & tiresome to walk & is hard on stock—especially horses. Mine has been *alkalied* for some days & is stupid. This dry road is also very hard on wagons, shrinking them. We water our hubs. Took soon after we struck the desert a cut off or river road (afoot) & our train took the main road. I was some miles from the train & could see no cloud of dust showing a train. Thought of Digger Indians[123] who hide in the willows on the river, followed a few wagon tracks through sand, dust & sage & reached the train after 3 miles walk through an intensely hot sun. Walked & rode to the nooning place which we reached at 2½ o'clock on the river & had no water over the desert. Was tired, hungry & dry almost to giving out when I saw the river regained hope & drank perhaps ½ gal of the warm river water. 23 miles to nooning place. Camped on river in bad grass and remained for the night. Passed an ox team from Michigan &c who left St Joseph on the 25th of April. Distance 23 miles.

THURSDAY 19. Left camp at 4½ o'clock & passed down the river over sandy & dusty road & hot sun. Nooned at 9 o'clock on this *hot water riley Humbug River* in poor grass & started on a desert of 16 miles which we reached after going two miles along this river (& on the right in places) are huge sand banks for miles 20 to 30 ft high & the valley wide here is closed in by high bare ridges of mountains. Found as is frequently the case human skull — this one extraordinarily large. Made a soup called *Lobscouse* made of a little rice sliced meat fine dry bread, flour &C. Our march over the desert was very fatiguing — mules of mess No. 1 gave out & teams came up to camp an hour after the rest. Stopped at 6 o'clock for night on river & drove mules 3 miles through river ravine to graze on poor grass into which lot of packers let theirs. Distance 28 miles.

FRIDAY 20. Left camp at 5 o'clock & entered upon barren & desolate road or desert & drove until 2 o'clock when we nooned in rushes & willows without water. Very warm, met a Methodist friend who knew several preachers of my acquaintance formed an acquaintance pleasant though short & am sorry I have forgotten his name. This grassless, desolate, dreary part of the road is tedious & disagreeable & tells on the tempers of men. All are dissatisfied & everything disagreeable. After an hours rest hooked up & went to what is called "the slough" at 3 o'clock where we found a lot of packers & Captain Winters[124] encamped. Captain Russell soon came up with his train, making the ground look all bustle & confusion or as we have it "business like." Drove the mules down the slough some 1½ miles into coarse grass. A fine little spring is on the opposite side of the slough, close to it the water is cold though a little brackish or salt like (much better than river water). Have news by more packers that just came in that Captain Harding of Kentucky had a few miles back shot a man who set fire to the grass after leaving camp & would not allow him to be buried. Found in Captain Winters train two Masonic brethren & was glad to see them as real friends. Captain Russell is lost on this road as regards camping places, water &c, although he has been through here before. An early Mormon train to avoid crossing the river have changed the road considerably. Have contradictory reports as to Captain Hunters company the distance back &c. Many of our company are dissatisfied bad camping places have had bad effects on the equinimity of the minds of men on the plains or in the mountains. Distance 17 miles.

SATURDAY 21. Was called from bed at 3 o'clock to assist in taking my horse from a mire hole into which he had fallen from a bank. Went to the place & found him again on *Terra firma.* Horses are exposed often in various ways. Lot of packers left camp at 1 o'clock close to our bed on the ground & nearly walked & stamped on by the mules who seemed to have but little respect for sleepers at their feet. Capt. Winters left camp last night. The table land on the road side of the slough is pretty high & level the slough 1 mile on the right of road. Left camp at 5½ o'clock & at 8 found on the left of the road among willow bushes quite hid from view excellent grass, turned out mules & filled in two hours, cut of it & took along. Entered on a desert & as approached the Sink125 the ground was encrusted with a parched alkali crust which sparkled & reflected the burning heat too uncomfortably for miles before reaching the Sink is a perfect level entirely bare & shows to be at times all under water, curious horseshoe shaped stones in one place. The Sink is a lot of water with no well defined end, the water standing along in pools & mud on the sides. Mules fagged & teams came in scattering to where Captain Winters was camped by a well which had water like lye & that in the river or Sink is fully as bad entirely unfit for man or beast. Nearly all our mules & horses sick of alkali & no grass at all here only Flagg & Rushes. Stopped & rested mules tying them to wagon wheels & left at 5 o'clock for some stopping place with grass & water. Soon the teams began to fagg the mules being sick & dry & hungry. Breyfogles, Stones & Waltons teams remained on road, unhitched and the prospect gloomy in the extreme, other teams advanced with difficulty, night approaching & the flat bare & inhospitable desert lay a wide expanse before us. As the sun gave her farewell glances on the gloomy scene (the most gloomy that ever set on us) I was attacked with palpitation of the heart & faintness & was only restored by taking of Dr. Zivils medicine I carried a little phial of. As night came on the words & cracks of whips urging on the fagged mules was heard often & the pitiful noise of the poor mules was frequent & still nothing but the bare desert & desolate mountain ranges with their dim & rugged outlines was to be seen. But to our joy after going a while a light was seen at a great distance ahead to which the road led & ½ mile on this side were told to our joy (by packers) that we were at the Sulphur Wells to which we hurried ourselves & dry mules & all drank gratefully although the strong sulphur taste was unpleasant — the water is much like that of the Delaware Spring the wells (3 of them) only from 2 to 3 ft to the water & the water is now used nearly as fast as it springs by the many camping emigrants & their animals. Four wagons came through together & the other three came in late in the night. Dr Boyle & Raney[126] who went in advance two days ago to overtake a lost mule (which Lunn found packed at the slough yesterday & the packers first said it was theirs) gives gloomy news as to the deserts ahead & the suffering on them, obtained from an acquaintance of his who has just returned to inform & assist his train through. Went to bed without supper, a Buffalo robe & pair of blankets is my bed & the room is bound by the horizon & covered by the canopy. Distance 25 miles.

SUNDAY 22. Our train laying by today to recruit (I & most of us) laid until the golden luminary cast her beams into our faces. Got up, felt rested, assisted Fisk in cooking breakfast (made slob-scouse) & coffee, the latter tasted sulphury. Had to cut roots of greesewood out to burn, there being nothing else, that burns poorly when all green. Made shade with wagon cover & spent the day comfortably there being a pleasant breeze but scorching sun. Dr Boyles friend, Wm. H. McFarland[127] of Pickway, Ohio, who had gone ahead of his train informs us that the desert[128] ahead is covered along the road with dead mules & oxen & men whose teams give out are too dry to ask for water & the suffering great. He has left the following notice here Viz:—

"I have been through the Mormon Cut-off & find it 45 miles 12 miles from here is Salt Creek—some grass —water salt—the first 30 miles of the road generally good —some sand—the last 15 miles very heavy sand. By all means travel the last part of this road in the night or early in the morning. Be sure to supply yourselves with plenty of water & as much grass as you can take for your animals. When through you strike Carson River— grass good. July 22/49. N.B. Please leave this for the benefit of emigrants."

The following notice was left by J. A. Gooding: "To James Gooding & Co. H. Howley & others.[129] The travel is now all by the Cut Off to Carson River—45 miles, last 12 miles very heavy sand. No good water after leaving Sulphur Wells to this River. Salt water & a little grass in 10 miles. Take all the water You can from this place, also plenty of feed—grass—rushes &c. Expect to find the *worst desert* you ever saw & then find it was worse than you expected. Take water, *be sure to take enough.* Drive as much in the night as possible — when safe over good feed & water. Drive clear through without leaving your wagons if you can. N.B. Be very watchful of your animals as the Indians are troublesome. Please let this remain."

These messages are of great moment when left behind. Captain Winters having a *roadometer* on his wagon informs me that it is 1720 miles from St. Joseph to the slough, our camp night before last. (by way of Salt

Lake).

The Iron City Rangers came in today & lots of packers who seem numerous as locusts in Egypt. We have kept up with several pack trains for 4 or 5 days past. The I.C. Rangers or rather Russells train to which some of these then belonged lost two men by drowning in Green River & one by mountain fever. Packers say that many emigrants have turned back & that some 400 wagons (ox teams generally) are on this river nearly in one train. There will be immense suffering here through the deserts for want of grass & water & the great heat. Some oxen lay down on the deserts & the teams can go no further. Went to my world large & twinkling canopy bed room amid the noise & confusion common in an army or numerous camp.

MONDAY 23. Compared with the heat of day nights are quite cool, got chilly before break of day under a pair of blankets. The hour to leave for the desert being set at 2 o'clock the whole forenoon was busily spent in preparing for it which all did with a hearty good will though with fear & trembling. We cooked a camp bucket full of thick Lobscouse & fried corn bread & emptying the tea cannister of its contents filled it with coffee. Everything that would hold it was filled with water, Viz:— Canteens, kegs, gum boots, gum sacks, life preservers, coffee pots, buckets (with cover tacked over), & on our wagon Fisk put in boat or sack shape Chadwicks rubber blanket & put in 5 buckets of water. Some trains sent ahead men to dig more wells which being done they guarded to have the benefit of them. Mules & cattle by hundreds, during the day came up & could hardly be kept from walking right into the wells (from 4 to 5 ft deep) & drank bucket after bucket without number. Men who just came in wearied & fatigued & almost suffocating came with peculiar eagerness to these golden treasures & it often did no good to hold out to them the first cup —the more used the better one likes this water, too much can hardly be used of it. Our Delaware[130] friends came

in with fatigued stock at 10 o'clock & even glad to meet
this lot of "good fellows" (generally). Hurd & lady
also came up his team much fagged & wife sick, his or
hers is a dreadful situation. I fear she will perish on the
road though seemingly not despairing yet. He is an imprudent driver. Clark & Webster formerly with our train
also came up & have packed (Clark sick). Took their
load in Breyfogles wagon for use of their mules. The
sun shines with great ferocity today. Grass here is crispy
with salt mules drink much water. The bare white desert
to the East & higher, sandy greesewood covered banks
around us walled by high desolate & perfectly barren
ridges makes up a scenery forbidding in its aspects. Hardly a bird or living thing is to be seen for the last hundred
miles except lizards, horn toads &c. Left camp at 2 o'clock
this afternoon & in 10 miles reached a slough like stream
called Salt Creek[131] that grass around which (precious
little there is) is crispy & the ground in places white with
salt. The usual desert appearance thus far for a few
miles as the golden banners of the setting sun penciled
the mountain peaks & twilight lowered her soft shadows
over the valley we entered upon a flat & perfectly bare
desert of 4 or 5 miles width by the road & in length run
down 12 or 15 to the mountain base on the south. On
the right at the distance of a mile it was bounded by sand-
banks. This is level as a lake & appears at certain seasons
to be under water & its lake like appearance is peculiar
when casting the eye over its extended bosom. The horse
John Bull we traded for at Fort Hall gave out on the
flat could walk no further — food for wolves one of which
trailed lazily from a dead ox — I took him by the wayside & shot him. Mules begin to fag, passed a very sandy
road for a few miles. While nearly over the above flat
found the hands (Cain & Rany) which we & other trains
sent to dig for water, they dug some 10 ft when they
reached a certain depth the water rushed in rapidly but
was too salt to use. Met lot of folk waiting for their
train. Found in a few miles another well with salt water.

Took supper, laid me on a bare sand bank & rested & dozed a little. Passed a wagon, men asked for candle to pack — being unable to go further with wagon. Had a sick man who when they put him on a horse groaned & who could but feel for him. Passed some 20 carcasses of mules & oxen, the stench of which was very disagreeable & bones scattered pretty thickly, some of these animal were killed by Diggers (Indians). Stopped near the commencement of the deep sandy part of the desert at break of day — fed balance of grass & rushes or flagg, took breakfast of warming pint of coffee & soaking bread in it. Have almost given out from fatigue of journey being almost disabled by a pain across lower region of breast which interferes with breathing, but eased it by tying hdkf. tight around the waist as a support or stay, felt disagreeable this morning as did all of us. Have much trouble to get all teams to this point, many mules fagging requiring changes. I walked some miles to urge along with my cane the leaders of Shades team. The train betimes miles apart & men required to push wagons through heavy places. Started again on road & soon got into sand banks & continual deep sandy roads one team after another bogged down. All hands pushing at wheels & pulling at ropes could not bring them further & 3 teams stopped 10 miles from destination (Carson River) came two miles further & another wagon turned out. Came a mile further & two now turned out. Ours the last so Dr Boyle & I remained with ours to guard[132]— guard left with each & the other mules taken to river to recruit. Barcus & Bryden team by manual labor forced ahead. Had 11 head of stock for our wagon & charged on, they fagged but could not go through. My horse "Bob" in team all through & stood it well. Having provisions & water here & bedding (the latter warm) we at home with the wagon, but have constant & urgent call for water & some provisions from men almost famishing. Our Delaware friends also in a bad way, got teams only to sand banks & other trains all along shore like ours, horses worn

out, their men & horses passing by scattered & like us
fatigued & have gloomy times. Give number of hungry
bread & thirsty water today. Hardly a train has got
through without first recruiting stock. As we came along
wagons & packs were strewn in great numbers standing
½ way up to hubbs in hot sand. Mules & horses pass
here with lank forms & glassy eyes topping greese wood
& eagerly smelling every bucket for water. 10 or 12 Snake
Indians from California passed our wagon & were quite
friendly, shook hands, knew Capt. Sutter said "heap more
there," much Spaniards, Americans & provisions. Had a
letter from citizens of California. One Digger naked
except for britch [breech] cloth. This evening teams
coming back from river for wagons some of which require
much urging to get along. The Dr. & I eat, sleep &
watch alternately tonight, Indians being bad here & our
force very small.

WEDNESDAY 25. Arose after the sun was up & glanced
into the muzzle of the two holster pistols by my side,
disturbed by trains passing & remarks about road. Cool
toward morning but very hot all day. Harris of Delaware folks came with water for his folks were glad to see
a familiar face. They lost 6 or 7 horses & must recruit
others a few days to take them through this sand, will
take only one wagon. At 12 o'clock last night Hurds
familiar voice urging on his fagged team that could
scarcely go further, exchanged a few words & he left for
the river but Harris tells me did not reach it but left his
wife alone with wagon & took horses to river to recruit,
his wife walked all last night. Said last night his wife
was regaining health. Am told she rode one of the Delaware Co. horses part of the desert & walked part until
Delaware Co. stopped. Trains, single wagons, packed
mules &c almost constantly passing, all requiring urging
on which also is the case today & men offer any amount
of money for drink of water. Poor suffocating horses,
mules, oxen not knowing where to go come to wagon &
put their heads in shade & cannot be driven off. Poor

animals. Man of an Illinois Co. passing by remarked he had found a linen towel on the Platte marked Columbus Ohio, which I lost — told him I valued it as a relic of my mother's handiwork & he promised to return it when his wagon came up. Found it a dull gloomy place to stay with wagon on this God forsaken desert with a little tepid, yes warm water. I have thought of home, friends & better or pleasanter days. The Dr. read Shakespeare nearly all day. I read Fremont's acct of California &C and sewed on buttons, mended suspenders & overhauled all my things. A man who packed from St Joseph says 3600 wagons had passed Fort Childs when he passed there & others still back. Also number of packers. He says in his company nearly every man had been sick & one died of Cholera after an attack of a few hours — thinks packing is unhealthy & disagreeable—says Cholera was bad in St Louis, St Joseph, &c when he left (left I believe 20th May). Says a number of emigrants died in early part of the trip of Cholera & numbers turned back discouraged. Webster (Webster & Clark) had his pack which he left by the side of the road when his mule gave out, rifled of all clothes, money &c & Webster has no clothes but the suit on him. Were about to make coffee of our little stock of water when our folks came a little before sunset for our wagon. Strong coffee quenches thirst best of anything (as men know who travel here). Passed over balance of heavy road without difficulty. Passed wagons, dead horses, mules & oxen by wayside, & up the river 3 miles where we camped under large & beautiful Cotton Wood trees at 11 o'clock.[133] Not having seen a tree for last 700 miles or since left Fort Hall, the sight of this wooded stream was an object of perfect delight. After desert life a tree is an object of *Social* interest & these scattered & beautiful trees do appear so cheerful & homelike. Carson River is a fine deep meandering stream 30 yds wide fringed with willow bushes & large Cotton Wood trees against one of which I laid my head & went to sleep satisfied although as our teams came in during the night we were in danger of being trampled on by mules turned loose. Drove mules across river into pretty good pasture on a bend of the river. Distance 9 miles.

THURSDAY 26. Got up late after a refreshing sleep. Wolves howled & barked much. Bradly out to scare them off & found Chadwick making breakfast for mess 2 & 5. Had slap jacks, meat & good coffee & he did the "honors" of the table agreeably & being hungry enjoyed breakfast. The sparsely timbered stream with clumps of willow bushes looks refreshing & forms a beautiful scenery. The Digger Indians are bad here—have shot mules & oxen. They are in the lowest state of human existence & shoot from the bushes in which they can easily secrete themselves. Two men in shade with only drawers, watching wagon, one played the fiddle & other kept time. Oh, "Life on the Ocean Wave." Dissatisfaction in our company & none who knows by experience can feel the misery of such a state of things. Left camp at 3 o'clock & went up the river 3 miles to a bottom of excellent grass, road heavy with sand. Over the desert are clumps of greese-wood bushes from two to ten feet high, seemingly washed or blown away, other places are sand banks as also along this river 20 to 30 ft deep. An ox of some train grazing with our mules drove into camp had during the day 5 or 6 arrows shot into him, one pulled out of his eye measured some 5 inches, poor animal is thus unfitted for use & not killed. Noticed an arrow pointed with a flint stone. Some boys met several Diggers in bushes pointing arrows at them & being without arms retreated & after going for them could not find the rascals, these Indians are in the lowest human condition most of them quite nude & others wearing britch clouts. Eat man or beast in short are real arabs & as I watched stock tonight among bushes could not help but think of the advantages they had over us. Had a company supper of Mess 5 & 2 & others of our company & several of the Delaware boys, some 20 in all. George did up the honors of the table quite satisfactorily in his peculiar way. Had soup of *Rice, bread flour & Sage Rabbit, Slap Jack Cakes, Coffee* &c. &c which were all good & much enjoyed by the company. Distance 3 miles.

FRIDAY 27. Weather warm but pleasant breeze which is common here. Lay in camp today to recruit mules which is dull & calculated to give one the blues if so inclined. Continued dissatisfaction among our men & the company will probably break in a row. Oh! frail man. Wickedness is complete here, law & common obligations are obsolete. Delaware folks with us have not yet their wagons in camp & must sacrifice much. Price appointed to go ahead tomorrow & look out quarters &c for us in the "Digins." A fine yellow flower[134] in bloom here which unlike flowers on the road generally, is closed by the first rays of the sun. Wild Sun Flower abundant here, they are smaller than cultivated ones. Here as at the camp, below us on this River we have the luxury of fine cotton wood shade trees. The breeze rustling the leaves is to us who have seen no trees for a month quite a charm, but no feathered songsters makes these trees & clumps of willows vocal with their notes. With the exception of a few doves which four of our boys saw I have not seen a bird for some days travel in fact but few birds are found in this God forsaken part of the world.

SATURDAY 28. Having taken my bedding (robe, blanket & coat) to spot for bed & left it awhile (last night) when I returned could find nothing of it & laid down on wagon cover spread with such a charity blanket over me & found this morning my bedding after much search & some contention among other beds. Waked in the night by the yelping of a lot of wolves near camp & after wishing them bad luck turned to sleep again & waked in the blaze of the morning sun. Ours is not only a large but pleasant bed chamber — perfectly dry & cool enough — have no dews here — the air dry & bracing & breezes at night. Price, Barcus of our Co. & Haines of Delaware Co. left last night horseback as advance guard to the

"Diggins" & Stiles left afoot. 7 or 8 Delaware boys started with an Ox train, (Capt. Eichelbergers) their horses being in bad condition will only take one wagon from here & a cart which they will make of another wagon. Left camp & the Delaware boys at 4½ o'clock P.M. for a desert of 20 miles. Find our mules have recruited much. Struck the river 5 miles above & then again in 15 miles, road in places heavy sand, but mostly very stony & dusty. Scenery barren & desolate, alternate banks & ridges of sand & black lava or volcanic rock. The low mountain ridges running in curious disorder indicate that we are ascending the foot of the Sierra Nevada mountains. Having grass with us stopped from 10 to 11½ o'clock to rest & feed mules & ourselves too. Our stopping place was on the dry bed or bottom of a lake of some 20 acres — level as water, hard so that wagon going over made but little impression — being a cement of sand dried hard as the water evaporated at certain seasons & leaving a delicate coating of alkali on top, it looking white & shone in the light of the moon like spotless snow & in contrast with the ridge or circle of hills surrounding this basin with soft outlines, looked beautiful in contrast. Got our supper prepared for the night trip & partook of the simple meal sitting on this clean table in the clear light of the moon, the stars begemmed the canopy a scenery below & above that fairies might enjoy. Some of the boys said this was the best tavern on the road as the floor was scrubbed clean. Took a rest or doze of an hour & we left. A very chilly wind blew up, rather uncomfortable. Struck the river[135] before day & being dark on a/c of the setting of the moon stopped till day light & moved to a pleasant grove near by in a bend of the river. Distance 20 miles.

SUNDAY 29. Was refreshed after the fatigues of a nights march by a goodly quantity of coffee &c. Laid me down to sleep but was called on to watch mules 3 hours, took my journal along & under a beautiful shade of the delicate foliage of these trees with a cool breeze made the notes for yesterday & today. Seclusion here where shade is acceptable, is sweet to relieve one from the contentions of camp. This is the Holy Sabbath day but with us the Sabbath is no Sabbath. Oft on this day do I think of the sound of church bells & my friends going congregating there. I say my friends & yet have no assurance but death may have snatched forever from view & enjoyment the dearest of them. None but he who is the great *I am* knows whether we shall meet again. Was informed by a packer via Salt Lake that the mail contractor on that road who left St Jo. on the 25th says that there cannot be less than 6000 wagons on the road to California. A great number of families — women & children, suffering will be great if this be correct. Not a spear of grass will the last half of trains get. Some might take Oregon road, dispose of stock there & go to San Francisco by water. Although grass is good on Carson River it will soon be all — the bottom places are small. At the head of the Humboldt River stock should be recruited to gain strength for the deserts at & beyond the Sink. Every day now makes our men more fidgety about the prospects ahead. This is the 91st day of the trip from St. Jo. ¼ of a year & most of us are anxious for a more permanent location or life—if possible. To me the time has withal the fatigue & vexation passed off pretty rapidly. Left camp at 3½ o'clock p.m. Had much running to do after my horse who would not be caught which was provoking in the extreme. The sun shining with a scorching effect & the road heavy & sandy to walk. Passed over a desert of 22 miles when we struck the river again at 1½ o'clock in the night after the most tedious stretch we have made except the 41 mile desert. I walked all the way & would rather walk 40 miles solid road. Walked ahead several miles at a time & laid down on sand to rest. Diggers might have scalped me. Passed over the baked bottom of any dry basin like last night which looked like a small oblong patch but after walking an hour on it & still quite a distance to make on it I con-

cluded it must be 4 miles across — a bed hard & level on
a floor as white as snow. The barren & now more elevated
ridges of mountains on either hand of the road & running
in various directions show that we are on the Sierra Nevada mountains. The air from the west is quite chilly
tonight, but an occasional breeze from the South is warm
& pleasant. Through the planes & mountains cool & warm
breezes might be felt alternately passing over one nearly
at the same time, when I reached camp being very dry
(not having water all the way) drank much from river.
Was much fatigued & hungry but after attending to
team &c rolled up in a blanket & went to sleep. Was
almost over joyed to see the line of trees indicating the
river course & soon found Rugg & DeWitt who had been
sent ahead to look out a camping ground. Distance 22
miles.

MONDAY 30. Arose late this morning a hot sun was
already promising her heat with fervency. I looked to
the West — saw plainly a ridge of the Sierra covered with
a quantity of snow which showed in strong contrast with
the scorching heat of the valleys. Two wagons of Lexington, Mo. packing here. Changed our racked wagon
for one of theirs. Have seen of the best wagons & furniture cut up for fuel & left by the road side. If only some
poor in the states had these things. Was in Capt. Eichel-
burg's camp just above here with whom part of the Delaware Co. are going. The Capt. is a good fellow. His ox
teams (5 yoke per wagon) travel well. Some cows in
the team look well & stand it better than oxen which I
find is the case generally. Left camp at 3½ o'clock (our
wagon excepted), our team having one mule strayed.
Our mess remained until after 6 o'clock. McCommon
went out and found it 2 miles below among the willows.
Went up the river 8 miles at twilight passed a glorious
scenery on the river. The level bottom of some miles width
with mountain ridges of rugged outline 100 to 1200 ft
high rising on either side, the river winding its meandering way through the bottom with the most beautiful trees

along its banks. The clear sky — pure atmosphere — still evening & shining moon added to the picture. Following this bottom reached the camp of the other wagons at 9 o'clock. Made a supper & laid down in the "star spangled" out door room, the milky way girthing the camp in milky whiteness.

TUESDAY 31. The wind coming from the snowy ridges in view chilled me toward morning — the air is quite cool this morning. Left camp (good grass) at 6 o'clock & soon crossed a ragged spur of the mountain runing up to the river. From this hill is a splendid scenery — being near the head of the valley of Carson River issuing through a canon or gorge between the mountains. The valley stretched out from this view for many miles a beautiful greensward with the river winding gracefully through it sparking in its rapid current & banks fringed with the most beautiful trees.136 The high & rugged mountains show a curious contrast in this view. The road today has been extremely rocky & stony & uneven. Broke Canfields wagon in part. Passed a broken wagon on this road. After ascending a little hill with a deep ashy dust of snowy whiteness we passed through sparsely studded grove of Pines & Cedars of various kinds, a few miles in length. Here are the Cedars common in the states beautifully tapering to a point. A kind new to me bears berrys large as hazel nuts & is a fine ornamental tree some 20 ft in diameter on ground, rounding like a haystack (wider than high) the limbs extend out regularly resting on the ground. A species of pine new to me is beautiful — small trees spread considerably of a pea green & leaves or twigs of curious prickly formation. The mountains are covered with a black rock of volcanic character with considerable quartz *opaque* & partially crystalized. Struck the river again above the canon in a fine & picturesque bottom with good grass surrounded with high mountains — the highest on the right covered with Cedars & Pines on sides & snow on top which seems to be perpetual. The old road passing by the canon way is very bad compared with the cut off we came today. Passed (afternoon) through a fine meadow like valley137 after passing a spur of mountain on either side with very large rocks. On our right soon after leaving camp was the (at present insignificant) lake called "Reed [Red] Lake."138 Following this picturesque valley until twilight we camped for the night near the foot of the main chain of the Sierra mountains crossed during afternoon. Several little rills of crystal purity with clear white sand & pebbles in the bottom, cold water one of which had hundreds of little fish some very tiny — appearing to be nursery of some larger stream. The scenery of this valley walled in by the highest ridges of mountains is highly picturesque.

AUGUST 1 WEDNESDAY. Arose early—refreshed by a good nights rest under as clear starry & moonlit a canopy as shines around. Got breakfast in a hurry & left camp at 5 o'clock. I will call this "Camp Beautiful." Starting out as the sun rose in gorgeous splendor casting her beams over valley & peaks I viewed the scene and was properly delighted & felt myself fully repaid for all the vexations & sacrifices made for & during this trip. From camp the road leads near the foot of the main chain of the Sierra which rises abruptly from 2000 to 3000 ft. The outlines or top is gently irregular in places beautiful peaks rise seemingly to a sharp point some of which are covered with banks of snow. The most beautiful tapering pine trees cover this ridge in most places nearly of uniform size & regular distance apart, forming fairy like groves at the foot. The slope is covered in places with finely jutting rocks of grey granite color. The mountains look light colored is perfectly clean & without dead trees at all. The slope or ascent is occasionally varied by ravines. The bottom or valley is from 6 to 8 miles wide. The ridges on the opposite side rise less abruptly one ridge above the other until lost to view in the blue distance. The valley is level & ornamented with the willow fringed little streams winding their way to Carson River which is marked by the bolder cotton wood studding its banks along its whole length. Grass of various kinds common in Ohio is abundant here. Clover in places grows thickly as it can stand. Timothy with its familiar looking head is also part of the spontaneous grass of this lovely valley. The scythe could be employed here in this meadowlike valley with profit if located in the states. The soil is evidently rich. Nearly every variety of grasses are on it & plants of kinds new & unknown to me in great variety. Sun flowers are abundant as well as other kinds of flowers, among which is a large white one of singular beauty, I suppose to be the "California Poppy." Goose Berries are also found here. The great mountains & beautiful valleys can hardly be surpassed in rugged grandeur & in the fairylike beauty of the latter. Passing a part of the mountain of clean surface & entirely barren found all along its foot for a mile hot springs smelling of sulphur & emitting steam, same are too hot to bear the hand in more than an instant. Along here is a large slough or lake hiding most of the water by "Bull Rushes" which grow very large. Crossed several pretty bad sloughs, crossed a number of cold & crystal pure rills running over pebbles & shining yellow mica looking like gold under the limpid current. These rills start from springs in the ravines above increased by snow water which falls down in romantic cascades. These little streams irrigate this whole valley which alone cause the rich growth of vegetation in this country at this season. Nooned in the valley near the foot of the main Sierra although we expected to get to the pass[139] or ascent ere this. Made some 16 miles this forenoon to a place which this morning seemed but 3 or 4 miles distant. Among these mountains distance is very deceiving, 10 miles appears like one mile in Ohio. The atmosphere is very clear & pure which accounts for it & views of landscape are on a large scale. The sky is here usually very clear or of a peculiar blue & hazy white. Saw this morning at a distance several objects in the valley looked like mule but on closer examination found they were Sandhill Cranes which are some 5 ft high while

walking & make the valley resound with their cooing or
whirring noise. Went to the head of this deceptive valley
in distance by twilight where we camped for the night
at the place where Pass Creek or the main stream of
Carson issues from the famous canon which deserves the
name "Camp Romantic" from the hill descending to this
camp is a fine view of the beautiful valley behind us — the
dizzy heights of the Sierra near on our right — the blue
chain on the opposite side of the valley which rises one
ridge above the other until lost to sight in the distance —
the finely curved hills studded with pines forming a beautiful grove forming the base of the snowy peaked heights
in front of us, & the Carson cutting in narrow gorge
through the main chain. Took a farewell look at the
valley rich in production of nearly all kinds. Shrubbery
is here in great variety as well as plants & flowers, Sage,
Old Man, Strawberrys, Apricots, a species of Peaches
& Cherrys an endless variety unknown to me. Found
here a card sent back by a Mr. —— giving an awful acct
of bad places in the ascent of the mountain through the
Carson. The Indians (perfect Arabs here—naked) have
for some days made fires at a distance. Distance 22 miles.

AUGUST 2 THURSDAY. Had rather chilly night & for
last two mornings (this included) had some dew which
has been uncommon for some time, doleful sound of wind
through pines & rushing of the stream. The morning
cool, & beautifully clear, wore our coats. Left camp at
5½ o'clock & soon entered into the canon of Pass Creek140
perhaps the grandest & most boldly romantic scenery in
America when we enter it & through its length (this
days travel 7 miles) it is but little wider than necessary
for the stream & road the former is crossed on bridges141
twice & once forded. On either side are the boldest &
highest ridges I ever beheld — in many places rising to
the height of 3000 to 4000 ft almost perpindicularly
their sides in places walled up perpindicularly for hundreds of feet but mostly jagged rocks of granite (all
rocks here are a brittle granite grey color) these run up

nearly straight leaning all a little the same direction.

This mountain scenery compares perhaps nearly with the Alps, forbidding in aspect yet as a whole its comprehensive grandeur is impressed on the beholder. The view is on a scale so large so wildly romantic, and yet desolate as almost to overpower the mind with awe. Contemplating this scenery (which cannot be described) & then turning to ones own dependent little self, a wide field is opened for useful reflection while "looking through nature to nature's God." The peaks in places rise up almost out of sight with their sharp points covered in places by snow. Others rise less abruptly to gentler swells or domes. Relief to the eye is only found in the softening influence of the ever green finely tapering pines of several varities from 4 ft in diameter downward forming in places curious contrast with the barren rocks of immense size through which they have sprung up seemingly without any soil to be a kind of specimen of that which is unfading on earth. Through this narrow gorge or canon runs or rather rushes Pass Creek or the main tributary of Carson River — a pretty strong stream which rushes in rapids among huge rocks now enclosed within a width of a few feet spraying current is forced, now forced among huge rocks in rapids & anon dropping its crystal current over a shelf or rock forming a fine cascade. But the gloomy part is yet to site. The road or rather the want of a road, I will call it a kind of blocked up passage winding in short angles among rocks large as common dwellings & over banks steeps, or pitches which no one would think an empty wagon had ever forced its way through save by tracks made when the wheels occasionally favored with a touch on "terra firma" (the ground). More than two animals cannot work to advantage in many places — more being apt to cramp the wagon. The wheels often strike rocks half as high as themselves over which men have to assist & this is no slight job often. In other places it goes over solid compact rocks for rods rough in the extreme & often too steep for ascents. Over these rocks up & down which animals sometimes have to force their way, often they fall & struggle in their weakened condition to draw sympathy from a heart of stone, but this is no place for sympathy! The first very rocky & steep ascent (at the foot of which many a stout heart has quailed) Ruggs mule fell (seemingly broke a leg) in attempting to force his way up a steep smooth rock. Coming up & seeing them unable to make the desponding animal attempt to rise save by the last resort for a mule (cutting him over the ear) I thought this was indeed going to California. Pushing up these hills (the wagons) is hard work. Our mess unfortunate having only one wagon & that heavy & loaded down (having worked 6 to 8 mules to it) could not proceed farther after having gone 3 miles. Having word from the light 4 horse wagons in advance that the road is "getting worse & more of it" we unhitched our team near where Capt. Walton had broken an axel tree (the hind spindle off) & knew not what to do except to go at once to packing the balance of the way. So we unloaded gave Walton our wagon examined our private effects & then our clothing, pistols, balls, &c that were least valuable. I have on 2 pr pants, 3 shirts, shot pouch, balls, & sundry other items. Having packed (without pack saddles) all we could sundry articles of value were left on the ground among which was 6 or 7 sides of as good bacon as I ever tasted. Proceeding on our way had much trouble to keep the temporarily arranged packs on the mules & dropped some Bacon by the way. Had things to carry in hands which added to trouble of arranging packs labor of ascending mountain &c completely exhausted all hands. I felt fatigued in the extreme when I reached camp. Passed several broken & deserted wagons, axeltrees, harness &c, showing the havoc of the Canon. Wagons stood with loads on until another day should find the strength of men & mules recruited for the struggle. Other wagons or teams were forcing their way through after having packed part of the load through.

The shrill noise of drivers & men pushing resounded & echoed along the heights relieving one from the doleful sound of wind among Pine trees. Passed Waltons wagon teamless, guarded by Krumm & Shade & soon met Canfield wagon in the ford in the curious juxtaposition of having the front axeltree stopped by a huge rock high on the wagon bed added to which were the disagreeable circumstances of having the wagon broken slightly & an exhausted team that could do no more. Never did man look more nonplussed & desponding than Canfield sitting on a rock by the side of the team in the stream of icy cold water which the men waded into to lift the wagon. Reached camp exhausted, dusted & muddy & hungry at 4½ o'clock having been without eating anything for 12 hours during which we labored hard but found Chadwick, Wood, Bryden, Moores, & others had coffee, meat &c prepared for us of which we at once partook freely. Distance 7 miles.

P.S. Canfields wagon came to camp an hour after us.

FRIDAY 3. Cool night, plenty of snow in sight on mountain sides, camp is in beautiful amid circular vale covered with fine grass & surrounded by high mountains studded with Pines forming groves in places unsurpassed in beauty. High walls of brownish black rock in places form a new feature in the geology of these ridges. Laying over for the day I washed flannels, socks &c, which is a "grand bore" to us men, but having a fine tree to shade & a fire already made & left by packers or Indians, did well enough for a washing place. A pack train from Mo. thinking we had deserted the Bacon, Powder & Salt left back yesterday bought it & divided among them but being informed of our intention to get it today delivered all up freely & would accept but little of that which I urged them to take as compensation for bringing it thus far. It being decided that our mess should make a cart of Waltons broken wagon left behind, Fisk, Crist & McCommon went back for it & made a cart which was the subject of much pleasant criticism & remarks. Waltons

wagon also (formerly ours) brought to camp. A train
of Californians142 just from the "Diggins" (from the
states formerly — some Mormons) camped above us (1
mile) some 8 to 10 wagons with ox teams loaded with
groceries & provisions for Salt Lake where they intend
wintering & will do well with their stock. We had many
questions to ask them about California. Their account
is favorable as to Gold, provisions abundant & compari-
tively cheap. The mines crowded, much business done,
liquor drank & cards played constantly, hard Society, say
they never left a place without regret except that. Having gotten ready left camp at 3 o'clock our mess last
having to pack four mules & 2 horses & four worked in
cart, proceeded over good roads except occasionally a few
rocks. Passing the California camp saw women & children which was a curiosity here. The women some wearing little ancient looking caps look like our grandmothers
"used to did." The men in minature the little flax headed
fellows made the grove vocal with once familiar childish
voices. Broke our cart (the axel tree in the spindle) in
crossing a rocky place after having much trouble to balance &c. Packed our things on mules & my horse which
were in it, & the others packed mules of our mess after
Walton & Boyle had taken them to camp & returned,
unfortunate indeed & now reduced to the compulsion of
packing reaching camp after dark took a cup of tea &
bread, thought & consulted as to our situation & laid
down under as clear a moonlit canopy as spans over any
country, with a chilly air, slept well. Distance 6 miles.

SATURDAY 4. It was by a meeting of the company
decided our mess should pack all they could & the wagons
take the balance. So Raney & Wood remained with our
mess & with McCommon made "pack saddles" & the
wagons left at 5½ o'clock for the ascent of the mountain
3 miles ahead which Dewitt who rode to it last night &
represents as being awfully bad. After much trouble in
arranging packs &c were ready & left camp with our little
"Pack Train" of two mules & two horses at 2 o'clock,

passed along a pretty valley[143] occasionally intercepted
by hills, reached a lake of considerable extent at the foot
of the most impassable passable hill that was perhaps
ever honored with a wagons pressure on its brow. At
the head of the lake as seen from the foot of the hill is a
bold wall of gray granite shelved upon each other in
huge masses. Here at the foot of the hill were trains
unloading wagons & packing things up the steeps. This
hill of hills is ¾ of a mile high. Our packs being pretty
heavy for fagged mules, my horse was packed pretty
heavy. I led him up ascending as the others were ahead
winding along at times could see them almost over my
head, this hill is called "the Devil's Ladder." The horse
It expected momentarily to fall back as he advanced with
groans up the rocky steeps in places walled some feet
height. Horses cannot climb mountains like mules can—
so I lost ground & led my horse alone & reached camp at
twilight an hour after the balance. At the foot of this
ascent many a one here found if not trouble & nothing
but extraordinary exertion of men & animals overcomes
the difficulties for this ascent is very steep in places
deeply sandy & then again obstructed by large rocks
which are strewn here in profusion some large as dwellings in the states. Passed a man with a Buggy half way
up seemingly despairing of ever reaching the summit to
which he turned his eyes wistfully. On the summit I
passed a two horse Yankee wagon with springs with a
real down easter aboard—"from Iowa last." Well, all
kinds of vehicles employed to get to the "Diggins."
Passed a snow bank near by the road & the air is chilly.
The road as has been the case since we entered the canon
is shaded with a variety of Pines, Cedars & Spruce. The
high ridges with many snow banks on their sides made
the upper scenery wintery while little vales hundreds of
feet below green with the carpet of nature looked summerlike. Occasionally pass a little lake mirroring on its
bosom the reversed forms of pine studded ridges these
are the collections of snow water thawing. After my

lonesome walk leading the horse alone I gladly hailed our folks from a hill. Camped in the most beautiful & picturesque valley144 of some miles in extent I ever beheld. The grass was finely carpeting it, at the end of a fine silvery lake145 with snow clad heights, around over all the declining sun cast her golden rays. Before reaching camp had to cross quite a stream & having no animal to ride jumped in 2 ft deep, water cold as ice (snow water) & the blood seemed to stop circulation I being warm, & for the moment felt as if death would result. Having Zivils medicine in pocket took a little & revived me at once. Reached camp & found Dr. Boyles alcohol for medicinal purposes, had been seized by the train when working up over the hill & some of the boys felt good. I took a little to counteract the effects of drenching. Washed myself & put on dry clothes & felt like myself again. Distance 9 miles.

SUNDAY 5. Arose after a chilly nights rest & being awakened by the cold operating on my head & feet uncomfortably. Had a meeting of the company & our Mess No. 2 ordered to go to the Fort or Diggins with their packs. Still remaining members of the Co to get all information to be obtained until the arrival of the Co. So after having the arrangements made, mules packed &c we give the word "good morning" at 7 o'clock & started with our little pack train consisting of 8 mules & one (my) horse — all packed but one (Sally). Fisk, McCommon, Crist & myself of our mess, Price being already sent ahead & Dr. Boyle remained with the Co. After driving our animals along this fine valley came to a little willow fringed stream running into the lake below, bad place to cross. I mounted the mule Sally to cross over & lead off when the packs crowded around me & threw my mule flat on the side on my leg but fortunately did not hurt me (how I escaped being hurt I could not tell). So we rushed them through & followed. Soon reached a long sand hill the road leading through thickets of pines & cedars & underbrush, constantly ascending or descending mountains until we reached the main or highest ridge[146] which is a long steep ascent with very ugly mirey places for the wagons. We struck to the right on the edge of a bank of snow to keep our mules from miring where teams were sticking fast & packing their loads up. This hill over the snow especially was very tiresome. It was steep & the irregularity of the snow made it difficult. I mounted Sally & forced her up part of the snow bank (which was 20 ft deep) nearly perpindicular to avoid worse road expecting her momentarily to fall back. Nearly exhausted (men & animals) we reached the top— the highest point of the Sierra Nevada mountains, called the Backbone. Stopping we looked around & here is a view too magnificently grand & wildly romantic for me to attempt to describe, although we have traveled nearly half a day from this point we looked down to the East & saw stretched out apparently a little meadow patch, the valley we left this morning, our wagons looked like white specs in the view. The view here is on a most extensive scale the bold ridges running in all directions with mighty valleys intervening covered with fine Cedars & Pines are apparently filling a world wide range in their unbounded lengths & variations running out of sight into undefined blue masses. Standing here we seem higher than any immediate peak save a black volcanic beehive shaped pile of rock on our right hardby the road which overlooks us some 50 ft. Here the sky was peculiarly clear — occasionally a snowy white hazy cloud passed apparently over our heads near by. For some days the altitude has affected us much, shortness of breath — walking goes hard, ones breath short especially today at this very high point. Snow in abundance covering in banks all the ridges around us & those had not already coats on put them on to shield them from the chilly wind which blows with some force seemingly from the Pacific. Here the road rises over a snow bank some 20 ft deep for some distance. Passed long a ridge that commanded a fine view of these American Alps. Saw on the left a thousand ft

below us a green vale which looked summerlike in contrast with the snowy regions around us here on the
heights. Emerged two or three times into prairie patches
of 10 to 50 acres, with but little grass & no timber, in
one of which we stopped to noon. Put beans over boiled
2 hours & were yet hard. Ate the soup & left determined
not to be detained again by beans that would not cook
(a watched kettle dont boil). Seeing our little caravan
of packs pass over this patch & ascending the rugged
mountains reminded me forcibly of my school boy days
seeing a cut representing packed mules about to cross
the Andes. We passed along over high ridges occasionally descending into ravines or valleys almost constantly
ascending or descending the roads in places being very
difficult for wagons. At twilight passed a newly made
grave with the inscription by it on a tree "Died/July
27/49 A - - - - -["] & Square & compass beneath inscription showing Masonic respect for a brother. Cedars
& Pines bend their twigs over it thickly. Traveled until
10 o'clock & before the moon rose we were in darkness
in thickets of pine groping our way on mules & afoot
hardly knowing whether our caravan were all together.
So each took charge of a part & anon the word passed
along "all coming up." A mule I rode being weak &
tired stumbled over rocks & took his own course in spite
of my efforts to guide him, not being "bridle wise." The
welcome moon arose at perhaps 9 o'clock throwing her
light over the highest peaks studded in regularity with
pines, the scenery was as I often imagined the Alps to
look. Looking under the limbs of surrounding trees the
scenery appeared like soldiers marching up & down steeps
in various directions as the trees stood apparently in lines
on edges of precipices. Reaching a camp of two wagons
of ox teams at about 10 o'clock on the side of a mountain
in tolerable grass we camped near by. Had to take our
mules down the mountain side ½ mile to water which
was scarce when we reached it through thickets of high
weeds & shrubs (brot to camp a bucket full & valued it

at $1). Made tea to soak bread & roasted fat Bacon at
the fire on sharpened sticks. Concluding to let the mules
take care of themselves did not watch, came after night
around our beds, fussing about. It was quite cold tonight,
a pr of blankets & buffalo robe hardly kept me comfortable after this hard days travel. Dist. 30 miles.

MONDAY 6. After repeating culinary performances had
in the evening, for breakfast — left this chilly place at
5½ o'clock. Saw woman with one of the wagons at camp
which was a novelty here & could not help looking at her.
Women seem to undergo the hardships of this journey
with uncommon philosophy. Our march today was through
the prettiest mountain scenery that could be imagined.
The road is nearly all the while shaded with the most
beautiful Pines & Cedars and Fir trees as well as Spruce
of many varities each. This forest scenery is by us enjoyed greatly after coming from St Jo to the main chain
without seeing a forest. Huge Pines 4 ft in diameter
occasionally shoot out of crevices of rocks where no earth
seems to be. Saw the most beautiful ornamental trees,
Firs especially. Pines 6 ft in diameter & 200 ft high
are common & always beautifully tapering often 100 ft
without a limb, standing regularly & of all sizes with
generally no underbrush, making the scenery grove like.
Met this morning Mr. Hastings[147] (author of a work on
California) accompanied with a Mexican Indian, who
goes to meet a train in which two of his brothers are. He
says gold enough for 1000 years in California. Provisions
abundant on the whole his acct is very flattering. Says
there is no grass for 25 miles & then none to the Fort.
Descended many long & very steep hills today often with
a reddish dust from 6 to 15 inches deep which when
water is poured on looks like rust of iron. Rocks are
granite & a black volcanic rock with occasionally quartz.
Had a long march without water & was extremely fatigued. Would have given my Gold in California for a
drink of water. Reached at 4 o'clock a lot of wagons
camped on the side of a hill in number making a show

like a camp meeting in Ohio, some cooking &c. Here went 3 miles to the left of the road into a fine piece of grass like a meadow where we found hundreds of animals & although a note was posted up stating a horse & 3 oxen had been stolen a few nights before we laid down after frying meat on sticks & making tea without watching. The road to this piece of grass is over hill & through narrow defiles winding among bushes &c difficult passes even for packed animals. Our fatigue was great & looked like negroes, sweating & the dust adhereing which when wet looks black. Passed going to camp a little stream the water of which seemed to be impregnated with iron. Distance 30 miles.

TUESDAY 7. As usual the sky is without a speck & the sunshine hot. Had the pleasure of meeting my friend Dr. Miley of Columbus who like myself looked fatigued &c. It is quite a treat to meet a friend here after a few friendly remarks he left. Cut grass to pack for the long barren road with our knives, it is coarse grass soon found it had cut my hands to draw blood &c. left camp & returned to the wagon camp on the road through the brush & over the hills & went on our way tho not rejoicing much having to walk this hard trip. Passed along over a ridge nearly all afternoon with valleys occasionally on the sides a thousand feet below again a valley or canon would turn at right angles with tremenduous mountain ridges running to points in it. In a word the scenery was varied & beautiful as this mountain alone is. After descending from this ridge by a long hill (hills & road generally deep in dust as yesterday) found on the left a small spring of sulphurus water of pleasant taste of which I drank 3 pints. At twilight entered on as beautiful a valley as ever I laid eyes on Called Pleasant Valley,148 grass & vegitation generally shows dry, the earth parched as by long drouth — being the dry season. The road is beautiful through this valley. Darkness overtaking us I led my horse ahead, all day found it more difficult to keep the road. Clouds of dust preceeding me. Groped our way till we reached a camp of two wagons where we halted & camped for the night. Fed some grass. Found here the offalls of shingles made near camp indicating civilization & I laid down fatigued but glad we were so near our destination. Good roads today. Distance 16 miles.

WEDNESDAY 8. Left camp at 5½ o'clock & traveled until one o'clock without water & the sun shining, intensely hot — would have given $10 for a drink of water. Missed a spring some distance from the road. The spring we reached is on the left near the road called Grass Spring. Grass is dead mostly but animals eat it pretty freely. Saw today the first "Diggins" by the roadside & pile of mud brought from dry digins & washed during the wet season in the ravines several of which we crossed, dry now. We have imperceptibly left the mountains & are now (today) passing over rolling pretty country. At the forks of the road we took the left to Sutters Fort at which Price before us took. The road to the right led to the mill[149] where the first gold was discovered by washing out the tail race. ¾ of a mile from the forks of the road is a grocery store. Rocks appear dark slaty & all stand edgeways, & a peculiar flinty stone with shiney clouded appearance when broken also what is called here Gold blossom a white quartz like stone of all sizes. Left nooning place at 4 o'clock — several companions from here went down a ravine to the left to Casmere River Digins[150] some 10 miles. We soon entered upon a kind of plain (occasionally a little rolling) the ridges melting together peculiarly which is beautiful in the extreme. Our march is through thinly studded groves of white oak trees, rather low & bushy that look much like an old orchard. We seem to be in the midst of a settled country. These trees occasionally stand regularly in rows like soldiers in procession, stems or butts very white & delicate. The sun set in splendor over this fine scenery giving one an idea of the beautiful in nature the better impressed by its contrast with the mountains just left. Mexicans,

Indians, & whites passed us on horseback on full speed with good horses, each having a rifle & pair of blankets. A little after dark saw with great joy at a distance two houses lighted with candles displaying themselves to advantage on the summit of a hill. The first house we had seen for the last 3 months (save the Forts). Coming up we saw a table set & ladies moving about it in the largest house. Near by it & in front stood a little shanty & occupied as a store room which though wide as a building & more so as a store.151 We stepped around on its ground floor feeling quite at home to be once more in the land of houses. The barking of a house dog sounded quite musical. Engaged supper for us four which being soon ready we sat down on benches on either side around a board well supplied & relished by us as the first regular or table meal we had for 4 months (save one I took at Fort Childs). Sitting at a table was a novelty & if our dirty black faces did not frighten the two women it was because they had seen the Elephant. We had biscuit fried bread, Salmon Trout, Bacon, Baked Beans, Coffee Sugar, Milk, Pies, Pickles &c., to which we did ample justice and paid the common price for boarding in this country $1.50 per piece a meal. These folks were Mormons. The old lady looked robust but careworn. The young lady (apparently her daughter) was rather pretty & communicative. Found in the store two New York miners had been here six weeks & had the blues, said mining was a humbug & put rather a damper on our folks, yet had not much less than $5.00 per day anytime. Left in the dark. The moon soon arose & had her silvery wand the balance of the night over as pretty a country as I ever beheld. Rows of oaks running along as if dividing large farms & occasionally studding it making fine groves. The country generally quite level roads excellent. Watered horses at a tavern where two men with wagon stopped they also gave a gloomy account of the mines — laid by the side of their wagon & swore freely as all do here, finally struck the American Fork a fine tributary of the

Sacramento. Here passed apparently an old established
*Rancho*152 which looked agreeable — pigs squealed here
& I thought it must be a farm & could be made a home
— buildings appeared permanent. The houses passed before were covered with willow twigs and muslin & enclosed by strips of muslin tacked on upright poles or
scantlings as weatherboarding. Was taken with vomit-
ing caused by eating salt fish. Marched this seemingly
endless road until the break of day, we found some grass,
though indifferent. Camped under a tree near the River
after the most fatiguing march made since we left St
Joseph. My feet were sore, felt unwell & could hardly
go further. Distance 50 miles.

THURSDAY 9. Having laid down at break of day over-
slept ourselves, did not get up until 8 o'clock, found
ourselves on a bottom of the American fork perfectly
level as far as the eye could reach with occasional large
White Oaks with bushy tops making beautiful shade trees.
Packed up & moved off 3 miles & halted at 10 o'clock
under a fine shade tree near the River 5 miles from "Sacramento City." Had much trouble to bring up some
stubborn mules & broke Crists rifle on one. In sight are
two ranchos or houses153 (on this side of the river) seemingly established some time since, also a fine one on the
other side, seemingly a very pleasant location. Fisk &
Crist went to the city to gain information, & see Price
but did not find Mr Price, they give a strange acct of
the city. McCommon & myself slept & recruited today.
The plain far as the eye can reach is covered with horses,
mules & cattle grazing on the rather poor grass. See in
all directions men riding at full speed after their herds.
Camps are pretty numerous along the road & Emigrants
coming in. Loads of provisions & mules packed are frequently passing by going to the mines apparently from
all nations. The Californians & Mexicans going on full
canter whenever they ride (& they live on horseback)
with good horses, gaily mounted with huge wooden stirrups covered with flaps in front—a kind of fender making

them look like large hats & wearing massive Spanish spurs. The sky is ever without a speck or clouds & looks beautiful. A constant sea breeze from the South West which is quite chilling at nights. Distance 3 miles.

FRIDAY 10. After soaking our hard bread in tea & frying fat Bacon on sticks as usual I left on Bob for the city of the "Sacramento." The road leading to it is the finest I ever traveled & over a level country with beautiful White Oaks shade trees. Found the Fort itself dilapidated some & is now arranged for other purposes (Capt. Sutter154 having sold out). Dr. Cragins155 I believe of Washington City has fitted up & is occupying part for a hospital. Another part will I believe be occupied for a Hotel & the blocks of adobe (sunburnt brick) of which it & the wall are built are (all not wanted here) taken up & used for other building purposes. A man painting sign here told me he made $12 pr day. Several little buildings nearby — some put up lately & occupied as stores. The situation of the Fort is fine being 2 miles from the junction of the American Fork with the Sacramento. Met here Price & Harris had a pleasant talk & proceeded to the City & together (with Barcus who we met here) spent the day in the City. Coming out on the pasture where we left Barcus horse & mine (larietted together) I walked over the level plain 2 miles before I found them, being passed & repassed by Mexicans & others on a lope after stock (with which this plain is covered for miles). Here I found the finest cattle I ever saw. No cattle in the States is as good and large as this having extraordinarily large horns (the oxen) saw fine milk cows also. Price & I going to our camp 5 miles out found the road crowded with passengers in all kinds of vehicles & natives passing like the wind on their speedy horses with gay blankets, the evening being quite cold, the wind pretty high. Passing the hospital noticed a small crowd (perhaps a dozen persons) bringing some one who died in the hospital — poor fellow put off this mortal coil perhaps far from home & friends & how glad would they

be soon to visit the grave under the tree near the Fort.
Reached our folks after dark, made supper by a fire of
a squad of 3 men & a boy from Oregon & just from the
mines who were real "backwoodsmen" but withal clever
& hospitable. Asking one how far he lived from Astoria
found he knew not that that place was in Oregon. But
for a description of *Sacramento City*. The City is situated
on a level bottom or plain of the Sacramento at the confluence of the American Fork. The City is now a grove.
The houses & tents being built among brush & trees. The
City is laid out regularly the streets crossing at right
angles (American style). The population[156] being floating can hardly be estimated. It is perhaps from 3 to
4000. Houses are going up that were shipped from the
States.[157] Many are also put up of lumber gotten here.
But most houses are mere poles drove in the ground &
muslin tacked on the sides & roof. Some roofs are covered
with willow twigs. Most of the houses are tents and many
live under trees in the suburbs especially Emigrants
(which is the case with us). It is essentially a "Calico
Town" & looks like a huge American Camp Meeting,
most people living outdoors & the streets crowded with
passers by, men from all nations, States & Races are
mingled Enmasse here. 15 ships lay in port their riggings
raising among trees & bushes on the wharf. It is truly a
business place & will some day be a great city. Lots now
sell at from one to $300 & change hands daily. Rents are
extravagant, one house $310 offered for. The Sacramento
is $\frac{1}{4}$ mile wide is the most beautiful stream I ever saw
timbered on this side with White Oaks, on the other willows & beautiful little delicate foliaged trees entwined
with grape vines looking rich indeed. One is at once
struck entering this city with the perfect confidence exist-
ing and security of property. Provisions which are very
abundant are scattered round in great piles as well as
all the other kinds of goods. Piles of thousands of sacks
of flour, hams, fish, liquors, goods &c are blocking up
every corner & nook and yet nothing is stolen. All feel

the necessity of this state of things in the absence of houses for protection. Wages is from 8 to $25 pr day, lumber $600 per 1000 ft. Brick $200 per 1000 water melons $4 to $6 per piece. Bread 50 cts per loaf, little pies 75 cts apiece. A ginger cake 75 cts per lb. Sugar 12½ to 18 2/4 (Brown) coffee 12½ to 25, beans 7 cts per lb, molasses to $1.50 per gallon, pork $45.00 per bbl. lard 30 cts per lb, flour $8 to $10 per 100 lb. Trade is without regulations & prices of the same articles vary much. Rolett [roulette] Fan Banks & all kinds of gaming concerns are abundantly patronized. You enter & all is quiet games going on all around you without a word passing thousands of dollars laying on the tables. I have known men to lose $2000 in an evening. The fat old Greaser (Spaniard or Mexican) sits behind the table and plays off the favorite Mexican game.

All appear unconcerned. Many liquor establishments and much liquor drunk & yet no quareling whatever. Business of all kinds done here, flaming signs up all around often put up before anything else against the house. Signs mostly brought from the States. "American Boarding House," "Miners Saloon," "City Bakery" &c &c. A New Yorker has a little 6 horsepower engine driving circular saw & he is coining money, charges $3. apiece for whip stocks &c. Blacksmith shops are under trees (sign against tree) $32. for 4 brand new shoes on a horse & other jobs in proportion.

Well we are now in California having been on the road since last April. A tedious irksome and disagreeable trip, made in about 100 days without an accident to any of our company. All came through lucky considering the exposures &c. We can only ascribe it to a providential goodness this favorable result of an undertaking fraught with so many dangers & dificulties.

Members of the Columbus California Industrial Association

E. Barcus
C. E. Boyle
David Bryden
Charles Breyfogle
James G. Canfield
Walter Cain
George Canfield
George Chadwick
Thomas Davis
Peter Decker
L. A. Denig
C. Dewitt
J. Shade Dungan
C. M. Fisk

J. Krumm
P. M. McCommon
G. Q. McColm
W. Moores
T. J. Price
H. Raney
Dayton Rugg
Theodore Rugg
L. H. Sherman
W. C. Stiles
J. P. Stone
Gideon Walton
John Walton
D. C. Woods

Route of the Columbus California Industrial Association

1849

April	30	Left the Bluffs (St. Joseph)
May	7	Passed junction with the Independence Road (200 miles)
	14	Passed Fort Childs
	23	Crossed South Platte at upper ford
	25	At Ash Hollow
	28	At Court House Rock
	29	At Chimney Rock
	31	At Scotts Bluffs
June	2	At Fort Laramie
	9	Second crossing of the Platte by ferry
	11	At Independence Rock and Devils Gate
	14	Wind River Mountains in sight of Sweet Water River
	15	Passed snow on Sweet Water
	16	Over South Pass, took Oregon road at the forks
	17	Crossed the Little Sandy and Big Sandy
	19	Crossed Green River
	21	Crossed Hams Fork of Green River
	23	Crossed Thomas Fork of Bear River (rapids)
	23	Crossed Smiths Fork of Bear River (wounded duck)
	24	Bear River—at Old Smiths
	25	At Soda Springs
	29	Crossed Pont Neuf River, a tributary of Lewis Fork of the Columbia
	29	At Fort Hall

	30	Crossed Lewis Fork of Columbia
July	1	At American Falls of Columbia River
	2	Crossed Raft River into L.F. Crossed Raft River several times
	4	Traveled on Raft River & left it & crossed hills into Great Basin
	5	Crossed Goose Creek
	9	On head of Humbolt
	20	At Slough of Humbolt
	22	Spent at Sulphur Wells
	23	Left for the Desert
	25	Reached Carson River
	26	Saw peaks of the Sierra Nevada
August	2	Ascended Carson Kenyon
	3	Traveled with a cart (our mess)
	5	Our mess left the Co.
	6	Crossed summit in the morning
	9	Near Sacramento
	10	Visited the City
	17	Dissolved Co. at Cold Springs
	30	Started for Trinity River
Sept.	13	Reached Readings Springs
	18	Left for Trinity
October	11	Left the River
	16	Reached Readings Springs again
	20	Left Readings Springs
November	1	Reached Sacramento
December	2	Left Sacramento for Fremont
1850		
March	18	Left Fremont for South Yuba

Remarks on an Outfit

BACON — Is not used in very great quantities

DRY OR SEA BREAD — One is apt to get tired of, but take

COFFE & TEA — Are used freely & are indispensibles

SUGAR — Should be taken in pretty large quantity, it is a real and very desirable luxury. Brown sugar to last to the S. Pass would answer well—after that the hot sun would make it run, so part of it as least should be crushed sugar.

CHEESE — Is excellent & should be taken.

Some vinegar is needed. It prevents scurvy and one has an apetite for it on the plains.

DRY FRUIT — Apples and Peaches should by all means be taken as you are cut off from all same or vegetables.

FLOUR & CORNMEAL — are indispensible

BEANS are good & should be taken in moderate quantity.

MOLASSES is excellent & should be taken

SALERATES enough to last all the way as the salerates of the plains is not very good in its natural condition

PEPPER & a little SPICE are wanted

BOLOGNY SAUSAGE or good smoked sausage would be good & handy

BEEF — Jerked, before starting would be excellent

DRY BEEF — Would be good & handy

CRACKERS & BOSTON CRACKER would be good for a part of the bread stuff

BUTTER or good lard would be desirable closely put up.

FRONT STREET, SACRAMENTO

Life in the Diggings

SATURDAY 11. Sold two mules (Till & Charley) for $130. (both). They are in rather bad condition after the trip. Packed up our plunder & left for "Sacramento City." At the Fort met New York Miners going up to whom we sold "Old Bill" our largest mule for $125. Camped in the suburbs of the City in a grove of & under an Oak Tree whose spreading branches is our only house. In town today paid 25 cts for a copy of the "Placer Times"[158] a 7 by 9 paper looks like a small beginning. This is a great thourgfare men on horses & mules moving to and fro on a lope & in wagons. Loads of provisions on wagons & packs passing out to the mines. Having now flour & molasses bake slap jacks, which is an improvement on hard bread.

SUNDAY 12. Went to the slew, washed myself, put on clean clothes & feel well though dressed very common. A

159

change makes me feel as though it really was Sunday. Went to church no, not church but to meeting for it was not at the call of the church going bell. Neither could I see the heavenward pointing spire through the trees, but found commerce had preceded the gospel when I looked at the masts of the ships crowding the Sacramento. Found the people convened under a roof used for shops where some 100 men & ½ dozen women were assembled (about the proportion of men & women in California). An Englishman was making a rather tedious prayer, had good singing by 8 or 10 persons when a rather priestly looking man arose on a stand & took the 2 verses 15 & 16 of 4th Chapter of Matthew & preached a very short good & very appropriate sermon, compared California to Galilee of old since it has a great work to do, being on the borders of Christianity. It must have a distinctive pious radically Christian people organized as a church around which all good influences would gather & radiate from. Need a church for stated worship &c. Touched a sympathetic chord when speaking of the mass here on a common level nearly all of which have parents brothers & sisters feeling interest for our welfare. The audience were quite respectful save two or three who left. No rustling silks & shining satins paraded the aisles, all left after it was over. Went to the River with Price & McCommon saw the shipping floating on the bosom of the Sacramento which moves in clear current over golden treasures. Nearly all stores open & about ½ the usual business done, some mules packed for the mines, hay unloaded & gaming done as well as firing of guns &c. But taken all in all there is more restraint shown than I expected to see in California.

MONDAY 13. Before break of day the Wolves perhaps a dozen in number howled in various directions some seemingly near our beds. Crist & I took our clothes to the Slough & washed. It took until noon I had some 20 pieces & washed them pretty well although it is a sort of "bore," but would have cost $10 to get them washed. Three graves digging under a tree for corpses now in

the City died of Billious Fever & Diahrea which are common complaints here. The water of the wells (not walled)
is constantly kept riled & is of a coperas impregnation
— though fresh is not so healthy as the clearer though
tepid water of the Sacramento. Wash being soon dry in
the warm sun & dry wind put it up & feel glad my "duds"
are once more all approaching cleanliness.

TUESDAY 14. Cool (at times chilly) nights are pleasant
after the hot days, the sun shines very hot here — though
always a cool sea breeze. McColm came in having left
the train going to the mines at the mill159 40 miles above.

WEDNESDAY 15. McColm in liquor. Harris & I tried
to catch fish in the Sacramento with hook & line but would
not bite although we see many play in the clear water.
Thermometer stands 98 in the shade. Price & I got
the written authority of Fisk, McCommon, Barcus and
Crist to act as their proxies to settle up the affairs of
our company and divide property for them. Left camp
in co. with Price and Dr Bryden at 4 o'clock P.M. (the
latter having been sent to request our attendance to divide
company matters & settle accts &c). Went out 6 miles
where Bryden had left his horse at a *Rancho* and made
coffee & broiled bacon on sticks for supper. Two Squaws
came to the *Rancho* with venison, appearing very shy to
approach. A young man met them & bot it of them.
Started on our way at twilight & four miles above at the
Rancho where we left the American Fork watered our
animals with some difficulty on acct of the steep banks.
It being very dark had trouble to keep the road getting
several times lost. Near this Rancho the Wolves struck
up close by in curious unison a shrill noise. The bushy
white oaks studding the vales appeared to give a pleasant
view to the dim outlines of scenery. Price thrown forward from his mule Sally on acct of weakness. Passed
a number of camp fires by the road, & a young man sleeping on a wagon by the way seemed to have come to an
unwilling halt in the darkness — was a down Easter came
via Cape Horn & found this a more novel life than that

on the ocean wave. Halted at 3 o'clock and turned our animals out to graze on the dry grass — laid down in blankets & slept until the sun was up. Distance 25 miles.

THURSDAY 16. The sky was overcast with clouds and threatened rain a few drops falling, at 7 o'clock started on our way. The sky soon cleared off before a brilliant & very hot sun. Reached Green Spring[160] where a Hotel & Store throw a civilized air around a beautiful little valley enclosed by forest hills and has several fine springs of cold water, where we halted and made breakfast at 9 o'clock. Paid 37 cts for a lb of Bro sugar. I enjoyed some pleasant remarks to flaxen headed boys belonging to Oregon folks. After leaving two Yankees under a tree who finding walking tiresome priced my horse Bob. Asked him $110. for horse, saddle &c & holster pistol or $80. for the horse — sold him the horse &c in the evening for $100 & parted with him reluctantly in bad condition as he was having done much hard service on the trip under the saddle in the wagon & packing. On such a trip treat a horse gently — use him only when necessary & you will get him through probably — American horses I would risk as soon as any — if not sooner. Though an entire stranger to me I took his order of $85 on his associates at Mormon Island.[161] Passed a ranch in a pleasant valley pastured by splendid cattle. A family from Oregon camped here — spoke with an old lady — & a rather pretty daughter of hers seemed interested considerably in our conversation. Met Denig & Stone camped (at twilight) 3 miles from our company whom their mess had left with their property — took supper here & left for the camp of our company. Stone was informed by a traveling companion of Mr. Legg's of Columbus that he died on the Isthmus of Panama). It being dark missed our way & reached 3 miles on our [way to] Culloma where there was no grass — priced barley the only feed for animals here — price of which was 50 cts pr lb. Watered our animals at the River fastened them to bushes to browse & laid down at 10 o'clock. Distance 30 miles.

FRIDAY 17. Got up & went to the Saw Mill162 which is running day & night & cannot supply the demand for lumber at $400. pr 1000 feet. The race of this mill is where gold was first discovered in California quite a brisk village has sprung up here scenery hilly & romantic (Culloma). Called at the shanty occupied by Mr Hurd & lady our former traveling companions — pay $600 rent a year & Mrs Hurd said among other ridiculous prices that nutmegs sell at $1 apiece. They get $25 a week for boarding. Returned & went to the company camp near Weaver Creek.163 This morning the sky was again over cast & thundered & rained & found it had rained quite a little shower (sufficient to lay the dust) where our camp was. Found here the first miners to work & was struck with the hard labor it requires. An old fellow after examining a hole he had difficulty in sinking stood in it & I asked him what he was digging for & answered me "for a living." He found no gold. Mess No. I & others of our folks at work. Balanced up my books as Secretary of the Company. Had them examined by a committee who found them correct. Had during the afternoon & evening meetings of the Company & after making settlement & division of effects voted each an honorable discharge and the Company had fulfilled its destiny. We parted in good feeling and hoped though we could hardly expect to meet again — each man now going to seek his fortune. The Flag granted to me.164 Distance 6 miles.

SATURDAY 18. After settling up the accts of the Company Price & I bot a cart & wheel harness of Rugg for $75. Gave the farewell word to all friends & left. Woods "hove" off of his mule to the amusement of the company who were Price, Bryden, Cain, Sherman & I. Camped an hour after dark. Distance 12 miles.

SUNDAY 19. Felt unwell, had bowel complaint yesterday afternoon & today. Left camp early & had very warm day. Price & I left road & went to the Mormon Island. Left McColm clothing & after enquiring at about fifty camps for the man I had order on for money for horse which when I found them was paid me. Several stores are here. A lady asked me an ounce of Gold for a Lariet. Returned to Sacramento road & met Bryden & the others at Willow Springs.165 This road is through a fine rolling country, roads excellent. Traveled until 9 o'clock were behind the wagons & tired out before reaching camp. Distance 28 miles.

MONDAY 20. Left camp & returned to the City at 10 o'clock where we found the rest of our folks who were here when we left and some of the rest of our folks. Having drank coffee only & avoided water feel better today. Our mess dissatisfied on acct of the division of the Company property. Distance 10 miles.

TUESDAY 21. Laid in camp & did nothing. Sold two mules of our mess for $184.

WEDNESDAY 22. Sold the cart Price & I bought for $125. Profit $50. Sold the 3 mules of our mess among its members. I bot Rough & Ready for $40. Capt. & G. Walton with teams came to camp. Wrote a letter to Judge Thrall & one to my Bro Charles. Price sick of bowel complaint as well as others of our folks. The well water here is not good is cold but impregnated with coperas.

THURSDAY 23. Had a long walk after our Sally mule & found her not. Sold my Revolver Pistol for $20. In my ramble after mules met a lot of *Spanish* or *Wild Cattle* which is in herds on the plains on the west side of the Sacramento where the Spaniards go & "lassoo" them, bring them here & some sell for beef & other times for milk cows & work oxen. This cattle is the finest in the world. Is easily known by the wild staring look — often run before you approach closely. When they hold heads up look bold — trot off freely like a deer & appear beautiful being usually in good order. Have large horns very thick & high hump, full quarters and look very round bodied. Sold my "Rough & Ready" mule for $55. profit $15. The young man of quick turn & intelligent appearance rode a good horse & full Spanish *rig* & had no doubt made of the *dust* before now in which article he paid me. Each trader has or ought to have a pair of Gold Scales as much of the dust passes in place of coin. Camp now under large tree.

FRIDAY 24 TO TUESDAY 28 INCLUSIVE. During the above four days continued in camp on Friday settled mess accounts and divided the property on hand and sold some among ourselves. The mule Sally being lost Fisk sold the balance of the mess his share for $5. We risking her recovery afterwards. I & Stone found her with some of his, and a treat of Claret wine paid the bill. On Saturday night the following of our associates left us for the "diggins" on the Middle Fork — Viz: Fisk & Barcus — Crist, Lunn & Stiles — Breyfogle, Stone & Denig. Thus our company scatter over this land to seek each his fortune & some of us may meet not again. On Sunday Dewitt, Sherman left for the McColamy [Mokelumne] "digins." Now but McCommon, Price & myself to occupy the old Oak whose wide spreading branches protect so well from the intensely warm sun. On Saturday Price, McC. & I bought two horses of Walton & his spring wagon for $125. & $150. respectively. This morning—Monday—I left camp early to hunt the Sally mule & two horses went out some miles east to a thicket where some Spanish Cattle started up wildly as they are wont to do when one approaches & soon a young man came to me on a mule full speed advising me to leave that grove or thicket as Spanish Cattle often attacked footmen & pointed out a Cow near by which had a few days before nearly killed his brother. He said new comers often thus exposed themselves imprudently for want of knowledge of the habits of this Cattle. Going some miles further in an almost scorching sun found the horses — took a dinner in Sutterville166 where an Oregon family camped. Hot biscuit new to me & stewed fruit a luxury & by the way an expensive luxury being worth 75 cts per lb. Came to camp in middle of afternoon after walking in all some 20 miles & found mercury at 104 degrees in the shade. Suffered much of heat today.

WEDNESDAY 29. Wrote a letter to brother David. Price, McCommon & I with Bryden, Wood[s] & Cain are going with a party of Yorkers to "Trinity River"[167] 250 miles N West of this is an unoccupied mine. Bot a horse of Hinkle[168] of Delaware for $50. to take on this trip with the two we have already. Price & I made purchases of provisions, tools &c for the mines. Hard bread at 17 cts lb, prime mess Pork at 17c lb, Flour 9c lb, Bro. Sugar 18c lb, powdered do 26c lb, dried apples 62 pr lb Blk tea at $1 pr lb, Hyson tea $1.50, saleratus $2.00 pr lb, bottle pepper sauce (small) $2.00, a little mustard jar 75c cheese 37½c. lb ½ lb ground pepper for 50c, corn meal 10c lb ginger 50c lb, Vinegar $1. pr gallon, rice 12½c lb. Every store keeps liquor & it is expected that you will drink. Found generally good fellows engaged in business here. McCommon sold the Sally mule for $80.00. Everything of the mess effects is disposed of & each share of proceeds of mess is about $130. Dr. Boyle took his share all in medicines excepting $28. which we paid him. Deposited a hand trunk & lot of clothing &c in a sack with messrs Black & Co. for safe keeping. With assistance of Mc & Price hitched up the horses bot of Hinkle — an Indian horse that never had worked before. He was awkward but I drove him with one of our others (Dick) & broke him in. The Yorkers expecting to start with 6 mule team with us at 4 o'clock & with the intention to cross the Sacramento & camp on the other side for the night. We left our familiar old Oak tree & found confusion around the "Yorker Wagon." It was loaded too heavy — but drove to the river at twilight to cross after each of 8 or 10 had given his private opinion about the load &c publicly. Halted at the first ferry[169] where a "drummer" for the upper ferry[170] was ready to venture the prediction that crossing on this ferry after dark was very dangerous. After the Ferry man (who was in opposition) had parlied a while we camped for the night without crossing. Mc & I got hay for the horses which was dealt out to us sparingly as gold dust. Price & I ordered our letters to Trinity River by Breyfogle & took a tolerable supper at $1. consisting of a sparse cool dish of Lobster soup — a slice of bread & a piece of Apple Pie, went to our wagon & made our bed on the bank of the Sacramento in the edge of the city among trees, the owls keeping up an almost constant hooting — ships lay near us & the unriffled Sacramento reflected her clear placid surface in the moon light like a mirror.

THURSDAY 30. Sleeping cold under a pr of blankets went early — waked up a clerk in Duey & Smith Store & bot a good pair of grey blankets at $10. Crossed the Sacramento early this morning at the upper ferry—steep sandy banks & had trouble to get the wagons off of the boat. Tide ebbs the water up the River as we crossed. It rises & falls from the ebb & flow of the tide about 6 inches. This River is a perfect mirror in appearance, its surface without a ripple indicating depth & is clear as ever was any river. While crossing the finely curving bank covered with a beautiful thicket of willows interlacing its branches and interwoven in places with grapevines & the vessels & boats reflected their show in reversed order in the silvered surface. I counted twenty vessels of various kinds in this new wilderness port where the owls hoot one to sleep & the Wolves howl one awake. Word came that the Yorkers had turned back for another mine. We determined to go on & were overtaken by Bryden who said they were still going to Trinity River but going up the east side of the Sacramento. At Chiles Ranche[171] Spaniards were lassooing horses with dexterity, one throwing the Lassoo around the neck & the other around the fore leg and throw them. Have seen Mexicans lassoo Spanish Cattle which they do on horseback where they delight to be with a Lassoo. Had some trouble to get wagon across deep ditchs with steep banks which were dug either as drains or for fences, years ago. After we struck the River again 8 miles above the road (or path) follows along its banks. This valley is perhaps the prettiest in the world — bounded on the right by the silvery sheet of the Sacramento — fringed with fine timber, & on the left bounded by the horizon — the gently undulating plain extends seemingly unbounded covered with good grass knee high, and occasional clumps of fine spreading oaks — groves of willows &c which with an "Italian sky" bending over it makes scenery delightfully lovely. Mc saw several deer & ahead of us start in wild scampering mood a lot of Spanish Cattle which like all animals on this plain look sleek & fat. Breakfasted with good relish at 10 o'clock. Left camp at 3 o'clock in great heat & camped on the river for the night at 7 o'clock. The river all along is pretty & beautifully timbered. Bryden caught 4 Salmon trout at noon & shot four partridges which we made a supper of, quite palatable. These birds were all but one shot with a rifle from one bush. They fly not off at the report of a rifle but sit still while their comrades fall by their sides. Swarms of musquitos in camp tonight. Distance 20 miles.

FRIDAY 31ST. And such another night, did not sleep 15 minutes on acct of the rascally musquitos, uncivilized scamps — wind nor cold would check them. They sang, presented their bill & took pay in blood (more precious than gold dust) Bryden & I curled down together. He declared they worked through 2 pr blankets. McC tried the wagon without evading them. Price flung his hat around him — now one would be up then another & ours was a hard lot. Owls made the woods that skirt the Sacramento ring with their hooting noise. Took breakfast before daybreak & after trying to get within Rifle range of a lot of Elk without success left camp (Musquito Camp) at an early hour & reached Fremont[172] on the west bank of the River at 8 o'clock. Approaching this village of a few houses is the finest bottom I ever saw with stock grazing on. Saw another lot of 3 Elk appear large as cows. Vernon[173] on the opposite bank of the river from Fremont looks from its location on the junction of the Sacramento & Feather Rivers romantic. The curve

of the River is fine here & altogether the view delightful.
Price & I fished without success & laid up for the day
at Fremont to await the Yorkers wagon from the other
side of the River. Roses of a small size light colored are
in bloom & a beautiful yellow poppy. 5 miles conversed
with an Iowa lady who wishes as soon as her husband
makes money to return to the States to raise & educate
her children better than she can here. A flock of several
hundred Geese flew over the River near camp & a man
shot one down which dropped heavy into the River &
the flock turned back in confusion.

SATURDAY, SEPT. 1. Dew had fallen to wet my head
& bedding & fog raised along the river this morning.
Bryden having been out yesterday to hunt up the Yorkers & his party & found one of the Yorkers lost — he
returned & we left early this morning for the "Trinity
Diggins" not knowing where we would meet them. Bot
a lb of Lead & paid 37½ cts for it in Fremont. Our
trail lay along the River bank for 5 or 6 miles to a
Ranche where it strikes off to the left to avoid sloughs
&c. Struck at noon on our left the dry bed of a stream
& having already suffered for water we camped & dug
two little wells & at 3 ft depth found good water to our
great joy. Had some doubts as to our being on the right
trail. A fellow who came out in Grahams[174] Command
& now employed in the Quarter Master department at a
salary of $3000, passed on horseback carrying an express
to Sonoma about 50 miles distant — is going with a Government exploring party to the head of the Sacramento
to see about new "diggins" & thinks with his salary &
the privilege of digging Gold & Rations in the bargain
he can live. A white & Colored man with pack mules
passed & got a drink of water & in turn passed the bottle
— the white man could give no information about roads
or miles & said he nor the Negro knew anything — but
the *darky* being the smartest & cleverest of them insisted
he *did* know & would tell, but did us no good. Drove an
hour after the full moon in all her splendor rounded up

in the East & the sun had set in the West like a ball of
blazing fire & camped by a pond receiving its waters
from a spring over which the water stands & is shaded
by some Willow & Oaks under whose branches we spread
our beds with each a Rifle or a Pistol by his side. The
Wolves howled & barked fiercely. On our way today a
young panther of 2/3 growth came up to the road within
50 ft of me when he discovered his strange company &
on a moments reflection turned back seemingly with more
of an air of surprise than fear. I was in advance of the
wagon. Game is abundant on this trail Deer, Antelope,
& Elk are almost constantly in sight, Wolves are no less
abundant, Partridges are in countless flocks & you often
approach them within a few steps. Doves also a good
many & a peculiar bird of white & grey spots. Squirrels
that live in holes in the ground are very numerous, instead of running up a tree to avoid you they run down
into their holes — are greyish rather small & unapproach-
able. Our trail led through as pretty a bottom land as
ever eyes rested on — stretching out in great width studded with large Oaks that frequently hang their branches
to near the ground as if gracefully to embrace & spread
out beautifully groaning under the weight of long Akorns.
The soil is rich — grass abundant & of best kind. In
places are fields of wild oats looks just like cultivated
stand thick & with filled heads — but shorter in straw
than cultivated. Along the roses & yellow poppies flowers
in full bloom also sun flowers. Noticed a few Sicamore
trees had sharp leaves, Oaks have small leaves which never
fall off as it is clean under the trees & in this country
have not seen a tree of any kind going to decay all appear
thrifty which adds to the beauty of groves & woods here.
Near the Ranch we passed on the river a lot of Spanish
cattle came running toward the wagon with threatening
aspects. This cattle is dangerous but did no harm to our
caravan. The middle of the day is unusually warm feel
this evening uneasy about the trail we go too far south
for our road. Distance 25 miles.

SUNDAY 2. Left camp early several deer kept at a distance this being a watering place. Passed a deserted Ranche. I was up for information as to trail (if anyone was to be found) House is several apartments built at various times to enlarge — built of logs. A clab board door fastened with a string of buckskin. Look in the departments — ground floors with a hide or two lying as a carpet & a few boards lay in disorder in one — rooms smoky filthy & forbidding. No windows — a pair of mill stones in an outbuilding. A pin drove in at hole of the runner answered to turn it on a kind of pivot in the center, 2 ft in diameter. A filthy yard on one side enclosed with picket logs fastened to strips with rawhide. Rode to a decent enclosure of some graves a few hundred yds off on a rise of ground — two enclosures of clab board paling. Here Antelope seemed to come from all directions in flocks, numbering perhaps 100. A fine location for a Ranch. Rode along dry bed of stream to left of road & found two deserted Rancheros of less pretensions than the first & in filth surpassing it much. Found hanging on a tree by a fire the hind quarters of an Antelope (fresh) which having been left for the public by packers who could not take all. I brot it along to the great joy of our little squad & we found it tender & sweet. Reached another deserted ranch by the trail wagon by it with jerked beef &c on it. Door was a dry hide set against the jambs to close the hole or doorway & things appeared as if inhabited — (saw here the first cat since I left the States). This was doubtless an American Ranche. Here to a certainty found we had strayed from the right trail, it seeming to run out entirely (or the road runs into the ground). Turned about & went back to the camp of last night having been 5 miles out. On return saw the finest Cattle (near the first Ranche of this morning), fit as could be. Bryden & I on horseback returned & rode to the right trail for miles along new paths where the stillness of death seemed to prevail save when broken by the feathered songsters, returned to the north for 7 or 8 miles on another trail which grew better as we proceeded & being right course concluded to return to wagon which we reached after a hard days ride an hour after dark. Distance (Bryden & myself) 40 miles.

MONDAY 3. Left early on our way back some four miles & struck to the north on a level bottom bounded in distance only by the horizon. On the left a range of hills or undulating prairies with a smoky atmosphere & scorching sun this was the days scenery. Antelope abounded. Nooned in the midst of this hot plain (having carried water in my rubber bag). Soon saw at a distance of 4 or 5 miles the "Lone Tree" to which we were directed for water. Found it 3 on left of trail after crossing bad ravine & ½ mile above found some slough water which a man drank of a few days since & died after a short illness. Dug a little well near by & got tolerable water. Watered & grazed horses, made supper & left for main trail which we had difficulty in finding being over taken by nightfall. Struck at random across the seemingly endless plain & fortunately found the trail. Traveled until 12 o'clock & camped in the plain without wood or water. Distance [blank] Miles.

TUESDAY 4. Had difficulty in finding horses, after walking for miles before & after day light found them & left camp at 7 o'clock, was by mistake left behind for some hours to look for Bryden. Overtook wagon again, saw two flocks of Antelopes 20 to 30 in each. Nooned at a slough from the river, dug for & got pretty good water in dry bottom of slough. At this place were many human bones & several skulls — apparently of Indians. The place wore a forbidding aspect. Had but little grass. Saw bare footed Indian tracks in sand & a Bears tracks of extraordinary size, had followed the trail for some miles which here is walled in by weeds & bushes high as our animals. Another large herd of Antelopes. Trailing after night had difficulty to keep on the trail. Rode ahead & lost road several times. Rode on side of road & found myself in the midst of an Indian Village surrounded with holes dug in the ground as is their custom. Thought I heard one grunt in his hole. This was on the bank of the River but I could not discover it in the darkness. Found the trail again & camped in an oak grove at 10 o'clock without water. Distance [blank] miles.

WEDNESDAY 5. Left at break of day. Had a chilly night. Struck the River again. Passed lots of fine cattle, saw Antelopes & Wolves without number, Wolves howled & came near to us at night. Grapes are beginning to ripen & there is an abundance of them. Bryden & I got very good & sweet ones. The vines are for miles clinging to & winding around the Oaks & cover the willows, some vines are barren & others loaded down with beautiful clusters of grapes, bluish & smallish. Nooned on the river. Saw large quantities of wild peas some speckled & others black. Have vines two to three feet. Acorns have nearly their growth & are fuller on trees than I ever saw. Many are from one to two inches long — are used by the Indians for food. Piles of Musscle shells are strewn along the River bank which the Indians get out of Rivers bed & eat. Also wasps comb or nests which they roast while the young are soft and eat them. They also eat seeds of grapes & roots. Are called California Diggers. Saw 6 or 7 diving in the River while nooning who came to the wagon, are perfectly naked. Have bushy black hair cut around, seem but a step above the brute creation. Have no marks of intelligence. Seem without shame standing before you & remind you of Adam in the Garden. Could understand nothing they said & consequently could learn nothing about our route. The valley along here beautiful. Rode ahead at dusk for camp through weedy bushes. Horses timid in such places. Met encamped on the river 4 men bound for the Trinity Diggins (Freeman[175] & others from Mass, & N.Y. had a sick man with them who had one mule & that very lame). Went back & brot our wagon to this camp after dark. These men like us look dusty & wear marks of outdoor life. Wear long hair & have but little modern Yankee left.

THURSDAY 6. Left camp after our simple meal which we had early. The night unusually warm for California. Were pestered continually by musquitos which is generally the case where camped on Slough as in this instance. These Sloughs often extend for miles into the bottom. Bryden & I gathered fine grapes which seem riper & more abundant as we ascend the river. Noticed a fishing place of the Indians seemed like rude fence across the river. They catch very large Salmon Trout which I cannot get to bite though they often shoot out above the water after flies &c. Saw another lot of Indians coming out of the bushes on the opposite side & sporting in the River. When these Indians have Gold dust they carry it among their bushy hair tied in rags &c. and cannot appreciate the value of it. Have given a lb of gold for a lb of fancy beads. The sun is intensely hot from 11 to 3 o'clock. Passed another deserted Ranche. Men living on Ranches have nearly all either gone to the mines or to the sea shore for health. Nooned with the 4 packers. Bryden & I tried to shoot Antelope of which we saw large flocks, but they make great speed for the clear plain & we got none. Camped on slew near the River among a lot of Oaks.

FRIDAY 7. Left on our way as the sun rose like a ball of fire in the heavens. The birds made the delicate foliaged trees & shrubbery skirting the river speak musical notes & the "Kinitas," Antelope, Squirrels &c held their gambols on the beautiful plain. Passed over bed of a dry stream which occur pretty frequently emptying Surplus water into the River in the rainy season. These beds of streams & washes as well as other places are covered often with the most fanciful stones & pebbles imaginable — being sand stone slate &c with delicate & innumerable veins of quartz running through the whole. Quartz is the most common of stones here & nearly all others mixed with it. Nooned on a slough & dug a spring the water of which seemed impregnated with magnesia, looked whitish & tasted of sulphur. Very warm day. Put in team as leader the Indian pony & worked as well as it knows. Indian horses easily broken to work. Saw numbers of antelopes in flocks, & droves of wolves. Price & I walked ahead, saw the finest lot of horses I ever saw were as fat as could be were lot of breeding mares, studs & colts of all sizes, some 50 of them colts looked like gingerbread colts, fat & sleek & seemed pretty tame. The team turning too much to the left missed the ranch. Struck across to a dry stream dug a good spring & camped, having been without water for some time looked for it anxiously beheld with delight the white arms of a Sicamore which seldom disappoints the thirsty traveler.

SATURDAY 8. Left camp in good spirits, our friends the four packers with sick man camped below at the ranch. Saw on the road Grizzly Bear tracks of great size, they love to travel on the sandy road & often follow it for miles, hardly a day but we see tracks. A bare headed Indian (as they all are here) came on a good horse in full California lope & rig, said to him Good Morning at which he laughed could not talk English so we let him pass soon returned in full speed with lot of horses & colts, the latter thus learn to lope as matter of necessity from youth up. Came to & stopped at Col. Ides[176] ranch who is absent on a tour of the States. His son had in the yard a fine mare, the fattest animal I ever saw — merely on the grass — asked $200 for her. Have 500 head of cattle, Spanish & American, prefer the latter for working & breeding. American cows often in 3 years have a progeny of 6 head — everything brings forth well here. Spanish cattle breed slowly look after their cattle but once a week & many only once in three months. Rain which occasionally falls about harvest time takes substance out of grass. Last winter more snow than before known in the valley, surprised the Indians much. Ide came out in 45. Of the family are digging above & employ Indians. A dozen or more Indians of all sizes about the Ranche, look filthy, are good natured & gamble off clothing if get any. Games are simple with bones & by closing hands with little sticks in & guessing which hand &c. Are timid about riding until broke to it by giving them instructions. Sell Beef here at $10. pr 100 lbs. Packers bot some & were jerking it, cut it into thin slices lay over a frame work 3 ft from the ground with fire under, dry it in 24 to 30 hours — use no salt on it & it keeps always after. Indians assist for the bones & fat or grits. Ides inform me that a single man has the Ranche below, curious life on Ranches. Two miles above Ides comes into a road which crosses the River by a ford. Nooned among rolling plains with narrow river bottom. Wagon of Cincinnati men just from the States passed — came in upper road past Lawsons.177 Passed over hills to the last watering place on the River for some distance & camped at midnight in a beautiful point of the bottom where the road leads up a dell or ravine. Oregon teams from the mines above are camped near.

SUNDAY 9. Filled gum bag & bucket with water the distance being without it being 18 miles. Traveled slow our team being weak. The bottom of River we left on yesterday. The scenery is now rather barren & desolate begins to appear like a Gold Region. Yellow brown hills & ravines in the distance see quite a range of mountains ahead to our left as well as on the opposite side of the river. Saw bear tracks today as usual, partridges as all along — abundant — on these hills the stones are small quartz mostly with sandstone. The road very dusty like brick dust. Oak trees more stunted but growing under loads of Acorns from 1½ to 2 inches long. Wild Lemon Trees or bushes abundant stems of which are brown & smooth. Has just shed old bark leaves thick & green — looks pretty — a nut grows also here similar to hazel nuts on bushes much like them. Wild rose bushes of large size. On top of a hill found a round hole 10 ft in diameter with water. Watered horses & nooned. Made the balance of the desert & reached Cottonwood Creek at 4 o'clock.

This is a fine little stream emptying into the Sacramento is constant, is fringed with fine Cottonwoods, Willows & Oaks, water fresh & has gold at the head. Camped McC. & Bryden went to Readings[178] Ranche 3 miles below. He was absent, lot of Indians about. The Yorkers wagon not yet here. Our 4 packer friends came to camp with another sick man, one of them had ague which Freeman said almost shook his horse to pieces. Rode up to the wagon & asked for medicines. I divided small quantity of Tartar with him & with my sympathy for sick man in this inhospitable region he left. How sickness tries a man, no medicine or physician in the valley, no accomodations, no proper provisions — & to sleep out at nights. Met an old Arkansas man & son just from the States, said he came over the mountains where no Antelope could come over, thought it beat Arkansas. His old woman told him not to come & is sorry he did not listen to her advice.

MONDAY 10. Finding we could take our wagon 25 miles further, left a note for our friends back to come on & left for the Trading Post[179] 12 miles above. Roads pretty good, struck the river again, watered, got grapes & soon met a man with an ox team who had been a mountain man, told us to turn back as the mines were very poor on Trinity, & the dry diggins on the Sacramento. This man & his comrade with a little son had a scrape with the largest Grisly Bear he had ever seen at the Trading Post where he camped last night. Thought it was another horse came up to his, tried to chase him off & growled at him. Said it was the first time he had been afraid of one. Treed all the men about, the father climbed a tree & his son run behind a bush. Thus it is not safe to lay as we do each night around the wagon. Reached the Post on Clear Creek (another fine constant tributary of the Sacramento) at 3 o'clock, camped. News unfavorable of the diggins here & emigrants without much & pouring in to them by the upper or Oregon road across the mountains which they take 60 miles east of the Sink of Marys River. Price was last night & today unwell on acct of having washed last night & not dressed properly in the cool evening. Met our Arkansas men here. The old man "Unkle Jo" we call him is a droll matter of fact funny old man & though he says he is religious at home & displays his Bible here he got *high* tonight & was sport for the camp. Came with his inexperienced son to take care of him but I fear sets a bad example. The Trading Post or house is poles placed upright. Miners are jerking beef here. It sells at 25 cts pr lb hind & fore quarters alike. Distance 12 miles.

THURSDAY 11. Left for the springs[180] from which point we calculate to pack across the mountains. Road for some distance level over bottom but before noon struck red hills again & mountains appear in the distance. Ascended & descended very bad hills & nooned at the foot of the worst on the river among huge rocks where grass is precious, on a kind of level corner between the hills & mountains which at a little distance ahead & to the left look picturesque & formidable. The river here falls some 2000 ft in 20 miles. Are in the midst of dry "diggins" crevices of rocks & beds of ravines are seeked & dug up to yield "the root of all evil" but the returns are not so rich as expected yielding only from $\frac{1}{4}$ to one oz pr day to a man. After nooning ascended another long & steep hill & on top met an Oregon man who informed us we were on the Oregon Trail which was extremely disagreeable turned back & camped where we had nooned & found our Cincinnati friends there too under the same mistake. Were told the road to the spring led up a ravine near by but could not find it. The Oregon man after friends of his camped with us was alone horseback & sick "said he had the Gold Fever" first & then the chills & fever. Might have done well enough at home has property but wanted some change & now goes home without it. Distance 16 miles.

WEDNESDAY 12. Left camp after a long hunt for horses on our back track. Price quite unwell today had difficulty in getting over the hills the road over being rocky & sandy

& very steep. Nooned on the River made gruel & black tea for Price as I had before. Returned on trail back probably 10 miles & struck in to the right over the bottom & ascended a long canon or ravine. Passed Price resting & could not get him to go along with me after going 2 miles with wagon & he still back we waited & I returned for him to the place I left him & found him not felt alarmed as to his fate in this country full of Indians & Bears either of which destroy life without scruple & this brot me to think of my situation 2 miles from wagon alone with no arms but a bowie knife. Returned to wagon & Bryden & I started back again (armed) & discovered Prices track on a trail used by packers a kind of cutoff — followed it for some miles & found him ahead of the train which soon came up. Being very weak got into the wagon at dusk. Soon overtaken by darkness among miserable hills & stopped ascending hill with gorges & heights around looking wildly romantic & a fit home for beasts of the forest, remained with wagon & Price while Mc & Bryden took the horses ahead in the darkness for water & returned after an absence of two hours with some of the precious liquid for which we waited eagerly. Were 2 miles from it. Laid down in this now forbidding looking place on the road & slept as men do who are fatigued caring little for comfort save as resting place.

THURSDAY 13. Had a chilly night in our desolate sloping "bedroom," Price quite sick made him gruel & black tea. Waked in the night & looked around me all hushed in slumber no sound save that doleful one which the wind made through the pine tops I thought of the changes in life, better days, friends I left behind and the dubious prospects here in this land of splendid overgrown fortunes, and miserable misfortunes. Had difficulty in finding the horses after found them at noon made two loads of ours (Price having to ride the hills being very steep) & with considerable labor reached the springs181 the furtherest point on our route to Trinity to which wagons can go. Here are two good springs, clear cold water but like nearly all California water has some mineral in it although not perceptible to the taste. Made a bed as best we could in the wagon for Price. Distance 2 miles.

FRIDAY 14. Found Price weak this morning I waited on him all day & was kept busy. Had quite a bad spell in the afternoon had taken cold first had a chill & today fever & has finally turned into an old kind of cholic complaint, which I relieved by a mustard plaster. Made during the day gruel several times, black tea, rice water, cream tartar & stewed peaches. McC. gone out with Bryden & Freeman & Severing on a prospecting expedition & returned at twilight. Are expecting the Yorkers & Brydens partners daily. None but Oregon folks camped here all summer nearly all sick during the season. Two men only died, disease seldom fatal in this country. These diggins opened last spring by the Oregon folks some did excellently occasionally made 6 to 7 dollars per day in Rock Creek and Salt Creek. Oregon folks good miners. In outdoor habits are well adapted to this country & the manner of living here. Are generous & have (most of them) taken the cream of the mines.

SATURDAY 15. Went out in company with Bryden, Freeman, Severing & Barlow182 prospecting. Traveled over many hills & valleys high & deep enough to make me quite tired carrying pick, shovel, pan & scraper. Were in several ravines got small piece myself in one when scouring got several in crevice, followed Salt Creek which is turned pretty well inside out. Met several digging who made about $10 pr day & felt discouraged. Found some fine grapes at an opportune time when we were parched with thirst. Barlow is the sick man who was with the others coming up the Sacramento, is still unwell & laments that he, fool like, as he says left the luxuries & conveniences of refined life in N. Y. City for this country. Has spent much to come out & left a family behind. Though perhaps not very rich yet nearly all the many ravines among these mountains have gold. Found Price some better this evening & am glad to find that the Yorkers &

Brydens men have arrived in the neighborhood & camped some miles back. Left 3 men behind, two sick & were nearly every one at times sick on their way up.

SUNDAY 16. Price mending slowly — waited on him today Yorkers had much trouble to find horses which have to be hunted each day for miles the grass being very poor. Washed, changed clothes, read some & felt as though it really was Sabbath which I could not lately or not more than two or three other times for the last five months. Ours is a romantic camping place on a hill with pine studded mountain ridges & deep dells around. Springs in this country usually on hills & outlet sinks before the water flows far. 8 or 10 camps under trees within sight. Freeman raised a small American Flag which reminds me of Fatherland & many stirring scenes, Freeman & Severing left on a prospecting expedition today, others camped here generally kept the Sabbath but hear reports of guns fired occasionally. Of the Oregon family camped below us the old lady & two or three daughters dressed up & the change of cotton drilling for calico which one of the girls made was quite Sundayizing the matter.

MONDAY 17. Freeman, Severing & partners left for Trinity give Barlow dust as a present. Barlow left alone unwell thinks this is "the climax of misery." Bryden & Yorkers found their horses some 3 miles from wagon. Price improving some but looks badly & is weak can sit up & walk about a little. Yorkers sick take hot coffee (very strong) with salt in it for fever & ague.

TUESDAY 18. Left early — divided provisions &c. Left balance not taken in wagon in charge of an Oregon family. Packed two horses (Dick & Hinkle) & Price rode one. Left in co. with Bryden & Co. at noon. Followed a packers trail winding around mountains through ravines & over steep ascents. Scenery wild & in places romantic — pines, cedars, wild lemon Black & White Oaks &c in way of woods. Had an almost perpindicular descent to Clear Creek 6 miles on the road. Camped on Clear Creek the water of which is unhealthy mineral. Distance 11 miles.

WEDNESDAY 19. Left camp & pursued our way which is a very poor path winding at times around mountains 1000 ft high midway up & animals constantly in danger of losing foothold. We followed Clear Creek all day, on its banks lay scattered a mans clothing & some bones I took to be human & nearby found a grave dug in the sand now rifled of contents probably by wolves. The stench being too great could not approach quite to it. This made a solemn impression on my mind. Passed huge black basaltic (volcanic) rock curiously shaped near by a substance resembling in appearance & taste Salt Petre oozes out of the earth — looks white an acre in size crust ¼ inch thick. In creek out of crevice of rocks oozes a white substance like Calomel supposed to be poisonous. Descended another almost perpindicular hill & many dangerous places along precipices. Brydens grey mare losing footholt rolled down hill with pack. The pack rolled to creek & got wet. Mc unwell today. Clear Creek dry where we camp but water ¼ mile above & also below. Scenery today was often grand always wild & rather desolate. 14 miles.

THURSDAY 20. Had a restless night. Bryden & Co remained back met lot of men who had done well on Trinity, saw a black tailed deer. Saw the starting point of Clear Creek now dry here. Head at the dividing ridge that we crossed today ascent & descent long & very steep scenery from ridge grand, detached mountains running in curious direction thousands of feet high studded with finely tapering pines & cedars. Through an immense gorge you see high ridges running in ends abruptly cut off. Mc quite unwell today Price not so well. I feel fatigued walking over those mountains which rise ridge after ridge in endless numbers & variety. Struck the Trinity & after crossing a crystal clear brook coursing its way over pebbles that sparkle in its bed like gems. Following down the river emerge on a beautiful bottom a mile in extent. Camped in a pleasant place 3 miles below where we struck the river on its bank river low 30 yds wide, rapid current & very deep in places though generally fordable, water clear & fresh. Distance 13 miles.

FRIDAY 21. On our way down the river (could not stop last night) had kind of fever & chills under a scorching sun & camped at 10 o'clock. All sick (I had fever) other sick men camped here, seems to be sickly here, cause probably sleeping on ground in low places along river bank & the water though clean appears to have poisonous mineral qualities, operates strangely on the kidneys. Bryden & Co. came to camp at twilight, Cain sick. Tells us one of their animals rolled down a hill 60 or 70 ft with pack. Have today unfavorable accts of these "diggins" and are all sick. Had an Indian alarm, sick man near by saw some Indians ste[a]l from camp here, have fears for our horses which the naked rascals eat. Fired a rifle & pistol to scare them & went to be with our usual bed fellows — rifle & pistol. Distance 5 miles.

SATURDAY 22. Had another miserable night & a chill & feel poorly. Left Bryden & Co. behind & went on our forlorn way sick & discouraged. Forded the river 3 times, rapid current & large rocks & stones in bottom make it disagreeable fording. Met two Illinois boys camped sick & without animals. Passed Readings Bar[183] which has yielded richly. Nooned on river bank where I was very sick. Had fever, my head seemed pierced by a thousand needles & my joints & back in particular ached to distress. Drank a pint of hot coffee, sweat profusely & got better. Crossed the river here & followed down & camped on bank near two parties in one camp — old miners, feel much fatigues. Price & Mc. still sick. 7 miles.

SUNDAY 23. Am weak indeed & no appetite. Price returned without finding horses. I had to go for them over great hills very pictures of desolation & returned after a scrambling walk of several miles without horses, tired indeed. Saw several Indian huts deserted with willow gold washers about, made artfully. All sick — horses gone — 50 miles from stock over mountains. These times "try mens souls." Men in next camp deserted soldiers, one regular, one volunteer, latter asked former "Had you regulars down there to desert or did you just naturally leave." We just walked off. Spent this day miserably in camp.

MONDAY 24. Mc brot horses to camp which we hailed with joy. Heard last night the shrill noise of a Panther. Tracks appeared in the trail this morning. Passed down the river what is called the Kenyon Trail over dangers steeps & precipices. The river walled in by huge rocks 10 to 30 ft high in places, water forced through gorge of a few feet rushing in sprayey whiteness. Met lot of men who had seen before making an oz pr day. Camped on river bank, bot fresh beef at 50 cts pr lb. Are all sick with chills & fever. Distance 6 miles.

TUESDAY 25. Have slept for few hours for 3 nights. Had miserable pain in head last night & fever, all sick. Had today a severe chill with distressing pain in my bones & head, am troubled with cramps and here we are distant from comforts & necessities.

WEDNESDAY 26. Feel some better today but spent a miserable night have to keep my head wet. Price & Mc sick with fever & chills & getting worse.

THURSDAY 27. Have slept but a few hours all the past week. Had a chill this evening, the balance still sick & prospects gloomy enough.

FRIDAY 28. Feel a little better had a hard night keep my head bathed in cold water. Had another chill have to go 2 miles over hills after horses which exhausts me much.

SATURDAY 29. All sick, Mc badly. I am gaining some little. Rode down the river a few miles a sick Missourian stewing peaches gave me I relished them much. Met a number of sick men. Prices horses in correll rate from $125 to $200. Met an old friend of the plains & took a little dinner with him. Four men & two Indians made this forenoon 4¼ oz gold. Met Freeman & Co all sick with F. A green sick young doctor had sent where sick

men were crowded in. Enough to draw sympathy from
a heart of stone. On my return felt my usual chill at hand
& could hardly keep on horse with a burning thirst & head
ache. After dusk an Indian with gig approached I pointed an old pistol at him which I did to scare him as it
would not go off & he as quick pointed his gig at my
breast being only some 20 ft off. I threw out my hand
in token of friendship & he desisted & passed on. My
pistol being a bad one he had the advantage of me.

SUNDAY 30. Have pain in every bone & my head.
Washed & changed clothes & feel better for it. Am very
weak. Price some better Mc. very sick. How I would
like to spend this Sabbath at home. All is gloom here &
prospects ahead no better.

MONDAY OCT. 1. Feel poorly. Mc. dangerously sick.
Agreed I should go for a Dr. two miles below. Walked
far in heat for horses to cross river. Found him not being
up the river. Passed camp in evening & give Mc dose of
Quinine & will call in morning. Also gave me a dose of
Quinine.

TUESDAY 2. Dr. Called gave all Quinine thought all
would be well in a few days & charged $16. a piece quite
charitable these medical men are (Dr. Peter Robinson,184
Seneca Co. N.Y.)

WEDNESDAY 3. Slept a little more than usual of late
but feel poorly. Mc is a little better, nothing to interest
camp hear nothing of Bryden & Co. or the Yorkers.

THURSDAY 4. Had a cold windy night could not keep
warm under 2 pr blankets. Feel like the rest — no better.
Bryden & two of the Yorkers came to camp this morning. Have all been sick. Bryden & Co. had tools Money
&c stolen by Indians who also stole a blanket from Woods
bed while asleep. All camped 6 miles above. Feeling like
eating Fried mush & boiled & fried some — the finest
good tasting dish I had for weeks. A man staggered into
& about camp under a fit of insanity & left again.

FRIDAY 5. Feel some better. Went two miles after
horses which we constantly fear losing to Indians. Bot

rib of fresh beef & pc liver at camp below. Fried liver tasted well & other made a palatable soup.

SATURDAY 6. Our precious little stock of beef & liver missing this morning. The Indians or wolves have it. Price gone to Bryden & Co. camp. Feel very lonesome being only Mc & myself in camp & Mc is helpless.

SUNDAY 7. I am very slowly gaining strength begin to have appetite. Mc gaining very slowly, has lost all energy. Price returned found only the Yorkers, Bryden & Co. having started for the springs.

MONDAY 8. Many persons daily passing up & down the river under favorable circumstance I would call our[s] a romantic camp surrounded by very high mountain ridges studded with beautiful Pines, Cedars, &c. Price & myself able to be about.

TUESDAY 9. Had as usual a long tiresome hunt for horses. Commenced raining at 8 o'clock a.m. & rained all day & times hard preventing us from moving camp today as we intended. Having no tent our things got wet & were chilly. Got room in a tent below for Mc to sleep & took him there. Price & I dried our bedding in part by a large fire & laid down on the wet ground. Gave our provisions (all we could spare) to some Oregon men & we to receive some articles from their wagon at the springs & 25 cts pr lb for packing to Trinity.

WEDNESDAY 10. Foggy morning & chilly winds. Moved down the river each riding, having part of a pack in addition, camped on a fine bottom. Got room in a tent of Indiana folks for Mc. Am told of Capt. Stidgers[185] conduct on the plains by these men who traveled part of the way with him. He went to Oregon they say. The mountain tops are white with snow & today an occasional flake falls in the valley. 3 miles.

THURSDAY 11. Left the river going by a cutoff trail to avoid bad places on the river. Passed over a steep long & very high hill from which is a fine view of the endless chains & detached ridges of mountains, many now covered with snow making the air chilly here while in the deep valleys the sun is warm & pleasant. Camped under a shelter made of twigs by former travelers, with a large fire in front we were quite comfortable. 10 miles.

FRIDAY 12. Hunted horses till noon & Price too sick then to leave camp. Remained in same camp with gloomy prospects for the future. May meet much delay by sickness & have very little provisions.

SATURDAY 13. Left camp & followed clear little stream emptying into Trinity. Reached the river by a tolerably good trail & nooned at the upper crossing of the river. Crossed the barren hills on our way for several miles & camped on a pretty large bottom with a lot of Yorkers who cracked jokes around a large fire being a whole pine tree in a blaze. 10 miles.

SUNDAY 14. Foggy morning as usual on this river. Indians brot a salmon to camp we were glad to get for a dime & little in the way of coffee &c. Have gigs 20 to 30 ft long very light & artfully made were good natured Indians & had some clothing on. Nooned after leaving Trinity at the foot of the main ridge. Price sick, started to cross & in ascent Price taken ill with difficulty reached top of main ascent. Had to camp on this height without water having a little coffee in a canteen quenched Prices thirst, made a fire tied horses to bushes (there being no grass) & thus camped in as uncampable looking place as could well be imagined. The stars in a clear field of sky vied with each other for twinkling beauty. Our camping ridge only about 20 ft wide had on either side ravines perhaps a thousand ft in descent too steep for a horse to go. 7 miles.

MONDAY 15. Moved off pretty early having had no supper or breakfast. The trail along here is dangerous as well as difficult descending the long steep hill of the main ridge. Price saddle (he & I rode on pack saddles) turned & he was thrown some 20 ft ahead of the horse into the dust which is deep to horses fetlocks here. Had some difficulty in ascending some of the steep hills with our heavily laden animals. Distance 18 miles.

TUESDAY 16. Wended our way to the springs. On Clear Creek noticed a number digging some have done well here. Could hardly recognize the springs as the same place, it being almost a city now.186 A great number sick here. Found wagon & things on it in good order. Oregon man give us a piece of light bread at supper which is a real luxury our living & fare is harder than that of the prisoners in the Ohio Penitentiary. Distance 14 miles.

WEDNESDAY 17. Mc & I bot a loaf of bread of Oregon woman for $1. & it was a treat. Sold off some of our provisions &c. Am informed that Ex. Gov. Shannon has purchased Readings Ranch on Cotton Wood Creek & grazes stock. Gives notice to that effect signed Shannon & Given.188

THURSDAY 18. After doing some trading left camp for the lower, or first springs to dispose of balance being pretty heavily loaded had difficulty in ascending a steep hill. Distance 3 miles.

FRIDAY 19. Arose early & went round among the numerous camps here to dispose of provisions & tools & by 10 o'clock had pretty well sold out. Prices irregular a/c of so many wagons returning to the city & sell at any price almost. Flour rates at from 30 to 75 cts pr. lb. Not being able to find the horses in time remained in camp.

SATURDAY 20. Saw curious meteoric display last night while in bed in my large & well aired chamber. Had an onion for breakfast first since I left home, cost $2. pr lb. Sold my gold watch at a sacrifice of $10. After being on the road 7 miles could not find my purse of gold dust containing from 150 to $175. Returned to the springs searched & inquired but found it not. Oh miserable luck. In a camp here a young man came in & weighed $45. he had dug in 2½ hours.

SUNDAY 21. Had a good supper with a clever lot of Missourians a mess of a joint stock company of 50. Capt. Campbell189 whose son in law lies dangerously ill here his flighty expressions about home &c are calculated to

draw tears. Lodged in good tent with some jovial Cin.
boys. Felt housed up too much in a tent. It has no stars
like my usual bedroom. After posting up two written
notices concerning my purse I left for Price & Mc who
I found camped near the Trading Post with some wagon
of the Yorkers who have all been sick. Inform us that
healthy looking jovial man Dake died at the springs,
surely life is uncertain. There being no grass or horse
feed at the springs my horse had but "Post hay" or
rather tree hay. Searched the wagon for my purse but
in vain. As I emerged from a ravine into the lovely
Sacramento valley the river winding through it like a
silver thread I felt a joyfulness which can only be realized
by one who has for a time lived in sickness among desolate
mountains — separated from communication with friends
or enjoyments of civilized life. Here the air is vocal with
the music of feathered songsters, flocks of wild geese or
brants wing their way from point to point in countless
numbers both day & night. Here the stately Elk the
fleet Deer & graceful Antelope roam in spite of the in-
trusion of numberless gold seekers who are going to &
fro in every direction & mode of locomotion. Here the
nude child of the forest in his native nudeness hunts the
salmon with his gig & the Sacramento yields of her abundance. Here the sleek cattle feeds (not upon a thousand
hills) but on plains bounded in view only by the horizon
and here are the habitations of men, evidences of civilization &c. Passed numbers of emigrants just in from the
States. Poor fellows looked fatigued & had a long hard
time of it. Camped on Cotton Wood Creek where Indians
from Ranches on the river stroll thickly. Had in sight
all day a snow capped peak on the opposite side of the
river while here in the valley it has been very warm. Had
the great satisfaction while going to bed this evening to
find the lost purse of gold dust. This pocket I had not
before used & it seems almost a miracle that it should
have been there. 25 miles from springs.

MONDAY 22. After a hunt till noon for the horses we

left camp (Price sick) felt fever & aguish today. Camped on river bank & had trouble to get water for horses on a/c of the steep high bank. A man with his all on his back came to camp & we being all unwell offered his services for boarding & carriage of his bundle. Entered into conversation with him & found he had been in nearly all countries on the globe, having twice made the trip around the world. Part of the time as a sailor. His name is Taylor. Left home 13 years ago & not seen his father since, & cares no more for home or friends, curious men in this world. Distance 20 miles.

THURSDAY 25. Have accepted Taylors proposition & he assists much. I am still unwell & quite weak. The journey thus far from Trinity has been laborious to me P & Mc being invalids I had much more to do than my strength allowed. Saw at a distance Indians gathering grass seeds. It looks novel the way they work. Camped on river with several Oregon families some of whom are on their way to the State & others to Oregon. Have done well in the mines. One of them had Indians to work, was here early in mining operations & made a fortune. Said he pack lot of Indians 50 lbs apiece & went over mountains 20 miles in a day. He made hundreds a day. Distance 25 m.

FRIDAY 26. I write by the light of a dim campfire after all the rest are in bed, as I often do being the only time to keep notes. Had a very chilly windy night one could hardly (keep) blankets from blowing off of bed & today is windy & cool. Taylor brot to Price & me in wagon a fine lot of grapes. These grapes are abundant along this river & good as cultivated grapes. Ascending from one of the many narrow ravines & ditches on this road the King Bolt broke & the hind wagon dropped. After two hours work started again & camped again with the Oregon families. There is a lot of girls in this Co. which will no doubt make good partners for some fellows who like they want to live camp life much as they are accustomed to it & look as though other accomplishments were vanities in their sight. Some horsemen of this party saw a lot of 200 Elk in a drove, Elk, Antelope &c keep off the road more than when we went up. Distance 23 miles.

SATURDAY 27. Did not start till noon for want of horses. Indians brot fine salmon to camp. Camped again with the Oregon families on the river. Today Taylor left us being offered $10 pr day to assist in driving lot Spanish cattle to the City. I could take an interest in experienced conversation. Distance 10 miles.

SUNDAY 28. Having hobbled horses last night were enabled to leave camp early. Suffer considerably from hard bed — makes one sore having only a Buffalo robe under one. Camped on the slough where we first struck it, the water stands in pools is green & full of insects. Made coffee of it which tasted bitter. Distance 24 miles.

MONDAY 29. Left camp early on our way over plain bounded only by the horizon. Fine Spanish cattle graze here. Reached the "Lone Tree"190 which is seen at a distance of 10 miles. Here the water is as bad as at the slough. Many have been taken sick after using it. Went to the head of the ravine — a mile & got some pretty clear but made bitter coffee. Distance 20 miles.

TUESDAY 30. Could not get a match to burn & left camp without breakfast on our way over a plain which the eye only finds relief when it rests on herds of Spanish cattle so sleek & fine looking, always looks wild. Reached a point where we dug a little well in the dry bottom of Cash Creek [Cache] as we went up where a Mr. Cochran191 is establishing a Ranche & who treated us kindly. Distance 16 miles.

WEDNESDAY 31. Had a blustery rain threatening night, chilly & windy today, & had sprinkle of rain. Took a cutoff trail very indistinct road & not leveled down yet. Passed a Ranche where a ladylike woman sat by the fire & gave me a lump of salt without charge we being out of salt. Bot a few lbs of fresh beef. Here horses, cattle and hogs seemed to overrun the plain. This Ranche is said to have 4000 head of Spanish cattle, 400 breeding mares & hogs plenty. At a distance of 10 miles volumes of smoke & crimson flames roll along & form with the clouds, being fire on the plains. Camped on river bank — feels quite wintry. Man with family camped close by said he was fool enough to bring his family to this country but said soon as he could raise it home would see him again. 4 or 5 interesting little girls enliven camp children are rather scarce here. Distance 22 miles.

THURSDAY Nov. 1. Price sick paid 50¢ for a pint of milk for him. The plain all covered for miles with stock belonging to folks in the city. On bank of river last night could at all hours and this morning too hear the fish leaping out of the water & large ones often splash in the water as would a man. Crossed the river on ferry boat after having had some trouble with the king bolt in our wagon. I counted 33 vessels of various kinds in port. The city has improved wonderfully, many good houses have gone up in the absence of our squad, about two months time. The streets are crowded with business & it looks indeed like a city noticed two or three buildings of zink & sheet iron. Felt great disappointment in getting no letters on my arrival here. Men coming from the mines are fond of luxuries, so we at once got light bread & pies & cheese. Found Barcus, Stone, Stiles, Bryden, McColm, Wood, & Cain of the Columbus folks here. Burke[192] of Columbus died on the Youba [Yuba]. Barcus, Stone & others buried him. Benj. Carpenter[193] died 160 miles this side Salt Lake of an absess. A Mr. Dimerest[194] of the Hunter Co. died on the plains. F. Breyfogle[195] & Denig left a few days ago for home. Capt. Walton[196] is a candidate for Senator & Mr Barnes[197] of Delaware for the House. The people behave & seem entirely satisfied without government but ambitious politicians must have office & therefore a self constituted government must be gotten up to spread the fame of some. Distance 3 miles.

FRIDAY Nov. 2, 1849. Price is sick is in tent with Barcus, windy & cool today threatening rain. Laid in camp nearly all day.

SATURDAY 3. Had a heavy storm & almost constant rain last night. Rained very heavy this morning, tents & calico houses had to take it some are blown down & water stands on the streets. Dr. Miley paid $1. for a dry sleeping place. The $8. Boarding House can't keep their boarders dry at all times. The mountains in sight are covered with snow. Cleared off in forenoon.

SUNDAY 4. Washed, changed clothes & felt better for it. Spent the day mostly in camp & it so occured that I could not go to hear preaching. A Methodist church sent from Boston is in sight & a pretty respectable frame church it will be when completed. Are organizing a Sabbath School & having preaching twice a Sabbath.

MONDAY 5. Rainy night & today still rainy, chilly & windy. Saw Booth & McCormack[198] of the Hunter Co. part of their Co. back yet. Mc. heavy black & fat is taken for a Spaniard at times. He says he saw as high as 10 funerals a day on the plains. Mostly of Cholera which disease came as far as Independence Rock & on this side. Says the road to California can be found by the graves on its side.

[Decker did not keep a Diary during the period from October, 1849 to March, 1850. From some fragmentary notes he wrote during that period, it is clear that Decker was in poor health. He spent this time recovering in the town of Fremont. His Diary resumes with the next entry dated March 18, 1850.]

PLACER MINING ON THE YUBA

Seeing the Elephant

VERNON MCH 18, 1850

MESSRS WILLIAMSON ROGERS, John Rogers[199] and myself having formed a partnership as a mess and prepared "an outfit for the mines" with a view of leaving Fremont some weeks since for that purpose, today (the weather being favorable) crossed the Sacramento by ferry at this place on our way to the South Fork of Yuba. Purchased a Gray Pony for $100 — and packed him with 100 lb for the balance of our things between 5 & 600 lbs is taken by Mr Brawley's team at 30¢ per lb to Deer Creek. Mr B has two teams & Mr White one, part of which being ferried across last week were not found here until late and we are here in sight of home for this night with a family by the name of Stewart.

Weighed myself & weighed 160 lb. Enjoying excellent health. Left many friends in Fremont whose Society I have enjoyed for some months with pleasure.

TUESDAY 19. J. R. and myself had a rather hard bottomed bed in a wagon, the cold wind blowing over us much as it would outdoors. Left Vernon at nine o'clock our road lay over the Feather River bottom which is gently undulating & apparently good soil, being covered with good grapes, occasionally clover a variety of the most delicate & beautiful flowers are profusely mingled with the verdure of this plain. The Sierra ridge with its snowy peaks presents a truly romantic scenery in the East, while the Butte[200] mountain in snowy garb runs paralel in the West, and the Sacramento & Feather Rivers course their winding way through the valley fringed with Oaks, Sicamores &c, making a scenery of fine contrast. Passed Nicolas[201] a town four weeks old on F. River, several ships laying in port. Road in places muddy and difficult. Camped on the plain where a scanty supply of wood afforded us sufficient fire to prepare a simple meal after which jokes and pleasantries engaged our company. Being all accustomed to camp life feel at home sleeping on the ground and cooking for self. The day was pleasant, the evening cool, but mosquitos on hand even though it be in March. Footed it myself **20** miles.

WEDNESDAY 20. Mr R arrived at break of day after a good nights rest on Tera Firma. Soon the east presented a singularly bright gilded horizon and a few moments after the sun was over the snowy peaks of the Sierra in her brightness gilding the scene in splendor. After partaking a hastily prepared breakfast the train moved on early & soon came to a very bad slew of Bear River,[202] but 10 or eleven yoke of oxen took over one by one of the wagons. Struck Bear River which we crossed by a kind of log built bridge. Toll $5.00 per wagon. Bear River is now some 30 to 50 ft wide timbered with white oak, Bucky in bushes & willow &c. The soil is apparently

richer than on the Sacramento and in places beautifully
rolling. Passed Johnson's Ranche[203] where they plowed
with 3 yoke of oxen. A few miles from the Ranche is
Dry Creek a pretty little wet weather stream timbered
as is B[ear] River with a nice little bottom covered with
good grass. Flowers abundant today & of various kinds
among them on the southern slope of some hills the Poppy
courted the sunny exposure. Squads of Indians watched
our movements from a hill & their conduct along here
gives us uneasiness as to our stock. Camped on a fine
sight on Dry Creek. Vegitation & foliage is more advanced here than on the Sacramento. Perhaps because
of less winds and chill in low valley surface.

THURSDAY 21. After a restless night witnessed another
beautiful morning. All nature here looks like the green
clad scenes of May in Ohio. Some trees in full foliage,
flowers abundant. Had an alarm last night thru presence
of Indians indicated by the cattle starting off. Brot them
in & all went to sleep again. Have reached the gold
region which is indicated by yellowish red soil on the hill
sides. Lots of grapes & Laurel bushes (or Wild Lemon)
with stunted white oaks and Live Oaks with Fir and
Pines. The view on the old emigrant road from a hill
after leaving the vallies is fine, presenting a rare com-
bination of contrasts in the bottoms and mountains between which one here stands. Passed a grave by the
wayside. Camped on a small wet weather stream which
rushes in places through kanyons and over falls formed
by huge boulders like some miniature Niagara. J. R.,
myself prospected here, the gold was very fine and not
abundant as desirable. As nightfall comes the Heavens
are overcast with clouds & the wind from the south, a
sure indication of rain. Our company all in good spirits.
Distance 10 miles.

FRIDAY 22. Having expected rain pitched & slept in
our tent on which I heard the rain spatter sometime before day. Rains in good earnest & all is gloomy & unpleasant in these mountains such times. Had several bad

hills & mirey places today. Crossed Deer Creek now
swollen by rains. Passed several camps & digins near
by where they make from 10$ to one oz per day but will
last only while the water in the ravine lasts. Ascended
and descended a number of bad hills. The scenery is
rather good mountain scenery. Stock chained up to wagon
being no grass as is common in the Gold Region and
Indians troublesome. Rained but little this afternoon
but threatening again. Distance 13 miles.

SATURDAY 23. Rainy morning & breakfast must be
prepared and camp labors performed unpleasant though
it be. Left at 9 o'clock our road wound around and lay
over dificult mountains, in places very mirey. Scenery
approaching the main charm of the scene in this region
is more like the Aleghanies than any other mountain
scenery in this country. Passed a lonely grave by the
wayside. Doubtless some emigrant. Broken wagons we
passed some ½ dozen. Left the emigrant road this evening. Have ascended much into the mountains, snow
lays here in places 6 inches deep & the weather cooler.
Most of the day drizzling, rainy & the fog would roll
along the shoulders of ridges & the lowering sky looked
so gloomy that it presented in full a specimen of the
Rainy Season in the mountains of California. Have
camped on Deer Creek204 the point to which teams will
take our things. Passed and saw a number mining washing with pans, rockers & quick silver machinery in ravine
along the road. Digging from one to 6 ft deep, disagreeable work, men much exposed here. Gold fine here. Beef
worth 60 cts per lb. Flour 75 cts &c. Our company all
in good spirits. Weather still foggy at times rainy and
gloomy. 15 miles.

SUNDAY 24. Rainy morning. Messrs Bradley & White
leave and sell their loads here — charge 30 cts per lb to
this point — Deposited part of our things here. Packed
the pony and ourselves and after a farewell to our friends
left Deer Creek Digins205 on our way to the South Fork
of the Yuba. The path when snow is away is muddy and

passes through mountainous country. Each of us packed
on our back from 30 to 60 lbs & it was toil of no ordinary character. Passed several ravines where men were
digging with various success. Met a number returning
from Yuba. Truly the miner has no abiding place. Constantly going from point to point. Reaching a point on
the mountain where the snow was in places 2 ft deep &
being fatigued pitched our tent for the night. Mr. R.
unfortunately fell from a log crossing a rapid little mountain stream of 2 ft depth, (Rock Creek),[206] making his
march yet harder. Distance 8 miles.

MONDAY 25. After mess council Mr R. left for the
Yuba to look for a claim. J R - myself proceeded on our
way to Deer Creek with the pony to bring another load
of plunder. It soon commenced raining & did so all day,
both of us trudged along coming back with packs on our
backs completely drenched in the rain. Met several squads
of miners passing & repassing with their heavy packs
there being no other way of getting provisions to the
Yuba on acct of the snow — Notice men at work in mud
and water & rain pouring on them. A more disagreeable
day has seldom fallen to my lot even in California. On
our return found Mr R had on acct of feeling unwell
& the bad weather stoped at the nearest tent on the hill
& was about moving our tent &c to that point, on reaching
the summit of the hill it rained rapidly all was wet the
wind blew & a more disagreeable time could not well be.
Pitched our tent near 2 men who keep a kind of movable
store. Snow all around us. Changed shirts & dried other
clothes by the fire in the chilling wind. After supper &
rain had ceased looked around for the first look at the
scenery, and was perfectly delighted with the view rare
as it was beautiful. Our camp is on the main dividing
ridge[207] (here quite warm) between Deer Creek & the
Yuba running here from East to West. This ridge is high
as any mountain peaks around in view & opposite to the
north are 3 forks of Yuba coming in between high mountains, the course of each fork (North, Middle & South)

being indicated by the immense volume of thick fogg which rise from each & the main stream and roll along the mountains beneath us forming a kind of basin of clouds in fantastic forms. Mountains lower than the point we view them from & all surrounded at a distance of many miles by very high ridges clothed in their snowy habliments [habiliments]. To the South also near by are the courses of Rock Creek & Deer Creek. The high & beautifully tapering Pine & Fir are the forest trees of these mountains with Laurel underbrush. All four had headache today caused probably by a coffeeless supper last night & breakfast this morning, our coffee and tea being on Deer Creek (distance 16 mi going and coming).

TUESDAY 26. Had a fine nights rest in pretty wet clothes & on very damp ground, pleasant today. Mr. R. left for Yuba prospecting. J. R. & myself went to Deer Creek again to bring the balance of our plunder. Passed some 40 packed men in squads for Yuba one asking whether we passed 4 pack jackasses just ahead, a quaint remark — a humorous expression or a joke is freely given & as freely received by miners here passing each other though perfect strangers. The words *how are you* seeming to be all the introduction expected by these men who have by this time seen much of the world & its ways. Passed along several ravines making into Deer Creek in which hundreds are diging & acres of gravel are dug up & laying in piles about. All kinds of washes are being worked — quick silver machines — common rockers — Long Toms & pans. Saw 5 men at a quick silver machine in a place where they made as high as 3 lbs $10 pr day — gold fine mostly — claims all taken up. In the tent where our things were deposited was left standing a cup with 3 or 4 ozs of gold dust & no one about. I am told 1 oz pr day is often made by rewashing dirt already washed — perhaps because laying on a pile exposed the clay is more cleanly washed a second time among which is the gold. On our way scooped up a pan of dirt from the bed of a little gulch washed out several particles of gold & much black sand. Had much trouble packing quick silver machine on a horse reached camp early & made a good supper of coffee biscuit & molasses. Had Mr. Epperson[208] with us all night & talked over our adventures on the plains, on Trinity and this country generally & gold making in particular. Distance 16 miles going & coming Deer Creek.

WEDNESDAY 27. Another fine morning & pleasant day. J. R. stayed in camp & washed our clothes while I made two trips packing our things 3 miles further it being found that animals could go that distance further on our way to Yuba. Worked my way with the poney 200 lb on him through snow from one to four feet deep — being in places drifted which seemed almost too much for man or beast to pass through, but perserverance overcomes many obstacles. Passed several tents on the way with banks of snow 3 ft around them. Passed several squads of men packing on their backs 50 to 60 lbs a piece. Pleasant day at times the sun shone warmly the snow glistening around me like a mass of pearls. Being a clear day could easily see the valley of the Sacramento with the timbered course of the river through it which is by our way here 98 miles distant.

THURSDAY 28. Another fine day. The sun hot at times. Packed on the poney & ourselves all our things to the point I packed the balance yesterday, met on the way two gentlemen to whom we sold the poney for $125. they taking him from the point of our deposits where soon after our arrival came to meet us Mr. Rogers. He had secured 3 claims on Lippards Bar.[209] The river being high little is known as to their richness. After a lunch packed ourselves heavy as we could carry & made for Yuba through & over snow in places 7 ft deep. The descent to the Yuba here is two miles[210] being about 4000 ft in places very steep snow half way down Yuba. Yuba is 40 to 60 ft wide running mostly in rapids dashing in spray over large boulders. The mountain closes it up on either side rising thousands of feet almost perpindicular the stream making frequent abrupt bends had many Bars on which tents were pitched by many awaiting the fall of the water to work. Some do well now. Crossed the rapid boisterous stream a little distance above rapids in a very clumsy log canoe managed by a green young man. Scrambled up an almost perpindicular hill with our packs, on hands & feet where a misstep might precipitate us into the depths a hundred feet below. From the crossing one mile above reached our Bar after scrambling over dificult hills & precipices & through brush & huge rocks. This has been a day of toil indeed on our arrival the men complained much of the digings. Distance from camp 10 miles.

FRIDAY 29. Although fatigued last night had but little rest — could not sleep our bed under an arbor of pine twigs. Felt the effects of yesterdays trip. Started again today to bring another pack. Felt more like enjoying the scenery than yesterday. The immense snows going from the heights rapidly raises the Yuba some 10 ft above high water mark. The river seems to have forced its way through these mountains which rise all along on its sides thousands of feet abruptly. Had a rather hard day of packing. Engaged to have 400 lbs packed to the river — 6 miles for $40 on mules. Met a packer with a mule fast in the snow shoved him out & floundered on again, ascending & descending the two mile hill is hard work. Were in danger crossing the river the canoe taking the start reached the oposite bank near the falls or rapids. Mr R. came up the heights acknowledging that he was scared having nearly lost his balance coming up with his pack & all hands agreed that I was scared yesterday in the snow situation. Weather pleasant today. Provisions not to be had at any price on the river. On top of the hill flour is $10 lb, pork $12. salt $1 &c, 50 cts for drink of liquor. Distance going & coming 16 miles.

SATURDAY 30. After a good nights rest got up with some evidence in my limbs of having acted the part of a mule in so far as packing was concerned. Prospected a little on our claims with no very flattering results. J. R. & myself went to the foot of the hill a mile below for our things engaged to be packed there. On reaching that point things not yet come on & quick silver machine can not be brought through the snow at present. On their arrival packed goods to the ferry & passed over loading myself when Messrs R. came & all took packs heavy as we could carry. Dificult & even dangerous path to pack. Cincinnatians are making ditch through the Ohio Bar[211] to turn the river out of its bed. Men on Bar below ours now make 2 oz pr day. Pleasant day 2 miles.

SUNDAY 31. Had a late breakfast & find ourselves the worse for packing. J. R. & myself went to the ferry & brought another & the last load of our things excepting the 2 machines. A Mr. Turner[212] went down to cross but would not risk it on the boisterous deep in a log. Washed & shirted & spent the balance of the Sabbath pleasantly after putting up our tent we once more feel at home. Cloudy today with a slight sprinkle of rain. Some & indeed all men here do more or less work on Sabbath — mining, prospecting, washing clothes, guning &c.

MONDAY APRIL 1ST. (All Fools Day) Had a comfortable nights rest, dreamed of home. After our usual breakfast of biscuits & coffee J. R. & myself started on our way to the top of the hill for the 2 machines on our way met men with provisions purchased 100 lb flour for $50. Passed over snow on hill 2 to 6 ft deep. Passed off rapidly. Arrived in camp with the machine (70 lbs) at noon (3 miles). Washed clothes &c. Pleasant cool day. On yesterday men made narrow escape crossing the river where we cross daily some jumped out of canoe & reached shore at the head of the rapids.

TUESDAY 2. J. R. & myself went for flour purchased yesterday & on way back sold it for $75. Some to mess of boys from Ohio. J. R. & myself did our first mining on this bar this afternoon with poor success making only $4.50. The river being too high to get to the Bar Rock.

Men on Bar below make 20 ounces & over pr day. Accidentally met a Mr Beach[213] (a peddler) from Columbus has sent home $2500.

WEDNESDAY 3. Quite a cool morning & pleasant day. On acct of hills we dont see the sun till 8 o'clock in the morning & sets again behind the western hills early. Mr. R & myself washed 50 buckets dirt & only got 25¢ so we quit that hole & prospected in afternoon making but $1.00 more. J. R. & myself on Bar above. Preparations making for turning the stream over this large bar of huge rocks. A kind of Kenyon here with a fall of 20 ft in as many yds. The water rushing in foaming sprayey whiteness through the rocks walling it up & projecting up in the bed. High water in this rapid river moves these immense rocks from bar to bar. Large Pine trees bear marks of falling rocks in floating down stream. Curious deep round holes worn in solid bed rock from one to 6 ft deep. The day closed with a delightful starlight evening. We look out of our Kenyon & hill walled stream nearly straight up to see the sky & see but little of it then.

THURSDAY 4. One year has this day elapsed since I left sweet home, friends & society for life in the wilderness — Many strange incidents have I seen in that time. Traveled about 5000 miles made some narrow escapes with life, undergone sickness & privations but never for a moment rued the descisin [decision] I made when I went on this uncertain journey, and now I am here in the Digins with plenty of provisions, good health & fine spirits. Felled a Pine tree across the river which the current floated off disappointing us in our prospects on the opposite side of the river. Weather pleasant made $5.00 prospecting & crevicing. Sold one quicksilver machine for $250. & took a common rocker at $40. which will sometimes suit us better. Our machine cost at Fremont $100. & freight here some $23.00 besides our packing. Made this trade with the Delaware Ohio boys, Moses Bodly &c.[214]

FRIDAY 5. J. R. with two others left on a prospecting expedition for a week to look out better "digins." Mr. Beach of Columbus passed here has settled on a Bar at the mouth of the kenyon on the Middle Fork of the Yuba. Mr. R. & myself worked at different places today making but $4.25. It is clouding up. Had a distant report of thunder which is very rare in this country & Oregon. The atmosphere being it seems not much charged with electricity.

SATURDAY 6. Rained most of the night & this morning pretty rapidly. The stream on the rise. A bootless & hatless fellow passed the tent enquiring for shoes or hat to buy. His feet in the rain looked soaked like a washerwomans hands. Few are the hats & less the boots on Yuba. Strange comedies might be formed representing "Life in the Gold Digins." Purchased a claim on the Bar below us of Dr. Ely of Dayton, Ohio,[215] for $25. to work on while J. R. is absent on the prospecting expedition. Dr. E. is going to the Middle Fork. He tells me Messrs Klegg, Ring & others of the Dayton boys are on the Feather River the American Fork &c scattered like the Columbus boys. Rained most of the day which will probably take much snow away. Am informed the Sacramento is quite high again. Spent most of the day in camp.

SUNDAY 7. Rained most of the night. This morning everything wet & disagreeable. A good specimen of the rainy season in California. The Fogg, in clouds moved along the higher mountain that encompasses us in curious curling forms. Washed, changed my clothes & more than all shaved off my Goatee preferring no hair on my face in the summer. Have as usual a large fire in front of our tent making a comfortable appearance at least. Mr. R. sung songs reminding me of home & the old Zion Church. Read in the Bible wrote some & the day passed off rather agreeably, in this lonesome vale. Rained pretty constantly.

MONDAY 8. Disagreeable morning rained until noon when the clouds broke away and disappeared in a few minutes time, making a pleasant afternoon. Mr. R. & myself did mining on our claim on the bar below this purchased of Dr. Ely. Made $14.00 in afternoon.

TUESDAY 9. J. R. returned from his prospecting expedition without selecting any place for our operations & brought $13.00 as the result of his excursion. Washed today 260 buckets of dirt which we got out of the bank 40 steps from the river & made $60.00 — three of us. We wash with a common rocker. The weather cool & pleasant although the sun at times shines hot.

WEDNESDAY 10. Since we do mining we get up at break of day & get our simple breakfast early taking biscuit along for dinner. Made today $49 by mining. The labor is hard one suffers this most in the back. Where we work the river runs in rapids & the roaring dashing water often prevents one from hearing another talk.

THURSDAY 11. Weather fine we expect but a few more showers to wind up the rainy season then for the heat & droughth. Added today but $36.00 to the volume of the metalic circulation by our labor in mining.

FRIDAY 21. Purchased today two more claims on the Bar below for $50. & now calculate on a summers work here on the Bar & turning the river. A claim is 30 feet fronting on the river, low water mark, & running back for as far as one chooses to work it. Made by our mining $40.00. Those amts. we make by our joint labor — three of us being equal sharers of profits.

SATURDAY 13. Moved our camp to the Bar on which we hold claims being more convenient than where it was on the Bar above. The Bar above (Lippards Bar) we gave up as it seemed to pay poorly. Made in the forenoon $29.00. J. R. & myself put up tent fixed things washed &c. & Mr. R. made $6.00 in the afternoon, making for the days labor $35.00.

SUNDAY 14. Our mess unlike many others have unanimously determined to keep the Sabbath & do no labor on this day. So this light of day found us yet in the embrace of Morpheus — a beautiful day. The birds make lively our camp on this Bar our tent is pitched on a rise & a kind of second bench back of the Bar about 60 yds from the river among a beautiful grove of Pine & Firs &c which rise in fine proportions to a considerable height, tapering in very regular manner. The river winds around us — its waters dashing over the rapids & rocks in sprayey whiteness while in front & back of us rise mountains the ascent of which is very steep for two miles. The snow on top is yet some six feet deep. Grisley Bears have lately made their appearance here again. The snows being away in places the[y] return from the valley, panthers are at times heard too. Feeling fatigued of the weeks work this is truly an acceptable day of rest & I enjoy it well.

MONDAY 15. The labor of mining goes better after a day of rest. I believe man gains nothing by working Sundays as some do here. Proceeds of mining today $75.00.

TUESDAY 16. Had a mess settlement of accounts this morning & a division of funds on hand after Mr. R. & myself had drawn out the amts by us severally put in. Made by mining $32.00. Wrote this evening a letter to Bro. C. S.[216] was up to 12 o'clock writing by a poor light on my lap.

WEDNESDAY 17. This is a cold morning Ice $\frac{1}{8}$ in. on water in bucket. Enclosed in letter to C. S. $2.50 in dust for each of Misses Mary & Martha Decker.[217] J. R. left for Deer Creek. Mr. R. & myself worked & made $55.00.

THURSDAY 18. Another cold disagreeable morning. On such a morning one dont feel like lifting rock about & washing dirt in water so cold as is this "Snow Water Yuba." J. R. returned from Deer Creek this evening. The man having left who was to take our letters to the States we mailed them. Added to the volume of precious metals today (Mr R. & myself) $52.00.

FRIDAY 19. Disagreeable forenoon and afternoon more so. Commenced raining at noon & did so till night being cold & disagreeable in the extreme. Made by work till noon $24.00.

SATURDAY 20. Cold morning. Ice on water in pails. To work early had much dirt to throw off from that fit to wash — panning out is a hard job in this cold water. Feel back ache considerably. Did the washing of my clothes after night always a disagreeable job made by mining today $43.00.

SUNDAY 21. Cold morning, feel stiff & tired in mornings. Shaved, washed &c. worked my way ½ mile up to very steep hill back of our tent & found pretty crystalized diamond flints or quartz mixed in curious confusion in flint rocks and separate pieces of which I brot a number. Here on this hill I am making these notes amid the music of feathered songsters, the roar of the waters & the plaintive sound of the wind in the pines; and in view of grand mountain scenery. Above me I see snow below me the heat of the sun is considerable. April so far is much as is this month in the States or at least as it was last year while I was on the Ohio, Mississippi & Missouri rivers and at St. Joseph.

MONDAY 22. Cool pleasant weather, worked hard today in a hole where much top dirt had to be thrown off of the lair [layer] containing gold — many very heavy rocks to lift which being rounded by the action of the water are hard to handle. These rocks are the principal part of my bar on Yuba & the rapid current when the stream is up move them about often making a noise of their jolting louder than the roar of the foaming & dashing current. Have seen an Indian on Trinity with no clothes on but a military coat, but today one of the party of Dr. Ely had an Indian boy here yet more grotesquely clad. Had a hickory shirt on with a vest over it & a pair of large old boots. His small legs with a pigeon toe knock knee gait looks ludicrous enough. These Indians will eat no pork. Bot a log for a rocker for $2. — made by morning $3.00.

TUESDAY 23. Worked in race. Armstrong[218] of the Hewleyt Company turning the river above came with a black eye requesting our presence on their Bar to see justice done between his company & claimants on the Frenchmans Bar concerning a river claim.[219] Seeing many other miners go did not deem move necessary & continued to work. Put up a notice today about turning the river — Beautiful moonlight nights.

WEDNESDAY 24. Am told Armstrong & Co. paid $600 for 30 ft square in the river concerning which the dificulty was, learn that Mr. A. did not get his black eye by a fight with those claimants but from a partner in their Co. Some Co. miners were present to see the settlement of their claims dificulty & all was done up peacably. Recd $2.50 for 2 meals of an old Georgian. Made by mining (Dist in race) $40.

THURSDAY 25. Worked hard, pleasant day, stream up. Proceeds of mining $57.

FRIDAY 26. Bot beef — the first we had since here — at 50 cts pr lb. A friend of mine James Flippin, paid $6. for getting boots ½ soled. Weather quite pleasant. Made by mining $37.50.

SATURDAY 27. Bodly saw Columbus boys (McCormack,[220] Lunn,[221] Stiles[222] & Bowers[223]) are all well & heard of Price[224] being at the Sandwich Islands & soon expected here & is quite well again. Washed clothes this evening after making by mining $38.75. Divided $375.00 mess funds.

SUNDAY 28. Had a good long sleep. We usually get up when the stars still shine yet on week days — A very pleasant Sabbath. The river up. Taking a stroll among the mountains saw fine specimens of rocks of quartz & slate of volcanic action. Have no variety of company here but do not feel lonesome in this mountain retreat in Yubas gorge.

MONDAY 29. Made by mining $68.50. Paid for 8 lbs Pork $6.00. On this river our Bar is now honored with a store which establishments on Bars are honored with that name when they keep flour, pork & liquors thrown on a pile under an arbor. Mr Hurley sold his claim on

Bar above where they were turning the river for $2000 & his son sold his for $1500. The old man started for the States at once. There are 10 shares or claimants to this river privilege.

TUESDAY 30. Made by mining $69.50. Warm pleasant weather. Work in bank back of the Bar which pays well for the height & distance from river. We take only the top dirt to a coarse white sand which holds no gold. On the bed rock is generally rich but the river being high & the bed rock laying deep here cannot go to it now.

WEDNESDAY MAY 1. Made by mining $65.00. In the bank at the lower end of this Bar at a depth of 10 ft they make some 40 cts to the bucket. This lead seems to have been formed by the eddy at the foot of these rapids. Took medicine last night & feel weak & unwell today but work all the while.

THURSDAY 2. Made by mining $57.00. Had this evening Spruce or Fir tea for the first [time]. Some use it daily as a preventative of scurvey. It had to me a not very pleasant taste but think it is healthy. It makes a colourless tea, looks like water.

FRIDAY 3. Made by mining $18.00 part of a days work. Mr Rogers is unwell I feel better today. Got 9 lbs beef on Cincinnati Bar at 5-¢ pr lb & a pound of soap for $1.00. The dry season seems to have fairly set in. The change from one to the other seasons in this country seems to be indicated by an occasional appearance of rain which passes off however without raining. The wind seems to change often blowing from every part of the compass during a day. Here however in this Gorge there is not much to be observed as to the wind for mountains influence it much in their course. Have for several days noticed a milk white cloud rising from behind the western ridge & spreading over a very clear sky in a curious circular manner for a kind of panorama like a huge umbrella. These white clouds at times curl in fantastic shapes along the sky in beautiful display giving a cheering aspect to nature after 6 months of gloomy rainy weather at 3 of which rained constantly & the change is welcome indeed.

SATURDAY 4. Mr Rogers being quite [sick] J R & myself sunk a hole 7 or 8 ft in the bank of our lower claim to prospect it but geting water did not succeed in finding the rich treasures anticipated. The sun hot, sweat freely & drank considerably of this very cold water. Made me sick toward evening — but taking no supper drank a cup of tea which raising perspiration freely I feel pretty well at bed time. Divided $255 of mess money.

SUNDAY 5. Had a rather disturbed night or restless sleep. Enjoyed bed well this morning until the light of the sun appeared on the mountain which is not very early in this lower region where the Golden Yuba runs. The birds twitered & made musical the grove of Pines, Cedars & Firs & Oaks we are camped in. All Nature seems to have put on her summer garb of green. The Oak & all trees & bushes that shed their leaves in the rainy season are now green & look cheering. Yet on the mountains but a mile from us the snow is several feet deep. I am told it is as much as 8 ft in places between this & the middle fork. Feel pretty well today. Having a beautiful & delightful day seeming truly like a Sabbath. Wrote a letter to Bro. David today.

MONDAY 6. Made by mining $34.00. Had toothache all day & at times fever—probably caused by tooth ache. Worked until middle of afternoon. Took a walk or crawling & scrambling trip up the river ½ mile to purchase a hat but could not cross river being too high to ferry. Saw several snakes on my rout. Rattle Snakes are getting rather plenty here, also a striped water snake and a spotted kind. These snakes at times curl up in beding in our camp. Lizards of all colors are constantly running in all directions as you walk. Some sit at a distance which insures them safety watching your movements slyly. These lizards are from 3 to 6 inches long & a rather uninviting *varmint* but said to be harmless. Water lizards of which there are but few are large 6 to

12 in long & said to be poisonous. Another kind of
varmint & I am done with this subject. A kind of fish
looking thing 2 to 3 inches long with claws & a tail
which it throws on its back with a bladder & sting in
the end which it thrusts savagly into a stick. The bladder is said to be poisonous & fatal. A young one of them
was nestling itself at the head of my bed not a foot
from my head — are found in the ground we dig at times,
& by the boys that were to Mexico called Scorpions &
Sentapedes while others call them Terantlus.

TUESDAY 7. Made by mining $36.00. Heard today of
a few boys on the middle fork making $100 per day.
While most of them are only laying by their claims to
work when the river falls. Snows 6 ft deep yet in places
on the mountains.

WEDNESDAY 8. Made by mining $37.50. Mr. Oats[225]
from Deer Creek tells me of rich leads running through
the hills where $40. have been obtained from one pan of
dirt — says a camp kettle & a womans shirt were found
six feet under ground where it had not been dug before
& old logs are found under ground where it had not been
dug before. He paid 2 oz. of gold for a pair of cow hide
boots.

THURSDAY 9. Made by mining $17.25. J. R. unwell
today. Some Mississippians brot a negro[226] a darkie to
work here & it reminds me of domestics at home. But
here every man is on the same equal footing. Here each
stands or falls by his own merits. This is the land of
men almost without children.

FRIDAY 10. Made by mining $12.75. Today we pros-
pected a claim of bank "digins" in the bed at the lower
end of the Bar. One layer of dirt 7 ft under ground.
Panned 75 cts to the pan, but being a thin layer & much
work to throw off top dirt did not purchase claim for
which 4 oz are asked. Heard of the Indian killing several persons in Grass Valley[227] near Deer Creek & burning house. Several hundred are said to be collected some
12 (mi) above on this river perhaps not for good purposes.

SATURDAY 11. Made by mining $29.75. Washed dirt in race. The weather has been for the most part this week very pleasant—a cool breeze stirring, the sun not very hot. Today a cloud rose in the west & at times thundered but passed off without [rain]. The sun shone at intervals pretty warmly. We have no thunder showers here.

SUNDAY 12. The birds played their musical notes in the pine branches around our tent before we were up this morning & the day as days are here now—delightful. Went ½ mile below to Cin. Bar in company with J R & Flippin. Found quite a store there.228 Got several papers of Mch. [March] date at the very low rate of 25 cts pr. ps. Contain debate in Senate on California Admission & Slavery. Even those from Slave States consider this no country for the peculiar institution. Have accts of Indian outrages on Deer Creek & some are for keeping a night watch on Bars here. Took dinner with Messrs Howard & Epperson229 who have their families on the Cin. Bar. Killed a large Rattle Snake — they are plenty & one is in danger of them here.

MONDAY 13. Made by prospecting $4.75. Built a log foundation some 4 ft high for our tent — put up our beds some 3½ ft from ground for healths sake & to avoid snakes & other reptiles.

TUESDAY 14. Did no work today the river being up — Read newspapers. Warm weather in middle of day.

WEDNESDAY 15. Made by mining in bank $12.00. Paid $1.50 for a mess of Ham which though evidently not so well cured as we used to have at home was a rarity that was indeed delicious. It reminded me of good living which is only a matter of memory with us as being among the "has beens." Would gladly pay $1.00 pr ps for a mess of eggs for once since I left home, but they are out of the question at any price here.

THURSDAY 16. Made by mining $17.00. Have sold the first claim we got on this Bar (of Dr. Ely at $25.00) to Messrs Howard & Epperson for $150. They with their families on coming here & we engaged to board with them at $20. per week. They are making preparations to come here in a few days. Hear of a Mr. Williams of Allen Co. Ohio, drowning at the ferry below when coming down the hill he told his partner he would die on the Yuba. Next day — Monday the two undertook — contrary to the wishes of the ferryman — to cross the river with the canoe, & on landing Mr. Williams partner jumped out on shore without taking rope along & giving the canoe a push in leaping the current took it with this poor fellow over the rapids — he sticking to it for 100 yds which was the last seen of him. Many lose their lives in this river — very few ever get out once in.

FRIDAY 17. Made by mining $15.55. Nothing new to-day — only additional Indian alarms.

SATURDAY 18. Made by crevicing today $14.00. Andy Sturgis found a piece in a crevice at the head of this Bar weighing $9.25. Mr. Fry a friend of Mr. Rogers' all night with us. Turns the channel of Deer Creek says that stream bed bars & all is every foot taken up from head to mouth. Mr. F saw 9 pounds of gold taken out of a rock at one time on Gold Run.[230] A claim sold there at $30,000. Tells of many coming from the States. He paid 3.00 pr lb for barley for his mule & $2.50 for a meal & 50 cts for a *horn* on Yuba above this. Money is easily got rid of here. Messrs H. & E. with their families are now on our Bar no doubt the first women that ever came to this point & how they scrambled up & creeped down the high steep & dangerous hills is to me a mystery — but they are here with 3 children giving a novel air of home & civilization to this Bar in the wilderness seemingly little in communication with the balance of the world.

SUNDAY 19. Commenced this morning to board with the families on the Bar at $20. per week. Am not yet well prepared for boarding. Today is rather windy though pleasant. The last week was generally warm which by melting snows keeps the river high. Visited the Delaware boys.

MONDAY 20. Made by mining $15.00. Sold to Messrs Dann & Co. a 20 ft claim for $100. Find it quite a relief to be rid of the drudgery of cooking & feel quite at home to sit down to meals. Truly "womans work is never done." Our boarding house is a roof placed on posts with a muslin wall on one side to keep the sun out. Benches on blocks form the seats. The air has free access to fan us. Women & men that cross the plains &c.

TUESDAY 21. Having no place to work mining made boards for Messrs H. & E. Canoe up from the Cin. Bar with much labor & crossed at the lower end of our Bar apparently not with entire safety. So our Bar has a ferry.

WEDNESDAY 22. Being out of a place to work while the river is up purchased a claim of Loree Mull & Co (Miamisburg) [Ohio] for $150 and are now working in the bank in Mulls lead formed by the eddy apparently. Made by mining $37.00. Sold Messrs Dann & Co 20 ft of our upper claim of Bar & River for $100. Cost us $32. Lent Messrs Howard & Epperson $101.00. Messrs Dougherty & Black in attempting to cross with the canoe here were taken down by the current & only escaped by jumping on to a log on the river side — a moment before the canoe was dashed in pieces in the rapids. There is much danger in crossing this rapid stream.

THURSDAY 23. By mining $43.00. Up with the Lark in the morning which a few stars are yet seen that seem to have belated themselves. This early to work before breakfast wash 50 buckets of dirt which we have to carry from 30 to 40 yds. 350 buckets is our days work, & we pan out about four times a day. A cloud arose over the mountain in the S. E. at 11 o'clock which soon overcast the sky & at twelve it commenced raining & blowing, hailing with an occasional indistinct flash of lightning & a number of rather moderate reports of thunder. Hail fell the size of Hazel nuts. A Yankee observed "it is a tryen to do as it used to do on it down East." The atmosphere seems but little charged with electricity — thunder

& lightning being very rare occurences, seemed much like home in this instance. Storm lasted two hours. Dr. Gardiner[231] (a Woolverson) arrived as a resident of our Bar & fellow boarder "at our house." Informs us it snowed on the mountain today.

FRIDAY 24. By mining $35.55 Having made a little on claims & worked while others lay idle a few envious fellows are endeavoring to create dificulty about one of our claims. Dr. Gardiner informs me that the thermometer has stood at 98 & 100 at Deer Creek — 20 miles from here, during a few days this month which is 20 miles from here & snow is laying between this & that point.

SATURDAY 25. By mining $37. J R & myself pd Mr. R. our part of Bradley's[232] acct. for hauling. 2/3rds of $172.80. This week with the exception of today has been cool & pleasant. Today was warm. Have noticed some mornings this week white frost. Felt rather unwell today after stooping down to dig my head seems to swim.

SUNDAY 26. Wrote to Mr. Anderson at Fremont for Howard & sent note for collection. Feel well & can appreciate the Sabbath today as a day of rest under present circumstances. Pleasant day. Since families here feel more at home. A boy & little girl washing gold on the Bar. The little girl wishing herself back in Oregon with her cousins. Thinks it too hard for people to come here & expose themselves so much. How natural this sentiment even to children.

MONDAY 27. Made by mining $36.00 Divided in mess $150. J R is unwell. John Epperson helped us in his place. Notice Howard's little girl rocking the babe in a Gold Cradle on this Bar.

TUESDAY 28. Made by mining $42.75. Messrs H. & E. with little boy working on the Bar. Dug — carried & washed dirt. Mrs Howard the best rocker & the jokes passed about it. Working a few hours they made $6.00.

WEDNESDAY 29. By mining $34.50. Mrs. H. & E. made by a few hours work between cooking times $12.00. Having ladies by us washing gold is quite encouraging

& pleasing. J R sick today.

THURSDAY 30. Made by mining $25.50. River claims are attracting attention some are being "jumped" & dificulties expected. Regulations here allow a company or one man all they or he can turn the water from. Water so clear that in eddies & deep holes say 20 ft deep the bottom is easily seen.

FRIDAY 31. Made by mining parts of day $15.50. Our lead in the bank formed by the eddy is geting poorer work down from two to twelve feet all formed by the river.

SATURDAY JUNE 1. By a few hours mining made $6.00. J. R. still unwell & Mr. R complains today. Made an unsuccessful effort with Doty & Co. to make foot bridge across the river. Have some idea of going to Oregon in the fall. Had a little rain & thunder this afternoon, hardly sufficient to call it a thunder shower. Went with Mr Epperson to Cin. Bar crossed the river over a dangerous footlog over which the dashing foaming current is at times thrown shaking it as if each moment was the last for the log & the one on it. It takes good nerves to cross — along the river in places one has to hold on to the crumbling slate rock with a footholt of half the width of one boots scrambling along when 200 ft below you perpindicular foams the restless dashing Yuba — many dangers are in mans path here — lately a man in this situation lost his hold & with great dificulty saved himself by letting go his blankets with a purse of $600 in dust — Met McCormack at the Cin. Bar bot a shirt of him. He deposited with Barton Lee[233] at the City $2000 in dust at 5 pr ct per month. All the Columbus folks are well so far as he knows.

SUNDAY 2. Enjoyed a fine nights & mornings sleep. Pleasant breezes make this day delightful — all last week was pleasant — at times pretty warm. May was a very pleasant month. I have seen warmer weather in Ohio & Pa. in May than here in the mountains. In places on the river the air circulates but little. Nature looks lovely though rugged here in many respects is perpetual spring, Pines, Cedars, Firs, Spruce & Live Oaks give it that air. Though the rainy season is disagreeable yet hard cold winters are unknown here & only in cold regions can home be truly appreciated. When a substantial warm & comfortable home is needed there is centered the real idea of *Home Sweet Home* & all the associations connected with social fireside as enjoyed in the Northern regions. Paid $5.00 for two letters from Columbus. One from Bro. Augustus a most welcome letter all well at home, written Mch 10. The other letter a curiosity in its way. How gladly I heard from home & friends.

MONDAY 3. Made by mining $15.00. Attended a meeting of Co. of 70 miners called to settle a title to a claim disputed between Mull Loring & Co. and some newcomers who have squatted or tried to jump this river claim now all under water. Intelligent men peacably settled. Alcalde M. Conner of Hamilton Ohio,234 took the evidence & is to decide on Sunday at 12 o'clock. Mr. Oats sold Middle Yuba claim for $1000. Bee project to Oregon. Hoffman & Little Express235 with 600 letters for Yuba at $3.00 pr ps. Mr. Little of Indiana & formerly of Lancaster Ohio.

TUESDAY 4. By mining $25.00. Mr. R. received letters all well at home. Many emigrants enroute to California — poor fellows. Recd letters from Mr. Anderson offers five per cent per month for my money. The towns in the valley (small ones) deserted nearly — folks gone to the mines as usual.

WEDNESDAY 5. By mining $20.50. rather uncomfortably hot today. A prospecting party found the Middle Yuba covered over with snow some 20 miles above, river here rises at night & falls in day time from 6 to 30 inches.

THURSDAY 6. Throwed rock out of race & washed dirt which had last fall been thrown off as not paying of which we got 19 to 20 cts to the bucket. Washed 200 buckets & made $39. River rose & took Dotys log bridge off. Warm weather though a breeze most of the time.

Hard work in race lifting out heavy rocks — back aches.

FRIDAY 7. By mining — washing top & refuse dirt made $39. Pretty warm. River claims are beginning to sell. A claim we could have taken up on Poor Mans Creek[236] when we came here is now valued at $500.00.

SATURDAY 8. By mining $30. Hard work — warm day. Have for first time in my life sore eyes. Many here complaining of the same.

SUNDAY 9. Fine draft of air all day — cool & pleasant. Read the Trial of Dr. Webster for murder of Dr. Parkman.[237] Sent by Mr. Little of Messrs Hoffman & Littles Express $500 in gold dust to Messrs Fall Anderson & Co. at Fremont where I am to receive 5 per cent per month for it. Am troubled with my eyes.

MONDAY 10. By washing dirt in race made $7.00. Cool day raise of water floated off our Riffle to the Cradle. Made another.

TUESDAY 11. Made by washing dirt in race $8.00. Worked in widening river heavy work, feel it most in my back. An expedition of 6 or 8 men is fiting out by packing several mules for what are said to be new and very rich diggings lately discovered between the North Fork of Yuba & South Fork of Feather Rivers.[238] The water being still high & but little can be made here at present I go with this expedition in accordance with the wishes of our Mess. I am not without hopes of doing something but enter on the mountainous road as one of toil without which gold cannot be obtained in the mines of California. Tomorrow morning we expect to be on this point for the new diggings some seventy miles distant.

THURSDAY 20. Our mule got loose but after short search found him. Had a cold night — make for sleeping apartment a kind of arbor of Pine & Fir twigs to keep sun off our heads. Left camp early after preparing a meal on a shovel being bread without saleratus & pork. Ascended a high ridge over the hard frozen snow from 10 to 20 ft deep. Followed the ridge or divide between

South & Middle Yuba heading Poor Mans Creek so that
kenyons were all avoided. Soon as we left the snow had
to force our way through thickets of chaparel, last 10
miles without snow & the temperature warmer as we descend the Western or S. W. slope of the mountain. Noticed some Pine & Firs 9 to 12 ft in diameter. Timber
on the mountain Pine, Cedar & Fir, Spruce etc. Noticed
in little valley above the Shaking Aspen. Company divided off so that today only Messrs Lippard & Baker &
myself came home together, Lippard as guide. Men we
met informed us Emigrants from the States already arrived in the valley having packed through in 75 days.
Found all well on Irishman's Bar (arrived fatigued &
ragged) & to my astonishment Mr Rogers (my partner)
offers his claim for sale at $250, having determined to
leave here. So I will be alone & cannot operate on my
claim well single handed & feel discouraged. How change-
able life & much more so in California than any where
else. Distance 20 miles.

FRIDAY 21. Cool weather, can bear a coat. Mr Rogers
sold his claim for $250. I have accepted a proposition
by J. R. Rogers to associate with him by refunding $100.
amt ½ paid by him to us for extra claim. So he & myself
mess together again holding 3 claims. Messrs Lippard &
Oats submitted the settlement of a dificulty between
them concerning a claim to Mr Rogers & myself. We
heard the evidence decided in Mr Lippards favor & both
parties seemed satisfied having agreed to abide our decision.

SATURDAY 22. Made a final mess settlement preparatory to Mr. Rogers leaving & closed up affairs as I presume satisfactorily. J R & myself having purchased most
of the mess property settled with Messrs Howard &
Epperson our board accts to date. Boarding henceforth
reduced to $18. per week. Pleasant cool day. Messrs
Howard & White & others of our late exploring expedition returned this morning having accomplished nothing.
Sold our mule to Mr Rogers for $140.

SUNDAY 23. Mr. Rogers wishing to leave today I went in company with Wisegarver & Dan 2 miles up the mountain for the mules. Shot a mountain hen, resemble a tame chicken much though some smaller. Mr Rogers packed his mule & bade us farewell — My best wishes are with him. Has to swim his mule below this bar is going to Deer Creek & perhaps to valley for work or business. Hope he may do well.

SATURDAY 29. By mining $4.25. J R made Long Tom this week & balance of time could not work on acct of sore leg. Mr Oats of Deer Creek reports Mr Rogers had lost his mule there, had not seen Mr. R. for some days. Weather quite warm every day this week. Worked in race myself forenoons & washed dirt when water was down in the evenings.

SUNDAY 30. Spent the day as usual, reading, writing &c most is the rest of this day. It is otherwise not really a Sabbath in the mines.

MONDAY JULY 1ST. 1850. [We have today traded claims] For the purpose of having two chances of claims in the river the more certainly to secure [a] good place. J R & myself today traded our lower claims of the two upper ones in the rapids on this Bar for 15 ft joining Armstrong & Co.'s claim being the upper ½ of Jas. H. Laughlins claim just below it. Messrs Flippin & Laughlin allow us $100. for the Bar of our claim when they take it out of the same. Held a meeting of miners on our Bar this evening preparatory to celebrating the 4th of July. I am on the committee on Toasts.

TUESDAY 2. By mining $7.00. Paid Lippard for ½ days work $4.00. Warm day river falling some worked hard putting rock out of race, preparing to dig.

WEDNESDAY 3. By mining $5.50. Paid Lippard for fraction of a days work in race $3.00. Prepared 7 or 8 Toasts for tomorrows celebration.

THURSDAY 4. The first glance of the sun over the mountain was greeted with 31 discharges of rifle, pistols &c. by a party of us. Revd Jolly,[239] Lady & daughter came, he officiating as chaplain. At 11 o'clock 100 men & five women were assembled Called to order by Chaplain. The Declaration of Independence read. The President (Dr. Gardiner) stated that on acct of the illness of his brother the Revd. Mr. Crummer would not be here to deliver an address as was expected. When at one o'clock the dinner being ready a beautiful table was set & filled three times after which 13 regular Toasts were drank amid cheers & many volunteer toasts, All appearing well pleased with themselves, and everybody else & the occasion, order being generally observed. Thus passed off the 4th of July 1850 on South Yuba. Toasts excellent songs by Yuba Glee Club.

FRIDAY 5. Had a Mr Moore to help us roll rocks out of race in lower claim. Work very hard, paid him $10.

SATURDAY 6. By mining $25.00. Paid Moore & his partner $20 for working in the race. Messrs Bradly & White240 here, glad to see them being Fremont friends of last winter. Tell us that all other streams are more crowded than this. Many engaged in making hay in the valley it being down to $40 per ton. Grass from knee to waist high on Sacramento bottom. Mr Little with mail came up & has no letters for me. Strange indeed. Got a Cincinnati Commercial for $1.00.

SUNDAY 7. Lot of men who went on mountain to watch a Grisly Bear returned at midnight & their discharge of arms created an alarm of Indians on the Bar. This Bear destroyed several hundred dollars worth of goods deposited by a tree to be brot to the Bar. The river low J R prospected deep down as he could on our lower claim in race & got from $2.00 to $2.50 to a pan of dirt —last few days & today a cool breeze & pleasant weather. Said to be cooler than common this season thus far. A meeting of miners of this District was held in accordance with a previous notice on the Cincinnati Bar, to elect an Alcalde & Sheriff for this District extending four miles up & four miles down the river from that Bar. The former excellent Alcalde, Mr Conner having moved to Middle Yuba. 133 votes were cast — a Mr Ross of Iowa was elected Alcalde & my friend Mr Lippard Sheriff.[241] I had the honor of being chosen Secretary of the meeting.

MONDAY 8. Made by mining $70.00. Struck the bed rock on our lower claim near the eddy found clay on it. The water interfered otherwise might have made twice as much. The crevices are sparkling with scales in the clay, a pint of dirt panned 50 cts. Had a meeting of the claimants interested in turning the river. I was appointed on the Committee on Race to see that it be put through rightly. Messrs Moore & Edwards working our race. Have mined there four days at $10 per day and we pay their dinner at our Boarding House ($1.00 pr meal.)

TUESDAY 9. Made by mining $53.00. Saw today Mr. Beach formerly from Columbus who sold his claim on the Middle Yuba for $1500 having taken out some $1200. He says he has made some 5 or 6 thousand dollars. Thinks our claims are very good in the rapids.

WEDNESDAY 10. Made by mining $39.00. Prospected our upper claim, the water is in the way but got 50c to a pan in clay below water. An Irishman commenced to work at noon on race.

THURSDAY 11. Made by mining $25.00. Paid Moore & Edwards for work $80. The Irishman & partner commenced work in the race. Not near as good hands as the others. An old Maine Yankee called "Bed Rock" is the best workman here.

FRIDAY 12. Made by mining $35.00. "Bed Rock" & his associates messrs Moore & Edwards called the miners together on the Bar above to settle a dispute between them & others as to a river claim. "Bed Rock" proposed paying me for my services to act as his attorney which I declined. A kind of court was organized (a popular court) Evidence received. The question debated put to vote & decided against Bed Rock & Co. Dispute arose because notice to turn the river did not set bounds. All the doings of the meeting were acquiesced in & settled.

SATURDAY 13. Made by mining $80.00. The water did

not interfere quite so much today as for last few days.
Had a offer of $600 today for our upper claim. $800
will buy it. Claims are changing hands now daily from
$500 to $4000. Sent Joseph White $75. Paid hired hands
$65.00. Have worked some in water this week & lifted
heavy rock which is hard work. The weather is pretty
warm. At 11 o'clock a pleasant breeze — after a wind
comes up relieving one much in the hot sun.

SUNDAY 14. After a long Sunday mornings nap, noticed the rays of the sun peeping over the mountain which
it don't do early to us in this Yuba Kenyon. Pleasant
day, nights getting more moderate.

MONDAY 15. By mining $44.50. Have Moore & Ed-
wards to work in upper race. Claims are daily becoming
more valuable. Water lots or river claims sell as high
as $50 dollars per foot running across where race is yet
to cut & dam to build and no way for prospecting being
entirely under water.

TUESDAY 16. By mining $35.00 Sold today our upper
river claim for $800. In cash $150. & a note for $650.
Have Moore & Edwards to work & finished race today.

WEDNESDAY 17. By mining $21.00 paid off Moore &
Edwards for work to date $40. Bought a common pair
of short legged stogy boots for $16.00. Wore my boots
from 1st of last Nov. to this day. Recd of J R White
amt of borrowed money $75.00.

THURSDAY 18. By mining $14.50. Committee on race
consulted with a superintendent of Dam. He asks 2
ounces per day for his services. The river to[o] high yet.

FRIDAY 19. By mining $42.50. Had hand half a day
to work. Borrowed $274.21 of Dr. Gardiner & paid Cook
amt due him of Griswold & Caintly $721.50.

SATURDAY 20. Did no work today but washing flannels
&c. Feel unwell. Water interferes in washing on our
lower claim being our only Bar Diggings. Weather has
been quite warm this week. The sun shines very hot
though most of times a breeze or wind blowing. Doty
& Gardiner at the head of the river make fine prospects

today — found one piece of $11.25 & other good prospects. Have their liquor with them & are excited & "corned" over their prospects. Some men cannot bear their sudden California fortunes. A piece was found 2 miles below weighing 32 ounces & it is said one now being exhibited at the City weighing 31 pounds, $1.00 a sight.

SUNDAY 21. Pleasant breeze makes this day agreeably warm only. Mr White here from Fremont — now living at Nevada City on Deer Creek. He says provisions are on the rise. We do no labor on Sabbath yet it is hardly a "day of rest." At any rate not a day agreeably spent here as a Sabbath. Mrs. Jolly & daughter on a visit at our boarding home. Conversed with a brother of Revd Mr. Jollys who came in some days across the plains from Wisconsin by the Carson route. He thinks as many more as were on the plains last year are coming this season, numbers have already arrived. Mr. Griswold paid today to Dr. Gardiner $140. of the money we borrowed.

IRISHMAN'S BAR SOUTH YUBA

JULY 22, 1850. Made by mining $16.00. J R worked for Danning—making purchasing. Bot a claim today of Miles Mark on the Gold Bar for $800. & sold ½ for $400, to Lippard whose note I took for $300 & paid Marks $200 cash. Doty & Co. are selling River claims at $50. pr ft — claims change hands much.

TUESDAY 23. By mining in forenoon made $40.00 on lower claim & sold it at noon for $600. in weekly payments of $100. Bought ½ River claim today of Dr. Gardiner for $500 — being 13 ft of ground on it $100 cash. Had a hand to work on Dam at $10.

WEDNESDAY 24. A Capt. Cook sued Mr. Loree for the lower claim we bot of Loree, on the grounds of a promise of gift am told they had a rather disorderly Court & seemingly prejudice against Loree. The case to be decided tomorrow morning. Had a conversation with Mr. White about Brady, Anderson & others at Fremont — & matters & things generally in California.

THURSDAY 25. The trial between Cook & Loree decided in favor of the former. Cook came & took forcible possession of our claim, was very excited & very unreasonable. I warned him off stating that I owned that claim by purchase & possession that he & Loree in their dificulty could not effect the right of our claim having a bill of sale of Loree. Told Cook how he must treat me &c. Saw Loree & he & his company give no satisfaction — bad case have no law to collect damages or money on Yuba.

FRIDAY 26. By mining in Co with Lippard on claim on Gold Bar & made $23.50. Loree in part promised to settle for our lower claim for $200 — which I agreed to take although we had just before Cook came sold it for $600 — & took it back when disputed.

SATURDAY 27. Divided money with Lippard dug yesterday our part $13.75 paid this amt to H. & E. Made today by mining $38.00. Had a hand to work — R. Woolfolk for $8.00. Mr Lippard sold him ½ claim by us on Gold Bar for $500. Had a very warm day. The sun shines hot today as usual. Men are crowding in from Middle Yuba in great numbers their River claims having all failed only the Missouri Bar claim is good. This is a hard case on these men & no encouragement for us here.

SUNDAY 28. Rather a sultry day for California — the river getting low. All are anxious to see the result of their labors in turning the river — a number of dams are partly in & much dificulty expected in back water & claimants located too close — some have their claims overflowed by other claims. This as Sabbaths are usually spent here was a day of partial rest, some business will always be on hand for Sunday — I wish I could see a Sabbath again at home where sounds the "Church going Bell."

MONDAY 29. Sold half River claim to H. Anderson for $250. In cash, $166.66, the balance we take in labor. Commenced work again in Gold Bar & made today $90. Deer Creek, Poor Mans Creek, & Middle Yuba having generally failed in the bed of the streams gives in here mistrust.

TUESDAY 30. By Mining $56.60. Divided $50. worth of specimens today — some of Poor Mans Creek.

WEDNESDAY 31. By mining $22.00 compromised with S. Loree at John's instance for $100 in consideration of the dificulty with Cook. Hands continuously work on Dam today, some 10 or 12 of them. Today was pleasantly cool.

THURSDAY AUG. 1ST. By Mining $57.50. Mull & Co. who have River claims above ours notified our men today noon of our backing water on them & for us to stop work which we did for the afternoon, & committee from both companys met to settle but failed. They listened to our companions reasonable & our work will now be forwarded & the *priority* of rights of locations of claims will have to be tested.

FRIDAY 2. By mining $6.50. Most of the day the dam hands were engaged diging the head of the race deeper to back up the water less on Mull & Co. and enable us the better to turn it in.

SATURDAY 3. By mining $8.50. Committee from Mulls & our company met again today, to settle the dificulty of our backing water on them but failed again to settle. Mull & Co will call the miners together on Wednesday at 1 o'clock to have the matter decided by a jury — hearing of evidence &c. Our dam backs the water through their whole race. Water backs much further than is generally calculated & a stream has not actually the fall it appears to have while high & water backs so as to make a sluggish current further back than a level.

SUNDAY 4. Nights are of late chilly — much cooler than a few weeks ago — but the sun shines very hot in day time making it only tolerable by the wind that daily rises at 11 o'clock & comes here pretty much from the North or North West. Had a pleasant dream last night of my arrival home among friends & former associates.

MONDAY 5. Very warm day. Did some prospecting

on Gold Bar.

TUESDAY 6. By mining $16.00. Made a prospect of $5.00 in a pan — a $2.50 lump. Rec'd of Griswold on note $328.00.

WEDNESDAY 7. Water interferes with our diggings on Gold Bar caused by the Cincinnati Dam. Washed 20 buckets dirt & made $8.00. Our Company & Mull Loree & Co. had a trial this afternoon as to priority of claims caused by our dam backing water on their claims. 100 miners were present Mr. Lyons of Iowa was lawyer — Mr Slater council for plaintiffs. Pease Moderator or Judge — rules as in court. Had 12 jurymen examined some 20 witnesses, agreed in written rules that a majority of jury should decide or when evenly divided the judge to give casting vote. Which being the case the judge decided in our favor. Trial orderly — formal and notwithstanding the parties bound themselves to abide the decision, yet Mull & Co much exasperated.

THURSDAY 8. Paid hand on Dam for 5½ days work $62 & J R & self worked on dam today. Old Kentuck superintendent or foreman. Recd balance due of Griswold $37.50.

FRIDAY 9. Prospected an hour on Gold Bar & made $2.00. A Mr. Moore [Morey?] of Schenectady N. Y. now from Middle Yuba tells me that Mr Beach of Columbus Ohio who sometime ago sold a claim on that stream $1,500 & got cash $1000 & a note for $500. was lately over to collect the note & the claim having turned out poorly the man would not pay it so Beach left for Marysville & said he would sell the note if he could. Some 20 miles below Snow Tent on the divide between Middle & South Yuba a man in his cabin heard the report of a gun & looking saw a man shot down by another. He (the man in the cabin) got his gun & shot the other man & on examination the first one shot was found to be Beach[242] & the latter the man he had sold his claim to. This news Morey tells me reached Snow Tent by men who said they saw the corpses. This occured about

4 or 5th of this month. Another report about Beaches
fate circulated here a few days ago which I first learned
today says that Beach & another traveler attacked the
landlord of a house they stoped with all night & Beach
was shot — this report however is contradicted. Beach
told me last spring he had sent $2500 to the Clinton Bank
—Columbus & he had I presume made as much more
since but what became of his papers & effects I know not
as Mr. Morey could not tell.

SATURDAY 10. Wrote letter to Bro. Charles — have no
diggings to work now. Had a meeting of company relation to Mull & Co. threats. Some prospecting done in
river bed here & is unfavorable — this is discouraging.

SUNDAY 11. J R & I went to Deer Creek with Mr
Flippin. Warm day — feel some unwell today. Mull &
Co. meeting today threatening to tare away our dam.
We are prepared to give them a warm reception. How-
ever it is now settled by us allowing them to cut a race
on the lower side of the stream where we turn it. Mr
Bodly called on me today & I am always glad of his
company.

MONDAY 12. Paid Messrs Doty & Gardner $117 —
which will entitle me to my note in case the claim is a
failure. The note left in Mr. Eppersons hands. Loaned
Mr Vanorman $22.00 many are leaving the river having
depended on river claims that have finally failed.

TUESDAY 13. All discouragements. Prospected on rover
claim with Laughlin & Flippin & it is a failure. Bed rock
smooth & hard & no clay on it. J R proposes to go into
business at Nevada & to take in Griswold with a capital
of $2000.

WEDNESDAY 14. Sold an old pick for $5.00. Prospects
dull many are leaving the river much disheartened. A
Mr. E. W. Dann of "Yankee Land" left under none too
favorable circumstances.

THURSDAY 15. Recd of Mr Howard on a/c of money
loaned him $100. Borrowed of Watson & Co. $60 and
paid Miles Marks $200 cash & Henderson note given to

Lippard for $400. Squaring accts for the claims bot of
Marks on Gold Bar for $800. Weather rather warmer
than common.

FRIDAY 16. Many persons here have boils or gather-
ings caused by bruises among rocks and the labor of
mining.

SATURDAY 17. Paid Lippard $117, paid Watson $60.
Recd of Howard $60. Worked with Flippin & Laughlin
in river bed panning out of one pan $12. & yet only
made $10 apiece in the day, it being only in spots as is
the case in all river beds where it pays at all. Had a
fight on Irishmans Bar at a gambling table between
Laughlin & a Dutchman. Dutchman whipped and was
called out by the Dutchman's brother they made an en-
gagement to fight tomorrow morning at 8 o'clock (Sunday).

SUNDAY 18. All expected the fight to come off this
morning but the tall Alabamian was found among the
missing & the affair was a "fizzle." Feel some unwell
very warm this last week & now sultry. Mountains look
now as at Trinity last fall — smoky & sultry & a little
sickness is beginning to show itself among the miners but
so far have heard of but two deaths.

MONDAY 19. Worked with Flippin & Laughlin on
upper river claim in the bank & made 11.50. H. Anderson to work in J R place. Like last season in the coast
range on Trinity — the atmosphere is smoky in these
mountains appearing much like an "Indian Summer" in
Ohio. But this smoky atmosphere appears about with
August & clears only by the commencing of rain.

TUESDAY 20. J. R. and others left on a prospecting
tour in the mountains for dry diggings. Paid Anderson
for work in J. R.'s place yesterday $10. I feel some
unwell today and dont work.

WEDNESDAY 21. Dr. Gardiner extracted a tooth for
me & part of root broke off & split piece of jaw bone.
My teeth in bad condition the enamel seems to come off.
There is much keen disappointment about failure of river

claims, some have been in debt for provisions & no money to pay with any other than flattering prospects ahead.

THURSDAY 22. J. R. & others on prospecting tour returned—report they found gold in many places in ravines between this & Middle Yuba but not enough to pay for work. The Cincinnati Dam a failure & is cut away today.

FRIDAY 23. Sold ½ claim on Gold Bar for $100. when taken out of the claim. The river claims at the Frenchmans Dam are about a failure & are put up as a stake at cards for 50 cts for which some of the company paid 2 month ago $4000 in cash.

SATURDAY 24. Tried to extract the fine gold from a lot of black sand & found quicksilver would not collect it on acct. of a rust on it of an iron kind — so we panned it out. Wrote to Spect[243] & Anderson at Fremont by Flippin who goes down tomorrow. Rocked out 100 buckets dirt for Howard & Epperson for $3.00 panned out of black sand ½ a pan only $6.50. Dull times.

SUNDAY 25. J. H. Lippard & F. L. Oats of Tennessee left for the States. I sent with them two letters addressed to C. S. Decker & Co. Dayton Ohio containing one for Charles one for Sarah with dust — one for Catherine with dust and one for Mary with dust. They expect to go by the 15th Sept. steamer. Heard of Delaware & Columbus Companies coming in divided up as I expected. Ohio company river claims also about a failure. Hard time on the river.

MONDAY 26. J. R. has a sore eye and is unfitted for work. I worked with Harvey in upper river claim in bank. Mr. Henderson, an Oregon man called Mr. Badger (of Alabama) a liar on which the latter knocked the former down & closed an eye for him drawing blood by repeated blows. Both are large & powerful men. It occured at cards. Mr. H. being too *tight* to fight at once threatened B's life & went & brot his rifle to shoot him which he swore he would but his friends persuaded him to let the matter rest until morning whereupon H. sent a challenge to B. to fight a pitched battle in the morning.

Mr. H.'s pride was hurt as he had not before been whipped. Mr. White came with a beef which will weigh 1000 lbs. Mr. Little with N. papers from which we learn the melancholy news of the death of President Taylor. I fear the States are in a critical condition have an entire change of administration not of a popular choice. Divided & had for our share of today & that dug before $25.50. Mr. Howard returned & found diggings to locate on.

TUESDAY 27. J. R. & others left today to take claims where Mr. Howard & Doty prospected & intend locating for the winter. It is dry diggings near White Oak Springs244 6 miles below Nevada. Harvey & I could make nothing & give up work. Mr. White killed his beef on Frenchman's Bar to which point I help to take him, it was dificult. The friends of Henderson & Badger settled their dificulty amicably by mutual acknowledgements being made.

WEDNESDAY 28. Nothing of interest today prospects on the river look gloomy & I feel like leaving. Tried to do something on our Bar but could make nothing.

THURSDAY 29. Mr Epperson returned from Nevada with a two horse team that had just come in across the plains they cost $280. I have some idea of going to Oregon.

FRIDAY 30. Had a dificulty with Mr Vanorman about money for a claim. Helped H. & Epperson to pack things on the hill on to the first shelf which is a mile up very steep from that point wagons *do* go. Also packed a load on hill of my things on my back.

SATURDAY 31ST. Helped H. & E. again & packed a load for myself — went on top of the hill with wagon & Mssrs. H. & E.'s families. Arrived at the top (3 miles) after dark & camped at the cold spring — a fine spring on the summit of this ridge welling out from under a large pine tree. A dozen wagons camped here just in from Illinois.

SATURDAY SEPT. 1ST. Had a disturbed nights rest under the open sky with cattle & horses making noises. Had

a camp breakfast reminding one of life in California
again as it is. The water of this spring very cold. Springs
are usually on top of mountains in this country. Here
are three houses, one a mountain cottage on whose register I saw familiar names. Gen. Moore, or Dr. Moore of
Moskingun Co. [Muskingum County] told me of Pilot
Breyfogle's[245] Company being in and splitting up on
the road. Came down the hill, folks have returned from
Mr Howard's diggings at White Oak Springs who say
they will not pay. So these families go first to Nevada.
Settled satisfactorily with Mr Vanorman & with the
Messrs Eddy could get no settlement of Adams & Co.
who worked claim on Gold Bar on conditions — to be
referred to J. R. In company with Miles Marks paid a
visit to Bodly & the Moses boys of Delaware Ohio.

MONDAY 2. Awoke this morning before the stars had
hid their twinkling & took an early breakfast & bid good-
bye to Yuba & the friends on it. With my blankets, &
sundries as a pack ascended the mountain at the Cin. Bar.
Met Capt. Cook on my way as they are along here on
Yuba. 3 miles to the summit is laborious indeed & at times
does one good for it is sure to start perspiration. Set
down on top of hill & look at the wonderful Sierra mountains with the Yubas in their Kanyons draining off the
snows. The mountains look smoky that is the atmosphere
giving if possible a grander view of the immense ridges
& kenyons fading away in the distant view. How free
one feels, yet as I sit down to rest in the thicket of huge
pines, cedars & firs &c there is a stillness that borders
on the deathlike giving rather a feeling of awe when considered in connection with the sublime scenery of nature
around. The woods in California seem like the original
or first growth. How seldom to be seen a dead tree
unless fired. It is very rarely that timber is laying roting.
Dust from 6 to 12 inches deep. Appearance of a volcanic
crater on hill took a lava rock as a specimen. Stores &
eating house along road, arrived at Nevada City at two
o'clock & put up at Augustines[246] Boarding House where

I found a good Cal. fare, milk &c (being extra). On Yuba the "Cows didn't come home." Bot a pr pants for $10. Mr Flippin from Fremont recd 2 letters from Bro. A. S. One brought by Mr. Spect & one by Mr Booth, also a note from sister Catherine. The folks being all well &c affords me news indeed gratifying.

SEPTEMBER 24, 1850. Had a rain storm all last night & the sky looked threatening this morning but noon presented a sky with only a few snow white clouds drifting along the Heavens in their peculiar California style. Went out to cut saplings for sleepers for laying floor in house & had dificulty to get them. Woods for miles are culled. Hosts camped about this place. While yet in bed heard a drunken Missourian utter his complaints against California & wishing himself back in "Old Missouri." How natural a feeling this with new comers when the first rains set in. Mr. Addison[247] & I agreed to finish the house at once not believing in having a ground floor & entirely open front. Hauled sleepers & hard lifts to put them on wagon.

WEDNESDAY 25. Engaged clab boards of Mr Wagner at $6. pr 100 in the woods. Hauled in 500 and paid Woolfolk for load. Received two wagon loads of goods this evening. Weather cool. Nights chilly. A town is laid out on Bucky Hill Kiota Diggins called Kiotaville [Coyoteville][248] Singular towns building country, hardly enough land to build all the towns on required here.

THURSDAY 26. Bot puncheons for floor for $64 & today hard to work Mr Addison & myself laying floor. Mr. Rogers & Mr. Edwards here & started for the Southern Diggings. Mr Rogers in bad luck dificulty with Judge Stamps.[249] Left acct. or directions with me to settle his claim acct. with Mr. Swingley. Lost his mule. Judge Stamps married to Miss Chord. His wife died in June last. They were *chivareed* by bell gongs &c by a large crowd who were in debt for liquor, over $200. Pleasant warm day.

FRIDAY 27. Seemingly more demand for flour still

selling at 20 cts pr lb. Mr Addison & myself finished laying floor & boarded up sides in part today. Laid the inside first with domestic. The day warm — nights quite cool. Have all the front open & sleep on counter.

SATURDAY 28. Shaved boards to finish the front of house. Brot in a load of boards — 400 & paid $5. for hauling. Had the pleasure of meeting with my old friend C. Breyfogle[250] & had a pleasant conversation about home & friends & old times. He says they had much harder times crossing the plains than last year. Pleasant weather today.

SUNDAY 29. Breyfogle talks of going into business here. His acct of the excitement people at home feel as to this country & friends here is glowing indeed. He left for Sacramento today. Mr. Rariden[251] of Columbus called on me this evening — was glad to see him he came in with Capt. Morgan[252] last season was on Feather River & made a failure is going into business at Rough & Ready,[253] is intelligent & good company is determined to make money before returning home. This is an unpleasant day to me stores all open & is contrary to my feelings to do business on Sunday, but could not close here as this is *the* business day of all others. So I spent the day in the store.

MONDAY 30. Mr. Rariden left for Rough & Ready was made a Mason on Long Bar,[254] Feather River. Had a bright Lodge there. Judge Thralls portrait. Shaved boards for front got Mr. Cloud to put up the front. Weather very warm except mornings & evenings. Mr. Cloud to work on front. Recd 2 loads of goods & 416 lbs flour.

TUESDAY OCT. 1ST. Finding this flour we got last night not very good. Made a sale of the whole lot to a baker @ 19 & made only about $82.00 on the whole lot. Mr. Cloud finished the front of house today. I now have a pleasant and comfortable business room & a tolerable prospect of business. Weather warm, nights chilly as usual.

WEDNESDAY 2. Mr. Addison left this morning for Vernon to purchase & forward more goods. Arranged cash & other accts today. Pleasant weather. Boys came in with purses of dust & make their purchases — talking about ounces as is common among Californians. They go out to dig & wash it themselves. Strange country where one can go & none to hinder him in replenishing his purse by the sweat of his brow in the banks & ravines round about Nevada. Men here are unfitted for society & how will these California boys be, many now bet at Monte freely — swear & bluster & talk of shooting at once if their dignity is insulted. All are here for money — men look in their countenances "Money" wanted for which every sacrifice will be made. The importance of the dollar & the might of an ounce are studied, sought for in every possible way. The cross cut saw the flout & the broad axe each bring $1.00 pr day for hire. To grind an axe first requires a fee of 50 cts to Mr Grindstone. The shoemaker says 50 cts for my flout to cut pegs out of your boots or go to & be d - - - - d, in short the sociable man is lost in the money seeking gold hunting selfish acquisitive miser & conniving millionare. Warm weather, white clouds occasionally but clear sky.

THURSDAY 3RD. Cool morning — warm day. Am alone in store doing a tolerable business. Am in a pleasant room in a pleasant street in a mountain city built or rather planted on ridges of a gradual slope drained by ravines that empty into Deer Creek where the main part of the city stands. The view is rather limited here but highly romantic aside from the idea of the hum of business. The crowd of a city on ground where six months before the natives of the forest were the sole proprietors defending themselves with the bow & arrow & located on a gold bearing soil. There are the beautiful tapering Pines & Cedars pointed Heavenward like Church spires, and spurs of mountains in view first reminding the initiated of the grandeur & vastness of the mountain scenery in the main line which these western slopes hide from view.

FRIDAY 4. Mr. Brady here. Loss of cattle & other stock in the valley & throughout California, by stealing &c. Many brot up here to these California Highlands. Spend my time tolerably pleasantly for California. Mr. Tucker stayed with me all night. Had a talk of Columbus &c. Warm day.

SATURDAY 5. Sent with Mr. Brady to Mr. Addison $100. in dust & letters to Messrs. Addison & Rogers. Brady gives a disparaging acct. as to Johns conduct. Warm dusty days & chilly nights. The shining of the sun in this clear atmosphere makes in time heat & the absence of sunshine is a chilly coolness at any time day or night, winter or summer.

SUNDAY 6. Had a busy day in the store today. This is the day on which many miners camped out of town come in to do their trading & all stores are open & could not do business otherwise. This is unpleasant to me but cannot under present state of things here be avoided. The M. E. Church South[255] have sent a minister here to take care of the part of the flock here which hold to the Church South & believe in slavery which has occasioned a split in the small congregation here when there was no occasion for it at all. It being a question which though practical in some respect at home is here a mere matter of opinion & spirit of domineering. The preacher wants to know whether they are working for the extension of the power and sway of the Church North or South. In this I fear is lost the great mission they should try to accomplish, the saving of souls. Pleasant day.

MONDAY 7. A fine warm & dull day for business. Mr Styles called in & tells of several Columbus folks and of their good health &c. and has news of the prevalence of Cholera in Columbus, and of the death of several acquaintances. This is sad news.

TUESDAY 8. Wrote a long letter today to Augustus (dated 10th) and expect to send it to the States by private means. Mr Breyfogle up from the city with lots of goods — stored some with me. Has a letter for himself and one for Mr. Cloud giving an acct. of the death of Mather Crum. Commenced raining moderately last night & has rained & hailed considerably today and is quite chilly.

WEDNESDAY 9. Had a heavy frost this morning and it was quite uncomfortably cold. But the sun is warm midday. The sky clear. A Mr Seymore of Pickaway O. called on me.

THURSDAY 10. Frosty nights & cool pleasant days. Houses are still going up without number & trains coming in across the plains. Poor looking men, women & children. At times sick, & emaciated — giving a strong picture of wretchedness — if not of despair. It is said of the Missourians that they were most sick & died more than of other States.

FRIDAY 11. Weather as yesterday. Flour & provisions advanced below from 8 to 15. pr 100 lbs. The demand in the fall seems to raise it.

SATURDAY 12. Weather cool. Two loads of hay arrived sent up by Mr. Addison. Old Oregon teamster out of humor about hauling hay. Left it with Mr White to sell for us at a reasonable compensation.

SUNDAY 13. Busy in the store. Warm day. Wrote by the teamster to Mr. Addison. Paid 37½ cts for an excellent large California Pare [pear] Grapes sell daily at $1.00 pr lb. Auction in town today.

MONDAY 14. Cold chilling S. W. wind but no rain today. This evening rains pretty hard. Young man from Zanesville Ohio showed me a miniature likeness of the girl he left behind which a grisly bear took up in his mouth in their camped and chawed it, breaking the frame or case & showing marks of his teeth. He tells me high up on Feather River & at North Yuba snows already fell 3 feet deep & men are preparing to winter there knowing that snow will fall 40 ft deep.

TUESDAY 15. Cleared off last night after a hard rain & had a white frost this morning. Breyfogle an attack of Cholera Morbus — a gentleman here in distress, came across the plains buried his wife 25 miles from here. Has two children one 7 months old & the other as many years. Mr Snyder of the firm formerly of McElvain & Snyder at Columbus called on me. He is strapped & in a bad way. Cool today. Many goods now coming in & flour still on 23 cts. Put up a little sheet iron stove which adds greatly to one comfort.

WEDNESDAY 16. A gloomy chilly day. Have accts of a few cases of Cholera at the city & at the Bay and further accts. of the destitution of Emigrants on the way in. Thousands being yet back.

THURSDAY 17. A clear pleasant day — times dull, teams selling out their loads at freight makes dull times for stores. Women ill from going about clad in mens clothes & thus travel from town to town in this country on horseback. Such is a specimen of Californias morals. Mr Breyfogle sleeping in the store with me, being unwell. I find him good company as an old acquaintance.

FRIDAY 18. Warm pleasant day nothing of interest today.

SATURDAY 19. Warm as yesterday. Had a good day for business. A Mr. Sweeney of Dubuque called & made himself known as a friend of Bro Davids. He has already made, he says, $200 & intends to go into business after a while, came across the plains this season.

SUNDAY 20. Fine warm day. Mr. Wagner took up an old horse saddled & bridled. Informed that he must have him appraised by 5 men & kept 30 days — if worth it, or sold & his expenses paid & balance kept 30 days for owner & if not then called for goes to county. A fellow called and claimed him.

MONDAY 21. Weather as usual. Kiota diggers doing well. Weigh purses at times that weigh 4 to 10 lbs of dust. Of three men that messed together two called one aside last night at camp & shot & cut him with a knife, leaving him for dead, took $1,800. in dust he had by him & fled & are now being pursued. The man they supposed to be killed had strength enough to crawl to a camp & his wounds were dressed & he will recover.

TUESDAY 22. Warm pleasant day a clearer atmosphere & a serenor sky can not be imagined than this of California. I went out on the street last night and read a newspaper readily in the light of the moon & could write a letter by it if I wished.

WEDNESDAY 23. Recd today of Mr Hunt (doctor) $250. I sent him a few days ago on Mr. Whites recommendation. Mr Kline sleeping with me in the store. Mr Wagner took up a Kiota claim No. 154 for me which I can hold until first of May next by being recorded in accordance with the regulations formed by the Kiota miners. Mrs Apperson256 very sick waiting hourly on her death.

THURSDAY 24. Pleasant day. The sky a little overcast after sunset. Fine weather for Kiota diggins. Men in the store who came in across the plains yesterday & who lived on mules & dogs for a week or so until relief came. One showed me a ball taken out of a wound in his shoulder, still sore, that was fired into him by Indians who succeeded in killing his partner. Many Indian depredations & much stealing by them.

FRIDAY 25. The sun cleared off the cloudy sky & have warm again. Mrs Apperson died last night. It is supposed a skillful physician could easily have saved her life, by timely attention. Funeral rites here. Dr. Wells sold his house joining ours & built like ours for $800. An old horse, or rather a worn out one was laying at my door this morning & had trouble to get him off. Those arrivals just in across the plains are objects of pity. Teams sell most goods & dull times are ours in trade.

SATURDAY 26. Cool nights & warm days. Am told by a friend who has a the[r]mometer in the Kiota Diggins that it stood this morning at 56 and at two o'clock today at 98 in the shade. The sun very hot here otherwise men can better endure heat here than any country I ever saw. There is no sultry weather a constant breeze relieves one from the heat.

SUNDAY 27. Another unobserved Sabbath is numbered among the past with the Nevadeans. Had a busy day warm and clear. Have news this evening that Cholera rages badly at Sacramento City[257] & almost in every instance fatal.

MONDAY 28. Cool pleasant day. Mr French[258] up with a train with goods. Dull times.

TUESDAY 29. Mr Addison came up this morning & reports several deaths in Fremont & Vernon by Cholera & over 100 cases in the City on Saturday. He attended to persons who had it. We expect it here soon. Dull prospects of business here & below. Fine weather.

WEDNESDAY 30. Weather generally fair but for two last weeks at times the sky overcasts with clouds, so it has been part of today.

THURSDAY 31. Cloudy & gloomy day. Mr. Addison & myself put up two very comfortable bunks for lodging which are the most comfortable beds I have had in California decidedly. Accts from the Valley relative to Cholera are gloomy indeed. Read a story "The Bell of the Bowery" & was very interesting.

FRIDAY NOV. 1ST. Weather cool & sky often gloomy & cloudy. Had a fine nights rest on good bed. Took a walk out, astonishing rapidity of growth of Nevada. Met Messrs Peters[259] & Esvonin are putting up a home.

SATURDAY NOV. 2. Cool & pleasant nights frosty. Two cases of Cholera in town today. Both men who came up from the city & were at once taken with it. Business dull.

SUNDAY 3. Gloomy day. Took a walk among the Kiota diggings in co with Breyfogle & Cloud. Had the pleasure of seeing Miss Morgan a rather pretty little "Hawkeye" girl. Mr Mooton up from Fremont gives an awful acct of Cholera & other sickness, there are several deaths. The Indians oposite Nicholaus & in other places have taken it & die in numbers. Cholera in the City as many as 100 cases a day.

MONDAY 4. Cleared off last night, & have this morning

a very hard frost. Ice ¼ to inch thick. Sun hot at midday. Report as to Cholera at city for Saturday 117
cases.

TUESDAY 5. Another very heavy frost. Ice on pan
of water at our bedside. Mr Stiles Jr is here bringing
hay from Vernon bot of Mr Addison. A teamster just
up from the city took Cholera so suddenly that he fell
in the fire by which he stood.

WEDNESDAY 6. Have many pleasant topics of conversation with Mr Addison. He a private in Mexican War
& was in Battle of Cerro Gordo &c. A high liver sold
his horse today for $75.00. Occasional creamy white
clouds floating along like haze.

THURSDAY 7. Cold frosty nights warm clear days.
Accts from below are sad indeed as to Cholera. Brown
& Davis Teamster died of it today here. Kiota Diggings
wishing continuance of dry weather & others with claims
in ravines &c waiting impatiently for rain to go to work.
Much time lost this way in mining. Mr Addison bot a
poney horse for $40. Peculiar characteristics of the Mis-
sourians, Neither South nor North, they are a peculiar
people selfish in the extreme. A Ten Pin Alley in full
blast next to our store & right back of it is no small
annoyance.

FRIDAY 8. Mr Addison left for Marysville on poney
& took $569. in dust along. Yuba & Kiota Dust — the
difference. Sold little sheet iron stove for $12. & bot a
large sheet iron one for $40. Very cold frosty morning,
clear warm day. Dull times.

SATURDAY 9. Heavy frost in morning, warm balance
of day. A gentleman here from the City states 58 deaths
occured the day before he left there and that but ¼ of
the population remain there. Hardly any business doing.
He played cards around a table with 4 others, one night
& before the seting of next days sun the four others
were dead & he had the cholera but escaped showed the
effects of it — says he saw 20 coffins laying in the grave
yard awaiting burial. Persons leaving the City are apt

to take it perhaps because of a change of climate as there is such great changes here in a few miles. Dull times.

SUNDAY NOV. 10. 1850. Am looking anxiously for a letter from home. Have my name on three Express lists & yet no letters. Cholera reports from below dreadful. Ships on the Sacramento stoped & laying at anchor for wanting hands to man them. Accts reach us of companies of 6 & 8 who started for home being cut off, every one by Cholera. Had no case in town here for a few days past. Cold nights. Frosty mornings, Faultlessly clear warm & pleasant days, with a gentle zephyr fanning one, quite delightful.

Nov. 11, 1850 — Pleasant day, smoky & without a prospect for rain. Indians say will have no rain for "two moons." Cholera abating some in Sacramento City. Commenced last night boarding myself & do so well & save about $2.00 a day.

TUESDAY 12. Frosty morning, nothing new.

WEDNESDAY Nov. 13. Weather as before. Folks going to Yuba again. Here all are moving to & fro & the quantity of clothing & other plunder left in points by miners to which they never return is great indeed. In this way thousands have goods, at various points in store never to see them more. Had the curiosity to look in at the window on a "Ball" the second of the season here attended by "Blacklegs"260 "Gentlemen of Leisure" & a few *gentlemen,* with a small sprinkling of Misses, young ladies, & married women which dance tolerably nimble for having crossed the interminable plains in their day. Some of the families look down upon these balls. True they are "no great shakes" no how.

THURSDAY 14. Frosty night after a hard wind of last evening, but a warm pleasant day today. Business very dull. A great majority of miners waiting for rain to enable them to wash the dirt they have thrown up in the ravines. Accts from below in regard to Cholera are now favorable.

FRIDAY 15. Cool & a little cloudy day after a frosty

morning. A Capt. Wallace of Clay Co. Mo. who brot a train across the plains this season loaded with bacon, died last night & was this evening buried in accordance with the rites and forms of Ancient Freemasonry.261 About 60 Brethren were out, myself with the number & buried at the same time a Brother Wood of Michigan.

SATURDAY 16. Feel today rather unwell. Have had no good appetite for some days & find that work is more suited to my physical condition than selling goods. Times very dull. Mr. Addison came up tonight by stage from Marysville. Says there has been no Cholera at that place and that it is about over at the City. But have it considerably at San Francisco. They're fewer at Marysville. Fall & Co. have sold out the two steam boat loads of goods brot up a few weeks ago. They sold $22000 worth of goods the last two weeks.

SUNDAY 17. Pleasant cool day. Sold $151 worth of goods today. A man shot in a gambling house again.

MONDAY 18. The peculiarly dappled & at times cloudy sky which preceeds the rainy season made their appearance today. Cool & windy. Business very dull.

TUESDAY 19. Mr. Addison left this morning on stage enroute for Marysville. A gloomy overcast sky at morn brought a rain by noon & this evening it comes down, "Alamode rainy season." Many are glad but *all* never get ready for a change of weather even in California.

WEDNESDAY 20. Had heavy showers last night at short intervals which continued through the day. Chilly, windy rain as usual here. Simeon Bodly staying here several nights lately. Mr. Breyfogle quite unwell.

THURSDAY 21. Sat up all last night with Mr. J. M. White's little girl Margarett who is, poor little thing, well nigh the end of her life journey. The family greatly affected by this misfortune. Rained considerably last night and almost constantly all day in good earnest. Mr. Watson just in from Yuba says it snows on the ridge & snow is six inches deep. My friend Mr. Bodly handed me the first and welcome letter from my dear brother David —

since I left home. This joyous news from home of Sept. 11th of good health &c. My gratification I cannot find language to express.

FRIDAY 22. Bodly & Co. left for Yuba. Rainy morning, cleared off in part at noon. Rained much last night. Road already bad. Business yet dull. Health good. Am reading an interesting book Title, "The Analogy of Ancient Craft Masonry to Natural and Revealed Religion" by Charles Scott. A.M.

SATURDAY 23. Rainy day & disagreeably chilly, but not more so than last fall on the Sacramento.

SUNDAY 24. Watched in Co. with Miss C. & Mr. Potter[262] at Mr. White's with their child Margaret Buckingham which after a severe sickness & suffering of two weeks yielded up her spirit at 20 minutes of five o'clock this morning and winged her away from amidst mourning friends to the enjoyment of society of Angels. At three o'clock this afternoon Revd. Mr. Owen being here on a Quarterly occasion preached a short but interesting funeral discourse at the house. Those usually mournful occasions are here far from home & friends doubly impressive reminding one of the mortality of those we love & who knows but their funeral service is now being performed in a distant land. Cool day & the sky clearing off.

MONDAY 25. Clear & cool & beautiful day. Frost this morning.

TUESDAY 26. Frosty morning & where sun shone not ice remained all day. Cloudy afternoon. Sent a note to Bakers in regard to balance due us, last night. "Short & sweet," for payment by Wednesday evening &c. Dull times.

WEDNESDAY 27. Small sprinkling of snow or sleet last night enough to cover ground. Cloudy & cool day. Recd load of goods of Fall & Co. Marysville. Teamster on way seven days says roads are very bad.

THURSDAY 28. Cool cloudy day. The Baker came in with one of his Alabama friends to intercede for him. My note created quite a flutter of interest in the camp

& on payment of $100 tomorrow promised to wait longer & soon they had raised $135.50 on it.

FRIDAY 29. Heard it rain during the night & is raining & gloomy today as rainy season is wont to be in California. Rain comes here either from S. W. South or S. E. and wind from the north or a clear northern horizon is a shure indication of clear weather.

SATURDAY 30. Rained much last night & continues rainy today. Gloomy indeed.

SUNDAY DEC. 1. Weather this is peculiar seems like clearing off for a few minutes then again clouds rise suddenly. This afternoon it snowed on the mud to a depth of five inches. Recd today a letter from Rev. John Burr which was open & that part written by Sister Mary was taken out.

MONDAY 2. Today we had the variety of rain, hail, & snow leaving a snow this evening two inches deep with a prospect of laying for a few days.

TUESDAY 2. Quite cold this morning & a clear day. Started a two mule train to Marysville for goods at 11 cts pr lb freight. Mr. Chapin called & I recognized him at once & had not seen him for five years. Miles Marks came up after 3 head stolen cattle & is unwell.

WEDNESDAY 4. This is the coldest morning by far I have experienced in California. Ice froze an inch thick at the foot of my bed during the night. A clear cold day. Ice dont thaw in the shade. Bot venison for my table use cheap as beef, 25 cts pr lb & is good.

THURSDAY 5. Another most uncomfortable cold morning thick ice, clear cold day. Sent a letter to Bro. David by Mr. Severance of DuBuque who is starting for home & is unwell. Prospects for business rather dull, much talk now of the Feather River Diggings.

FRIDAY 6. Cold, frosty clear night, pleasant day & dull times indeed & little profit on goods in town. Many people have left & are daily leaving for other diggings. Feather River & vicinity will next spring be the place for thousands to crowd to & who can foretell the fate or doom of overdone Nevada. Houses were built without number & now no house in town would bring 1/3 of original cost. Thus goes money & labor on *clabboard* houses. All (or nearly so) are now labeled "For Sale" "to Let" &c.

SATURDAY 7. Fine clear weather ground freezes hard at nights & remains so during the day in the shade. Was provoked today by arrival of train I sent to Marysville for certain goods, coming with any other than those wanted.

SUNDAY 8. A delightful day. Business tolerably brisk yet everything is much duller than formerly here.

MONDAY 9. Made a bill to Hogues & Co. for $129.90. Weather is pleasant, cool & frosty last night but warm & clear today. Sent a line with Cochran to Fremont for my rifle & an order to Marysville for a few goods. Mr. Augustine & family left Nevada this morning for Iowa.

TUESDAY 10. Some frost this morning but pleasant day. Clouding up this evening & a little sprinkling rain as I go to bed. Times very dull. Mr. Larsh left for Marysville.

WEDNESDAY 11. Cool & pleasant a little cloudy at times. Rain is much wanted by the miners. Mr Chapin in & had quite a long talk with him. Times duller than ever.

THURSDAY 12. Rainy today, though moderate only.

FRIDAY 13. Cloudy at times a little rain. Lot of Frenchmen had a spree last night at the French Restaurant on acct of good diggings. They panned out of one pan dirt $909. on Buckeye Hill, 55 & 65 ft shafts. So they told Mr. Chapin & me. This raises French to a high pitch.

SATURDAY 14. Had a heavy rain all last night & today it rained moderately all day. Miners are at work in rain fearing it will not last & improve the water. Clouds business of Long Toms good. Had long conversation with Davids friend Morgan on Masonry, Mining, etc.

SUNDAY 15. Cloudy & cool today. Mr Stillman furnished me with a table of observations of temperature &c. This evening in solitude I love to think of the past, home & friends, & many occurences of the past now interesting to review.

MONDAY 16. Rainy all day. Had uncommon hard blasts of wind last night, felled some trees which are now so thined out.

TUESDAY 17. Another rainy day. Rained much last night. Cool & chilly as rains usually are here. Snowed some for an hour this evening. Had a dull gloomy day.

WEDNESDAY 18. Cleared off last night. Have a frosty morning & clear sky which before evening threatened rain again. It takes but little time here to "fix up for rain." Nothing new or of interest. Wrote a letter to Amos this evening and enclosed Kiota dust & a picture of Seeing the Elephant.263

THURSDAY 19. Frosty morning clear day. Several ladies passed & repassed through Broadway today. Such as are Ladylike. Had a good business day though times generally dull.

FRIDAY 20. Weather unsettled change from clear to cloudy &c frequently. Nights cool. Times dull.

SATURDAY 21. Sent a letter to Bro. Amos by a gent going to Illinois with a specimen of Kiota dust &c. Frosty last night. Cloudy & clear in quick succession.

SUNDAY 22. Cool day, heavy frost this morning. Good business day. Old Father Horn "The Divine" concluded to go home if money raised for him to go which will be done more readily than it would for his continuance here.

MONDAY 23. Cold nights & windy morning but clear. Miles Marks here again. Nothing of interest.

TUESDAY 24. Clear pleasant weather. Men & boys this evening endeavor to usher in the Christmas of 1850 by making the hills resound with the report of rifles, pistols &c. which though inappropriate cannot but remind one in connection with this Christmas Eve celebrated among the Sierra Nevada Mountains, of the nature of the event. The merry doings of boyhood & the religious observance due or appropriate to the day.

WEDNESDAY 25. Christmas beautiful clear day as May days are wont to be in the States. In company with Miles Marks took dinner at the Oregon Hotel. Very ordinary dinner. Had auction today in town at several places. The streets crowded with the usual motley mixture of "Black Legs" miners, traders &c. and an unusual large proportion of drunken men. Two balls came off this evening $10. a ticket.

THURSDAY 26. Another beautiful day after a frosty night as usual miners want rain very much. Business stagnant. Paid $40 for one of Colts Revolving Pistols264 for my own use. Had a $12 pair blankets a $10 pair pants & an $8. coat stolen from the door last evening. Some still on a Christmas spree today. Shooting & noise going all last night.

FRIDAY 27. Frosty night & clear pleasant day as usual. Nothing of interest today.

SATURDAY 28. Weather as yesterday. Dull times. Dangers of a credit system in California.

SUNDAY 29. Beautiful day. Mr Cloud & I took a walk, went into tunnel runing into hills on Deer Creek. Got three (letters) for C. Breyfogle — postage $7.20. No letters for me. J. Moore & Co. Methodists formerly class leaders hold auction today. Wrote a letter to Bro. A. S. to send with Marks & Co.

MONDAY 30. Fine weather, dull times.

TUESDAY 31. Pleasant weather wrote a letter for Mr. W.— Sent $500 in dust to Messrs Fall & Co. for Gen. Moore. Miles Marks started for home, took letters to Rev. A. S. for me & $20. in Yuba dust to pay dues in Societies. Also sent Plum & Gooseberry seeds. Tonight the city & neighboring hills & dells echo the sound of all kinds of fire arms proclaiming the close of the year '50 & ushering in the successor '51.

WEDNESDAY JAN. 1ST 1851. Another year is gone & one too of many momentous incidents with me. 1850 was spent in California. May the new year of 1851 be one

of happiness peace and plenty for the human family.
Mr. Addison came up today on a collecting trip & has
succeeded badly. Tells of Mr. Ebrights being mangled
by the explosion of lot of gun caps so that life is dispaired
of. Wormbough, Anderson & the Brawley case. Pleasant
day. Last night a farce perhaps unequaled in any country came off in town. A lot of "Black Legs"265 succeeded
in planning & consumating the marriage of a "Green
Widower" to a lude woman of the basest kind (formerly
from Galena). The green groom not knowing but all
was right bot her $300. worth of clothing & a fine suit
for himself. Had a public dinner costing $300, & a free
drink for all. Paid a Blackleg 6 ounces for a sham license
& paid another gambler $50. for marrying them. After
the sucker was thus fleeced his Deary told him he was
a fool, swore he should leave the house or she would
shoot him with a pistol she flourished. And not until
then the truth flashing on the astonished victims dull
apprehension after paying about $1000 — thus far do
Demons go.

THURSDAY JAN. 2, 1851. Frosty nights, clear pleasant
days. Mule stolen from Capt. Moore. Stock very in-
secure much thieveing going on Lynch law best for
California yet civil process too slow uncertain & expen-
sive & has no dread where are no jail & penitentiaries.
Worse state of moral now than when lynch law prevail-
ing. Mr Addison left this morning for Marysville. Mr
Brandt of Zanesville, Ohio, leaves for home. Seems to
know of good diggings near Siars [Sears] diggings,266
Feather River would not tell exact plan.

FRIDAY 3. Pleasant day. Heavy frosts at nights.
Times very dull, many going back to Yuba to do mining.
Spent the evening at Mrs Whites very pleasantly. She
is a lady of very good sense has claims to considerable
experience. Lived in Tenn. Oregon & here & a family
of excellent reputation. Mr. Smith's romantic "Love
Scrape" with Miss Susan Combs the only woman that
has lately broken in on the usual *ennui* of Broad Street.267

SATURDAY 4. Weather as yesterday with a few clouds skirting the horizon. Dr. Knox house on fire, helped with water on it. Dangers of fire great among these wooden houses of pine and cedar.

SUNDAY 5. Occasional showers pattered on the roof during the night & today it rains pretty steady, giving new hope to ravine miners. Cantley, Massey & Co. came in this evening drenched, just from Feather River. Report poor diggings in vicinity of Tolls'.268 One of them been up on Nelson Creek.269 His companions lost & froze in the deep snows. One had his toes to come off & several died enroute. Reports he worked haf a day on Nelson Creek & made $9.00 per hour in the banks, but would not go there again for such pay.

MONDAY 6. Heavy rains last night & frequent showers today which gives more stir to things in town — nothing of interest.

TUESDAY 7. Had a rainy day with moderate temperature. Miners at work in rain, making gold while water lasts. Had a meeting of Odd Fellows this evening Bro. Barcus formerly of Washington Lodge No. 1 Cin. O. acted as Chairman who on my introduction paid a high compliment to my Lodge &c. Appointed a Com. to draft a Constitution & By-Laws for an Association to report at adjourned meeting Saturday Eve. Institution of a Lodge deemed impolitic at present. Had on Bidwell Bar270 a wandering tribe of Odd Fellows organized last summer same as this organization is contemplated. They have a chief & Associate Chief &c.

WEDNESDAY 8. A clear cool morning auguring a beautiful day. Business very dull making time pass.

THURSDAY 9. Frosty morning, clear beautiful spring like day.

FRIDAY 10. Fine clear weather with a clear Italian sky. Called to spend a social evening at Mrs. Whites. The ladies present made me phrenologise their heads & thoughts. I told them more than they thought any one could as to their dispositions. An old fellow, a traveler, played slight of hand games to our amusement & the evening passed off pleasantly.

SATURDAY 11. Another warm beautiful day after a frosty morning. Nights are clear & light. Attended Odd Fellows meeting. Passed on a Constitution only will meet again to perfect the organization of the Nevada City Society of the I.O.O.F.[271] &c.

SUNDAY 12. Fine clear day. Had a delicious breakfast got warm bread of Mrs. White had tripe & pretty good butter. My appetite fine & health good.

MONDAY 13. Pleasant day. Episcopalian Preacher sent here from New Jersey as a Missionary is now gambling, swearing & drinking, so says Capt. Moore. A Methodist Preacher from Alabama this summer peddled Monte cards on Nelson Creek.

TUESDAY 14. Fine warm days, nights now beautifully clear & moonlight. Accts of murder, robbings &c. are rife daily. Many desperate men now in California, Sidneyites[272] &c.

WEDNESDAY 15. Mrs White whose husband is absent informs me that a man got into the room where herself & a female friend sleep during last night & only left when a man who slept in an adjoining room made alarm. This bold rascal entered at a front window into the room where a pretty large lot of money is kept. Mr. Arnold — family of Columbus was here today. Sent $350. to Messrs Fall & Co. by him expecting to return home soon promised he would call on Augustus in Columbus &c.

THURSDAY 16. Pretty thick ice froze this morning, but warm pleasant to day. Some excitement as to the entrance of Mrs White's room. Sent a transcript to Dayton containing accts of emigrants of 1849[273] &c.

FRIDAY 17. Pleasant day. Men coming again to this place to go into the Kiota Diggings. Much jumping of claims & dificulty about claim regulations.

SATURDAY 18. Cloudy today with a good prospect for rain. Spent a pleasant evening at Mr. Whites Thursday evening.

SUNDAY 19. The sky clear again this morning & a fine day. A goodly throng of people in town today. Goods selling at almost nothing at auction here & in all California towns now. Spent the evening at church. Preacher not coming a prayer meeting held & had peculiar & affecting thoughts of home & friends while at church. How dingy & uncomfortable the churches here & how well fited up the Gambling Houses.

MONDAY 20. Fine pleasant day. Dr. Lenix[274] was shot last night while siting in his house. The balls passing through the window. He died in a few hours & today two men, Messrs Bess & Fitzpatrick have a trial. Bess having had a dificulty with the Dr. on the plains & a trial about it after their arrival here.

TUESDAY 21. Cold night & pleasant day. Trial of Messrs Bess & Fitzpatrick going on & will probably take a weeks time. Bess came in court arrived with revolver & knife. Court held in bar room of the Placer Hotel — much excitement prevails. Bess manages his own case. Is a desperate hard featured looking old desperado.

WEDNESDAY 22. Fine weather. President's[275] message &c. Here nothing new of interest.

THURSDAY 23. Spent last evening pleasantly at Mr. Whites. Feel at times very lonesome, and am seemingly forgotten by my friends at home. Get no letters & can see none advertised at any office for me. So I cannot but conclude that they write not neither care much for me.

FRIDAY 24. Warm & pleasant day. Striking Kiota Diggins in this vicinity that pay pretty well. Am discouraged about business. All looks gloomy for the future.

SATURDAY 25. Warm as usual. The sky clear as field of ether can be. Indians — the root diggers pass through the streets in gangs with bows and well filled quivers with best of arrows. These Indians though but mere animals are mostly of good physical development, rather less in stature than whites of a brownish black — bushy heads, rather flat noses broad faces & low foreheads. Walk erect & have an extraordinary expansion of the chest — much better chest than any people I had seen before. This they develop doubtless by much swimming & diving while young. Can hold breath — that is remain under water long as I can hold my breath with several efforts. They dive & swim like a duck & then come out & roll & billow around in the deep sand & dust of the river roads for the pleasure of washing off again. Then sit around each other & pick lice from one anothers heads and eat them. Thus are performed their ablutions.

SUNDAY 26. Clouded up today and had some rain. Mr White & two parties, Potter & Freeman[276] divided off. Business dull.

TUESDAY 28. Somewhat cloudy without rain.

WEDNESDAY 29. Clear & pleasant day. Feel ill at ease in my confined situation & dull prospects for business.

THURSDAY 30. Cloudy gloomy all today. Mr Knapp left for Kanaka Creek to prospect. Mr. L.—a preacher took a note given his partner & burnt it calling for $500. or more. Oh preachers how you do act in this California.

FRIDAY 31. Pleasant day frosty morning dull times. Breyfogle & Cloud trying to settle up business. Much excitement about Gold Bluff[277] on the Pacific, must be a great humbug.

SATURDAY FEBY. 1. Frosty morning & fine day. Had a singular dream in regard to the illness of Bro. Augustus' child.

SUNDAY 2. A very pleasant day & dull times. Goods are selling all morning at auction, 3 or 4 auctioneers hammering off at once. Goods bring often less than in the States. Asked Mr. Henderson for amt for Miles Marks. He says he has no money now. Will never pay anything unless he has it presented him when he is about to leave California, then he may pay $50. more. Has written to Oregon not to allow it to be paid there. Bot me a coat today for $12.00. Stiles here today. Today as I oft have done before I stood under the door taking "items" for an hour or more & now I as artist might

give curious pictures. The ¼th mile which Broadway
shows to the eye has her group of two, three to a dozen
men passing in squads each encumbered with some essen-
tial to "camp life" such as a piece of steak a side of
bacon — a ham a sack of flour a jar of pickles a pan a
pick & shovel coffee pot or camp fixtures of some kind
going along apparently merrily each bears the peculiar
exterior which tells to what "manor born." Then it is a
group of men from the States. They walk so free appear
so independent. Here is a squad of Cornwall miners.
They look, act & show out the miner. There are a few
rugged sons of "Erin" really "Paddys." How that dozen
or more of representatives of the "Celestial Empire"—
Chinamen trudge along with their gownish trousers worn
so low & brown flat faces, so inexpressive in countenance
but peacefully disposed. Yon hard featured "Villain"
like fellow is an Australian or rather a "Sidneyite." Why
are those Sidney convicts allowed to be landed here?
Here comes the slow plodding Dutchman with his little
greasy bundle followed by the broad faced Norwegian.
Look at the Mexican riding by on a lope & picking up
a whip that lays on the ground without checking the
horses gate. Thats one of the sort that old Jack gives a
"little more grape." Yon dark group are a lot of "Ka-
nakas" peculiar as their native Islands. What are those
Frenchmen gabbing all speaking at once & constantly
emphasizing so much quite different in their customs &
habits from the Chillians just behind them. That col'd
Gentleman dressed so gay is one of those bondsmen of
the South whose promise to the contrary has not restrained
him from asserting freedom on the far shores of the
Pacific. Last, yet first here is the little company of Indians passing along in Indian file, bows & arrows in
hands & the Squaws & their Papooses cribbed on their
backs, how nimbly they walk & how little intelligence
the Digger Indians countenance displays almost hid by
the bushy thicket of uncombed hair. Such is California,
a perfect "Confusion of Tongues."[278] The most opposite

habits here mix in to make up the grand whole. The bringing together of a worlds productions of the human species. Surely *Gold* thou hast a Talismanic influence. What but thou could do these things?

MONDAY 3. Had a fine day. Two Englishmen fought last night with knives. One lays on the hill dead & the other badly wounded. A coroners inquest held, the live man taken by the Sheriff & the dead one left lying on the ground, so a few miners buried him. Civil law is no law here. A poor fellow long sick died today at Whites. Had a faithful cousin to wait on him. Took an acct of stock & find business has not paid at all.

TUESDAY 4. Warm today as summer days in Ohio. The man who died yesterday at Whites followed to the grave by four persons. But little respect for the dead here & less for the living. Hard country & worse times, no news &c.

WEDNESDAY 5. Cloudy today with a fair prospect of rain. Took a walk out this afternoon up little Deer Creek & over Kiota hills. Many sinking shaft with great labor. Much as 90 ft deep hindered with water greatly. Du-Buque men mining a level or tunnel into western hill to drain it. Horse power established to draw water. Water for washing brot on to the hill from Rock Creek279 & another ditch in making 5 miles long from same Creek. Also a large ditch by Young & Co. bringing in part of Deer Creek on the hill for washing. Clear water cost $8 pr day for a Tom & 2nd & 3rd class already muddy $5. & $3. for a Tom pr day.

THURSDAY 6. Weather rather unsettled, a little sprinkling of rain this evening. Tonight Mr. Apperson [Epperson] was married to Mrs Brondurant. He a widower about 4 months, & she a widow some six weeks.

FRIDAY 7. Clear warm day. Persons passing through here on their way to Feather River daily. Bot me a Colts Revolver 4 in. bbl. for $40.00, No. 9770.

SATURDAY 8. Clear fine day nothing of interest today. Appersons shivereed last night.

SUNDAY 9. Business going on as usual. The town crowded goods selling at auction at 1/3 what they would be worth in the States. Had a beautiful day, warm.

MONDAY 10. Clouds up a little occasionally yet a fine day. Nothing of interest.

WEDNESDAY 12. Had a cold night, frosty morning. Dull times.

THURSDAY 13. Messrs Flippin & Laughlin came over from Yuba. Messrs Byerly, Scharm & Cryder also came over today.

FRIDAY 14. Fine day. Dull times & nothing of interest today.

SATURDAY 15. Had a fine day.

SUNDAY 16. Clear cold morning & fine day. Mr. White preparing to go home to Tenn.

MONDAY 17. Pleasant day, nothing new.

TUESDAY 18. Had a rainy day with occasional snow, quite disagreeable.

WEDNESDAY 19. Another rainy, snow day.

THURSDAY 20. A clear fine day, frosty morning.

FRIDAY 21. Pleasant day after frosty morning.

SATURDAY 22. Pleasant weather. Lent Mr. O'Brien coat for Ball tonight which comes off at Besses Hotel. Am making arrangements to sell at auction tomorrow. Had a disagreeable day.

SUNDAY 23. The sun rose clear & the day rather pleasant. Sold goods at auction. This is the only auction day. Goods brought less than City cash & house which cost $505. brought $210. Mr. Breyfogle left today for home took a letter to A. S. Decker for me. Had to pay tax or rather license.

MONDAY 24. Rain & snow fell nearly all day quite disagreeably. Am settling up my affairs here fast as I can & find it dificult.

TUESDAY 25. Snow & rain most of the day & get little snow lying — falls in mud. Am cleaning up my business. Paid Doctor E. E. Gardner $75.88 being amt due for picks sold.

WEDNESDAY 26. Had a very pleasant cool day. Rode out to Rush Creek[280] to hunt up a Mr. Thompson who owes Fall & Co. & after enquiring at about 100 cabins & as many tents found my way to the said Thompson & made him "fork over" *some*. Closing up goes slow. The Irisipalas[281] prevalent & fatal here.

THURSDAY 27. Commenced raining at sun rise & seems to have set in for a long steady rain. Settled with Kohlman[282] for the house. Had to move my flour.

FRIDAY 28. Snowing and rainy all day. The streets muddy & very damp & chilling. Have no good place to stay & time not spent in bed is spent disagreeably. My friend Mr. Knapp is here. Am closing up my affairs to leave by first opportunity.

SATURDAY 29. The sky is clear this morning & frosty. The sun takes the snow off rapidly & this evening cloudy again. Mr. Knapp & I took breakfast at Gregorys Hotel, where his daughters wait on the table. Had a fine breakfast warm biscuits coffee butter molasses stake hash &c. Am selling flour good article at $1000 pr 100 lb which cost me $2550 and an inferior article I sell at $300 pr 100 lb which cost $1750. This is making a "Pile" fast over the left.

SUNDAY 30. Rained & snowed at intervals today. The snow six inches deep but passing off rapidly in the mud. Called at Morgans this afternoon. Mr. Knapp left for Rough & Ready. Spent the evening with Potter Freeman & Smith.

MONDAY 31. Clear frosty morning & the sun shining — has taken nearly all the snow off today. Made arrangements to go to Marysville tomorrow.

TUESDAY APRIL 1. Somewhat cloudy today — yet pleasant. Left balance of my business yet unsettled with Mr. R. W. Cloud & left Nevada with Mr Cochran & his col'd man 3 mule team. Had some trouble to get up the hill from Deer Creek. Road bad — driver complaining about the mules & roads. Slashes his [whip] about our heads keeping one in constant dread of getting it

applied harder than the mules. Out of one rut or track
into another out of mud into mire &c. Stopped a few
minutes at Rough & Ready. Took a new & bad road
to avoid the boggs of Penn Valley. Stopped before dusk
at the Miners Hotel[283] kept by a Mr. Berry & Lady —
He is just recovering from a spell of sickness & has
buried all his children in California. Is discouraged with
the country as is natural under the circumstances. Snow
at Nevada four to six inches deep & eight miles below
is no snow — quite a difference in the advance of foliage
&c. Have some $2000. dust with me which it is necessary
to watch closely. Distance 20 miles.

WEDNESDAY APRIL 2. The ground floor of our Hotel
& adjoining sleeping apartment was damp & disagreeable. Had a restless night on acct of ones exposure
with money. Hear that the men taken at Nevada for
stealing of Mr. Nappa $2500. are having their trial &
will probably be hung by the enraged citizens. These
thieves had come to Nevada with the Circus. The weather
this morning the sky is cloudy. Met Mr. Cowles here
whom I met in the Mountains on Feather River. Started
for Marysville at which place we arrived at two o'clock
when a drizzling rain commenced falling. Mr. Addison
has gone to Nevada & we missed each other on the road.
Fall & Stombough[284] here & will have me stop with them
— Distance 25 miles.

THURSDAY APRIL 3. Had very heavy rain all last night
which has continued to fall today at intervals & the wind
blowing hard. Mr. Addison came back from Nevada &
we had this evening a settlement of our business. He &
the balance of the firm *Fall & Stombough* are kind &
liberal toward me. Our Nevada business has resulted
in a small loss to us — but less than I had anticipated.
This is hard but I will "hope on hope ever" and *try* again.
This loss & bad success is the result of fluctuations in
prices since last fall & the fair winter & the consequent
overstocking of the mines with goods. Saw Ed Moses
today & Marshal Bryan of Columbus. Mr Sites & other

acquaintances. Several steamers landed today — the Tehama, Capt. Sutter & Dana.285

FRIDAY APRIL 4. This morning the River Yuba is
quite high. The weather unsettled — cloudy & rainy at
intervals. The sky gloomy. By Falls pressing invitation
I stay with them. Fall does the cooking generally — of
which Col Jones & I have relieved him today. We are
cooking beans. Mr Fall has bought out Addison &
Stombough. They are going home the first of May.

SATURDAY APRIL 5. The morning pretty clear & had
a beautiful day. The rivers continue swolen — nearly
bank full. Fall had a busy time today — sold $4688 worth
goods. Mr. Kennedy of the City up this evening. Fall
made an Oyster supper to show as he said "hostility"
[hospitality] to Mr Kennedy. Mr Babb286 showed me
a specimen of gold — *pure gold* belonging to Mr. Stombough which weighs $1250.00 or 6½ lbs. Was taken
out of Poor Mans Creek on Feather River. Mr. S. in-
tends to take it home to Lancaster Ohio.

SUNDAY APRIL 6. Had a clear cool & beautiful day.
Mr Fall started for the Bay takes a load of dust for
one man to carry. The stores are all open & doing business. The Plaza is filled with about 200 mules with piles
of goods among & Spaniards mostly packing them. They
can pack with great facility. Have saddle weighing 60
lbs & are best to pack on although heavy. The Council
here is about passing an Ordinance to prevent the opening of stores on Sundays. In Sacramento City there is
hardly any business done now on the Sabbath & gambling
is much on the decrease. This is a great change since
1849. Have taken a walk a mile out from Marysville
on the bank of the Feather River am sit[t]ing by an in-
closure — made with brush — which is called a garden.
Potatoes are six inches tall & the Peas look fine. Farms
are already an object. A claim on Bear River worth
$12000. The late rain encourages farmers.

MONDAY APRIL 7. A beautiful warm day. Feel ill at
ease having no business to occupy my mind. Wrote a

letter to sister Sarah & mailed it today directed to C. S.
Decker & Co. to be delivered to her. Several steamers
land here every day.

TUESDAY APRIL 8TH. The sky is cloudy the air moderate & pleasant. Commenced raining at noon — dull day.

WEDNESDAY APRIL 9. The sun dispersed a few clouds
along the horizon & the day was warm and beautiful.
Saw Mr. Lunn & had news from several Columbus folks.
Had a pleasant walk with Addison this evening to the
country — a log house of moderate size standing ½ mile
out on the plain nine prisoners in & only 3 apartments.
Saw where some "outsiders"— friends tried to break out
the prisoners several were in for mule & horse stealing
— others for breaking into stores & one for murder. How
hard is the way of the transgressor.

THURSDAY APRIL 10. A few clouds stealing along the
horizon but the temperature is warm. Falls goods came
up I assisted in arranging them. He has more than can
be crowded in to his room. He is decidedly a business
man on a large scale and takes care of small things—does
the work of two men & never gets tired. Borckman —
his clerk says he is up doeing business till 11 o'clock
catches rats till two o'clock at night & then calls all hands
for the days business.

FRIDAY 11. Had an extremely warm day. Sold a great
many goods at Falls. Got a fine dog pup — paid an
ounce for it — & it hung itself an hour after he got it
by the string it was tied to.

SATURDAY APRIL 21. A beautiful clear morning &
warm day. Am taking a mixture of Cream Tartar &
Sulphur to purify my blood as I think it needs it. Had
taken no medicine for a year previous. Thermometer at
94 today.

SUNDAY 13. Another very pleasant day. My friend
Shannon[287] called here today. Mr. Lewis [Levi] Hite[288]
— formerly member of the House in Ohio from Fairfield
Co. is here & I find him quite well informed. Mr Fall
gone to the country. The boys got Wickizer drunk. Ac-

cording to an Ordinance of our City stores &c are closed
up — prevented from selling goods on Sundays. Many
are dissatisfied & it will hardly stand so long.

MONDAY 14. Had a very busy day at Falls & I assisted them. Sent some days ago to the City of San
Francisco for letters & the return is — none there. I now
feel quite confident that my friends take not the trouble
to write to me.

TUESDAY 15. A few fleecy white clouds along the horizon were dispelled by the bright shining sun. At eight
o'clock I left Marysville for Long Bar[289] — on Main
Yuba — 15 miles from Marysville. Gentlemen with a
young lady & myself were the passengers in the stage —
a fine coach — a ride of 10 miles up Yuba bottom brot
us to the foot hills. This plain is covered with the finest
verdure intermingled with a profusion of the most deli-
cately tinted flowers of many varities, with occasional
open groves of Oaks which with the view of the Butte —
Coast Range & Sierra mountains presents scenery as
beautiful & romantic as can well be imagined. My fellow
passengers were from the State of New York. The old
gentleman an aristocratic looking German & his young
wife a fine looking intelligent & modest New Yorker
who I was almost sorry to see rejoice in her companion
in the relation of husband — the pair being so unequal.
Have poor accommodations for a lady at Long Bar.
Called on my friends Bodly — Swain — Wood & White.
Went to Parks Bar[290] & stoped with Levi Hite at Stomboughs store. Distance 17 miles.

WEDNESDAY 16. This morning cold & rainy which
continued all day. Took invoice of J. Stomboughs goods
in "Cheap Store" which I was authorized to do by Fall.
Being assisted by my friend Levi Hite formerly of Lancaster O. At noon started for & reached Roses Bar[291]
after climbing hills in the rain for four miles. The River
being swolen nothing doing at mining & trade dull &
overdone. Teamsters sell most goods at very reduced
prices. Barton's Bar[292] is the same which lays on north

side below Roses. At all these Bars companies contemplate turning the River again. Returned completely drenched to Parks Bar in time to see two Englishmen (half tight) fight in a room where a woman screamed & the men around would have them fight it out which they did to the no small discomforture of noses & eyes. Rains hard tonight. Distance 8 miles.

THURSDAY 17. Had my collections made & business arranged by 10 o'clock. Left for Long Bar where I stopped a while & started for Marysville *afoot* which place I reached for an early supper a dozen ranches or farms are passed on the way some with good improvements & with these late rains have a fine prospect. The day somewhat cloudy & pleasantly cool. Distance 17 miles.

FRIDAY 18. With the dull prospect up the River for business I am now considered whether to accept a clerkship here at $125.00 pr month & boarded or go to mining. Cloudy cool day.

SATURDAY 19. Had a clear & pleasant day. Recd from Mr Cloud a letter & $68.15 on acct of Dr. Weaver & gives acct of robery on *Charles* of his $400 — & $200 — of Charles own. Messrs Addison & Stombough proposed to sell me their interest in a share in the Canal Company on Parks Bar 4/9ths of a share at the rate of $800. for a full share — which I purchased & am to pay when taken out of the claim. At the suggestion of Mr Fall I have also concluded to take Mr Stomboughs goods on the same Bar — amt to $1100.44.

SUNDAY 20. Cool & cloudy today. Mr Fall left for San Francisco. Col Jones & I had Masonic & I.O.O.F. conversation. The steamer West Point[293] came up tonight. Had a general space on her she is a large vessel.

MONDAY 21. Cloudy & cold this morning. Selected a bill of goods for store at Parks Bar. Got a team & left Marysville with my goods at noon. The chilling wind soon brought on rain & hail which pretty well drenched us by the time we reached the Bar. Business prospects are dull.

TUESDAY 22. By the assistance of my friend Levi Hite I had the room cleaned up of the cartload rubbage & dirt. Weather cool & cloudy. Am quite a stranger here there being no person on the Bar whose acquaintance I ever had previous to my visit here a week ago to take the invoice of stock.

WEDNESDAY 23RD. The weather is clearing up a few white fleecy clouds only speckle the horizon. Find my situation here alone in the store (with the exception of Dr. Steward who stays here) quite unpleasant on acct of being an entire stranger & unacquainted with the goods & prices. I find many Ohio folks here but none I ever knew before. Examined the Canal Co. claim in which I hold about ½ of a share. The Co. has 33 shareholders some hold them now at $2000 a share. My ½ cost $400. Working under disadvantage last season did not make much although the claim is rich. Furgason & two comrades left this Bar last fall with 700 lbs gold dust.

THURSDAY 24. The sky is now quite clear & the day warm. The nights are only moderately cool.

FRIDAY 25. Messrs Hite & Steward gone to Marysville leaves me quite alone. A Mr. O'Brien died night before last & a Catholic Priest was sent for to Sacramento. I suppose his will be better than *ounce diggings* as the deceased has a PILE & no friends so I believe the partner of O'Brien & the Priest divid spoils.

SATURDAY 26. The Parks Bar Co. & Connecticut Co. are now having a third trial about River claims. The former gained it this time & had a spree over it this afternoon. The weather quite warm the sky entirely clear.

SUNDAY 27. Today is less brisk than I had anticipated. The weather is very warm. The dry season seems now to have set in. The river water is already pretty warm & no springs in this vicinity will be disagreeable this summer especially when the river is once being turned & worked much. Met a Mr. Hosier of Dayton Ohio who knew Bro Charles & Amos & had seen Father at Columbus seemed to me like meeting an old friend.

MONDAY 28. The nights are only cool & the days very warm. The sky clear as usual in dry season. Business rather dull. Feel more estranged here than any place I have been at in California, no associates except new acquaintances.

TUESDAY 29. Another very warm day quite uncomfortably so. Find several families living here — but some are "sidneyites" some are of doubtful reputation & others are of the Pioneer sort. Gathered a beautiful "Boka" of flowers of many kinds of which the hills here are full.

WEDNESDAY 30. Clear sky & extremely warm day. This morning a corpse came floating down the River — none seemed enough interested to try to recover the body from the water & it passed on. It would be dificult to get it out. Many men drown in this stream some are put in by "Highwaymen" some fall in by loosing hold on rocks scrambling along the mountains or banks while many are drowned at the various crossings. Such a rapid deep & boisterous stream hardly any escape from when once in. These many dangers to brave in California.

THURSDAY, MAY 1ST 1851. A delightful day — a fine breeze & clear sky. The scenery about this place Parks Bar is a modification of the valleys & mountains. It is moderately hilly studded with stunted White Oaks & clumps of bushes & a profusion of flowers among which is the California Poppy. The general appearance is barren in the dry season although the foothills are covered in places with pretty fine Grapes. Heard today of Mr Cloud at Nevada [City]. He is well & doing very well. Nevada is pretty lively — I went there the wrong time & left the wrong time.

FRIDAY MAY 2. The day some cloudy & pleasant, cool evening — giving a refresh-time after the extreme heat. Six Chinamen drowned at Bartons Bar yesterday by a boat capsising all had money. As bodies of drowned men are discovered & taken out the one so taking it takes the money — the body sometimes remaining unburied.

Business dull & goods selling low. Discontinued notes for want of time to make them out.

WEDNESDAY MAY 28, '51. Two Spaniards had a trial with a Mr McAdams in Marysville a few days ago for a mule which each party claimed & there being no satisfactory decision the parties met on this Bar & at the St Charles Hotel had a meeting & another trial. The Court decided that the case could not be put off for a week as the Spaniards wanted without them leaving the mule as security or a deposit of money or other security for appearance. Whereupon the Mexicans leveled their pistles at some of the men & they being taken from them. They in the scuffle used their knives & wounded Judge Barnard294 in three places. One of the Spaniards was knocked over with a rock while runing. The other one was overtaken on his mule & surrendered after several shots were fired.

THURSDAY MAY 29. The Spaniards had a trial by a "Citizens Court." The decision was 30 & 45 lashes which were inflicted on bareback this afternoon. The excuse for this mode of punishment is that the ends of justice are seldom meted out at Marysville. Had a little row too about whipping. This morning a sad accident occured here. The Ferryman was taking twenty one men across at one load when in the centre of the stream the men rocked the boat & she dipped water turned around & eleven men were drowned. Ten only saved themselves. Five of those drowned from Mansfield, Ohio. Crossing these rapid rivers one runs no small risk. I cross once a week at night to attend Canal meeting.

[END OF THE DIARY.]

Notes to the Diary

1. John Walton, Captain of the Columbus California Industrial Association. He was a resident of San Francisco, a Deputy Collector of Customs, a member of the State Legislature and belonged to the Society of California Pioneers.

2. G. Q. McColm, a member of the Columbus California Industrial Association.

3. In 1849 Cholera swept over all the river courses. It originated from ships docking at New Orleans who discharged passengers who were infected with the disease and these people carried it via the river steamers to St. Louis and other ports and to the towns where emigrants were outfitting for the trek across the plains. Many of the river steamers stopped at night to bury the dead in unmarked graves along the river banks. So serious was this scourge that in July, 1849, President Taylor decreed a day of prayer to stay the disease. It is said that 20,000 persons died of this disease enroute to California during the Gold Rush years.

4. H. B. Scharmann makes the statement in his *Overland Journey to California,* that in Louisville "prices of all commodities ranged very low; thus a dozen eggs cost five cents."

5. James Porter, the Kentucky Giant, seems to have been one of the main attractions of Louisville. He is described by various travelers. He was 38 years old, 7½ feet tall and weighed 160 pounds.

6. L. A. Denig and Dr. Charles Elisha Boyle were members of the Columbus California Industrial Association. Of Dr. Boyle, considerably more information is available. His account of the trip to California was printed in the Columbus, Ohio, *Dispatch* Oct. 2 to Nov. 11, 1949, from the original diary in the possession of a granddaughter, Mrs. Charles E. Webster, Columbus, Ohio. The Boyle diary was edited for publication in the *Dispatch* by Myron Seifert. Dr. Boyle remained in California about one year, and returned to Columbus. While in California, Dr. Boyle mined briefly, giving up mining for the practice of medicine. He is said to have rendered a considerable service to the miners in the practice of medicine. Dr. Boyle excelled as a linguist and is reputed to have mastered 32 foreign languages. During the Civil War he served as a surgeon of the Ninth Ohio Regiment. He later practiced medicine in Columbus, until the time of his death, in 1868. He is buried in the Greenlawn Cemetery, Columbus, Ohio.

7. Jedediah Allen of the Delaware Company. This company was on the river boat *J. Hancock* with the Columbus Company. He is men-

tioned in the Diary of Joshua D. Breyfogle, who was also with the Delaware Company.

8. There were several Breyfogles, Charles of the Columbus California Industrial Association, Joshua D., Charles C., and Israel of the Delaware Company. It is difficult to untangle just which Charles is meant when Decker makes reference to that name. Dr. Boyle, in his entry for April 7, refers to him as "Charley Breyfogle." He writes: "Charley Breyfogle was extremely well pleased with his first trip on the Ohio so far down. He and Decker sat with me on the forecastle. Chadwick, Fisk and others had, by permission of the captain, a dance to themselves on the hurricane deck, and they did 'go it' in the peculiar style in which they perform everything they undertake."

9. H. B. Scharmann, *Overland to California,* describes the land here as level and barely cultivated, but observes that the fine stand of trees, especially oaks, indicated good soil for agriculture.

10. Joshua D. Breyfogle mentions this incident in his *Diary* (original in Baker Library, Dartmouth College) under the same date as does Dr. Boyle. He writes of the incident: "McColm, in attempting to draw a bucket of water for the mules, slipped into the river. Price seized him by the leg, but was unable to hold him." Not only the *Hancock's* yawl was manned for the rescue, as the Steamer *Atlantic* was passing downstream, and sent out a boat which was the first to reach McColm. He was, according to the Captain of the *Hancock,* only the second man ever saved from falling into the river.

11. Mentioned by Breyfogle as being on the Yuba, 8 miles from Foster's Bar, Feb. 28, 1850. J. Elza Armstrong, from Albany, Ohio, kept an overland diary on his trip to California, which has been published, along with others by John Edwin Banks (*The Buckeye Rovers in the Gold Rush,* edited by Howard L. Scamehorn, Athens, Ohio, 1965). However, as Armstrong's diary ends upon arrival in California, it is not evident that he is the Armstrong mentioned by Decker and Breyfogle, though he could have been at St. Louis and on the Yuba at the times mentioned according to the evidence available.

12. Dr. Boyle recorded the following comments for April 10: "About noon I and Decker and Price ascended the cupola of the new Presbyterian Church, and had an excellent view of the city and the surrounding country. We also visited the rotunda and the Catholic Cathedral at which latter place we heard the morning service. During the entire day was moving about. . . ."

13. No indication which Breyfogle this is although it may be assumed it was Charles of the Columbus California Industrial Association.

14. C. Dewitt, a member of the Columbus California Industrial Association.

15. A. B. Crist, member of the Columbus California Industrial Association.

16. P. McCommon, member of the Columbus California Industrial Association.

17. Goldsborough Bruff mentions stopping at the State House in Jefferson City and remarked on its similarity to the Capitol in Washington. Bruff was there April 20, 1849, a week after Decker and his company. (*Gold Rush Journals of J. Goldsborough Bruff,* Ed. by Georgia Willis Read and Ruth Gaines, N. Y. 1949.)

18. Independence was on the south side of the Missouri River and was a flourishing town made more so by trade with the migrating parties. In 1849 it was a town of about 1500 permanent population. Many of the houses were constructed of brick around the public square.

19. Edwin Bryant was born in Massachusetts, and became a journalist in Louisville, Kentucky, from which place he started for California April 18, 1846. He arrived in California the following August, became Lieutenant in Co. H of the California Battalion and returned east with General Kearny in 1847. He came again to California in 1849 and remained a few years. He died in Louisville, in 1869. His book (*What I Saw in California,* N. Y. 1848) gives a fine account of his overland trip to California, via South Pass, in 1846.

20. Col. William H. ("Owl") Russell, who accompanied Bryant to California in 1846. He was an ordnance officer in the California Battalion and returned east in 1847. He was one of Fremont's most ardent supporters during the Fremont-Kearny controversy. He returned to California in 1849 and practiced law in San Jose, Sacramento, and San Francisco.

21. Jedediah Allen and Moses Bodly were members of the Delaware, Ohio, Company.

22. Fort Leavenworth, established May, 1827, about 30 miles beyond Independence.

23. Major Winslow F. Sanderson, Co. E Mounted Riflemen, 1846. At Fort Laramie in 1849. Died in 1853.

24. St. Joseph was the jumping off place for the parties bound for California. In time it overshadowed Independence. On May 5, 1849, J. Goldsborough Bruff observed that as far as the eye could see there were tents and wagons. In a letter to his sisters, Catherine and Sarah, dated at St. Joseph April 27, 1849, Decker wrote: "I am about fourteen hundred miles from home. . . . We are camped some four miles from the town of St. Joseph. . . . The town has about 2000 inhabitants and but one church. . . ."

25. Dr. Boyle described this day with the following entry: "Came in sight of St. Joseph. . . . I went in town with Charley Breyfogle, who still, according to his account, is laboring under cholera, and endeavored to find lodging for him. I found the town full and had to take him back to the boat. When I got to the boat, J. G. Canfield hurried me into the cabin saying there was a man there nearly dead. This I sup-

posed was McColm, who I was fearful was about to be seized with cholera, but found that the sufferer was John Walton, who had received a very severe kick from a mule as they were taking the mules off the boat."

26. Evidently Mr. A. Pake was a resident of St. Joseph. History has not recorded him.

27. T. J. Price of Columbus California Industrial Association. He and Decker were close friends and he and Decker later went to the Trinity mines together. Later he went to Honolulu, where he made a small fortune shipping hay and grains, and then returned to California. Decker mentions elsewhere that Price was in Marysville in 1853 to attend a dinner given by Decker for friends and associates.

28. Dr. Boyle wrote: "Walton was very restless and in considerable pain until nearly morning when he fell asleep, and was up and about this morning although somewhat weak from loss of blood. Breyfogle was better, being kept busy. McColm was quite ill. . . . Breyfogle went some four miles into the country with his brother of the Delaware train."

29. J. Shade Dungan of the Columbus California Industrial Association was born in Pennsylvania. He was a post-office clerk in San Francisco, 1856-1865. Member of the Society of California Pioneers.

30. J. Krumm, a member of the Columbus California Industrial Association.

31. "Rattlesnake Hill" from which could be seen St. Joseph and the fields dotted with tents of those waiting to start for California.

32. J. C. Lunn and J. P. Stone were both members of the Columbus California Industrial Association.

33. Joseph Hunter, Captain of the Franklin Company that left Columbus, Ohio, April 2, 1849.

34. E. Barcus, Columbus California Industrial Association.

35. "The flag you presented us is waving in the breeze near by and looks well and reminds me of the time Mary D. and you had in putting it up. I am very glad we have it." Letter from Decker to his sister April 27, 1849, St. Joseph, Missouri.

36. David Bryden, member of the Columbus California Industrial Association. Later in 1854, a resident of Nevada City and Grass Valley.

37. There were two men by the name of Rugg on the train with Decker, Dayton and Theodore. See list of members of the Association on page 156.

38. Probably the same company of Swiss and Germans mentioned by Bruff and others. They were encamped on "Rattlesnake Hill." The Captain, or leader, was a Mr. Abbott from Baden, Germany. With his family of a son, a married daughter and her husband, and three children, they were on their way to California. Abbott died on the

Platte River.

39. George Chadwick, Columbus California Industrial Association.

40. H. Moores, Columbus California Industrial Association.

41. There were many varieties of wolves common to the prairies, the Buffalo range and regions farther west. The big white (Buffalo) wolf was shaggy, brown or black. There were also gray prairie wolves and the coyote.

42. These "Missions" or "Stations" for the Christianization of the Indians were supported partly by funds contributed by the U. S. Government, and partly by church donations. Bryant (*What I Saw in California*) describes the one run by the Methodist Episcopal Church, which may be the same one that Decker mentions.

43. Possibly this is A. W. McCoy, who started overland from Cincinnati early in the spring of 1849.

44. The Nemaha in the southeastern part of Nebraska empties into the Missouri two miles below the town of Rule.

45. C. M. Fisk, Columbus California Industrial Association.

46. The Otoes were a tribe on the Platte near its confluence with the Missouri.

47. Walter Cain, Columbus California Industrial Association.

48. Dr. Boyle also commented on this party, but fails to identify them with any detail: "Having made today a treaty of alliance offensive and defensive with a company from Illinois we proceeded onward with a good and willing heart, and encamped in a plain in a very pleasant place near a small stream where wood and water were abundant. . . . The train now consists of 15 wagons, five belonging to our allies and 10 our own company, and makes altogether an imposing appearance. And we suppose we will be well able to protect ourselves from attacks by Indians."

49. E. E. Canfield and George Canfield are very likely the same person, variously referred to as "E. E.," "Edgar," and "George." He and James G. Canfield, most probably brothers, were members of the Columbus California Industrial Association. He is listed in Decker's roster of Association members as George Canfield. The Columbus *Ohio State Journal* refers to him in its article of April 2, 1849, as E. E. Canfield. J. G. Canfield, his brother, refers to him as Edgar in his letter of August 21, 1849, after their arrival in California.

50. The Big Blue is an affluent of the Kansas. It rises in Nebraska and runs southward into Kansas.

51. The joining of the St. Joseph and Independence trails was eight miles beyond the Big Blue. The long lines of wagons to be seen both backwards and forwards were the cause of much worry to some travelers. They feared there would not be enough gold to go around.

52. The Buffalo (*Bison Linneaus*) traveled the prairies in great herds, and were one of the chief sources of food. The Buffalo hunters

were a breed of men peculiar to the prairie. They, the Indians and the emigrants, as well as the military were responsible for the extinction of this beast. The professional hunters were only interested in the hides and tongues, both of which had a high commercial value.

53. The Little Blue rises in southeastern Nebraska and empties into the Big Blue in Marshall County, Kansas. The emigrant road followed up the north side of the river for 60 miles. It then turned northwest striking the Platte a few miles below Fort Kearny.

54. The Delaware Company had also been apprehensive about hostile Indians in the area. J. D. Breyfogle, passing along the same route May 1, had written: "The camp looks warlike tonight. The boys are all loading guns and pistols. There is a band of Pawnees near us and they may wish to borrow a horse, which we are not disposed to let them have. We are nearly the foremost and must stand the brunt, but we are well armed and ready for any emergency."

55. Dr. Boyle also gives a detailed account of this episode, concluding his remarks with the following: "They told us they were Cheyennes [Sioux?] and were somewhat indignant at our supposing them to be Pawnees with whom they were at war and whose country they were invading. There are many personal incidents connected with this meeting which will not soon be forgotten. D—— was discovered under a wagon. C—— was unable to get his gun in order until informed that he would be assisted into the rank by some of our men. F—— stole my pistols and drank half a pint of whiskey to keep his courage and some few knees might be seen shaking and rattling as some supposed that a battle was inevitable. We had seen about 100 Indians go over the hill and did not know how many more were in the vicinity."

56. The Cheyenne (Shian) Indians were driven from their original habitat on the Cheyenne River by the Sioux. They ranged westward and were to be found between the North Fork of the Platte and the Arkansas where they banded together with the Sioux against their enemies the Pawnees. Decker corrects the mistaken assumption that these were the Cheyenne in his entry of Sunday, May 13th, when he finds that it was the Sioux who were at war with the Pawnees.

57. In 1848 a post was established named Fort Childs in honor of Brig. Gen. Childs, U. S. Army, who had distinguished himself at the Battle of Cerro Gordo during the Mexican War. The Fort's name was changed to Kearny for Gen. Stephen Watt Kearny. This was the first military post on the Oregon Trail. When Decker was there it was commanded by Capt. Charles Ruff.

58. Decker was not the only one impressed by the Mormon family by the name of Knowlton. Niles Searls mentions them at some length and adds to the menu "Doughnuts and all the little etceteras." (*Diary of a Pioneer and Other Papers,* typed copy, Society of California Pioneers.)

59. W. C. Stiles, native of New Jersey, and Superintendent of a mine in Nevada City, 1871. Died October 10, 1899 in San Francisco. Member of Society of California Pioneers.

60. Decker's language here is confused. Dr. Boyle writes that the squaws were making moccasins and beads. The "white husband" is probably one of the "two Frenchmen here who had lived, the one 15 and the other 24 years, among these people, and were married to squaws."

61. Ash Hollow, Nebraska, two miles from the North Fork of the Platte, was so named because of the ash trees growing in it. It was 20 acres in extent and was encircled by steep bluffs. The descent from Windlass Hill was very difficult to negotiate.

62. Dr. Boyle described the difficulty as follows: "At this place [Ash Hollow] a proposition was originated in Mess No. 2, of which I was a member, by T. Price and C. M. Fisk to move and leave the balance of the company because some of the messes had bad teams. I told them I intended to go into California with the hindermost wagon, and was kept in the dark about the plot thereafter. When they had got up a party made up sufficiently large as they supposed, they then told the captain what they were about to do. He told them the first man who left the company without orders he would shoot and that honest men enough could be found to shoot the balance. This put a stop to any farther proceedings in that way."

63. Called variously Castle Bluff, Castle Rock and Cathedral Rock.

64. This would be Miles M. Goodyear. Decker gives the impression that Goodyear was traveling eastward from Salt Lake, whereas in fact he had left St. Joseph around the last of May, heading westward. Goodyear and his company were in the vanguard of the westward emigration for 1849, and it was apparently his third trip across the plains. Goodyear arrived at Sacramento about July 21, 1849. He died that same year on the Yuba River, about November 12, at the age of 30 years. For an obituary notice, see the *Alta California* for December 31, 1849. Dr. Boyle mentioned Goodyear in his diary entry for June 2: "We met Goodyear here who left St. Joe with mules and horses for trading purposes. He had passed us not far from Ash Hollow where we bought a horse from him."

65. Chimney Rock or "The Wigwam," was one of the most famous landmarks on the old Oregon Trail. Joshua Pilcher who led a company of trappers up the Platte Valley in 1827 is said to have been the first to record the name of Chimney Rock. In 1860 there was a Pony Express station named for it. It was a popular camping place because of the fine spring of water.

66. Court House Rock, 20 miles from Ash Hollow. It was often mistaken for a building. These monuments from Fort Kearny to the crossing of the South Platte, up the Sweetwater and to South Pass,

were of particular interest to the emigrants. There is scarcely a Diary kept on this route that did not mention these landmarks, and many sketched them.

67. This was J. Shade Dungan, to whom Decker refers. He mentions him as Shade rather than Dungan from here on through the Diary. Probably because he was called that by members of his mess.

68. This is somewhat obscure. Probably Decker meant that he rode the horse "Bob" on his return from visiting Court House Rock, and on this journey saw his first Sage Rabbit.

69. Scott's Bluff named for Hiram Scott, listed in 1827 as an employee of Ashley, Sublette and Smith, fur traders. Scott disappeared in 1828 from the company presumably led by Sublette. He was never heard from again. In 1829 Sublette again leading a trapping party, is said to have found Scott's body. There are many legends as to how he met his death, the most popular being that he was deserted while ill by his companions, who were, themselves, starving. He was left to die at the foot of the bluff that now bears his name. His body was buried there. From this point it is about 559 miles to Salt Lake.

70. This was the blacksmith shop of Joseph E. Robidoux, son by his first wife of Joseph Robidoux, founder of St. Joseph, Missouri. He established himself and his half-breed wife and children in a trading post near Scott's Bluff. Antoine Robidoux, Joseph Robidoux's brother, was at Fort Robidoux, his trading post on the Uintah River. It was Antoine who, by his eloquent description of California, in 1841, inspired such men as John Bidwell and Joseph B. Chiles to come to California.

71. Here again we are met with the problem of names. This may have been either Dayton or Theodore Rugg, both of them being with the party.

72. Fort Laramie (first called Fort John) was established in June, 1849. At the time of Decker's arrival it was just being prepared for the occupation of troops. Joshua D. Breyfogle of the Delaware Company arrived there May 27th, and on the 28th recorded "We lay opposite the Fort lightening our loads. . . . We intend staying over today and going on with four wagons." Decker arrived at the Fort on June 2nd. According to some accounts the first train from St. Louis arrived May 22nd, 1849. (*Frontier Guardian*, June 27, 1849). Breyfogle seems to have been the first diarist to describe the post.

73. The Dutchman told Dr. Boyle he had started overland with a company from Ft. Smith, Arkansas. They had traveled to Santa Fe —"then fearing to go on, on account of the rumors of danger to be apprehended from the Indians, they left Santa Fe and started for South Pass. . . . When near South Pass, they had quarreled and he had left the balance of the company and started ahead, and unexpectedly came upon us."

74. Probably La Bonte River in the Black Hills.

75. La Prele (or La Prelle) Creek—sometimes called "river"—was the first big stream reached after La Bonte River. It boasted a natural bridge.

76. At this point Decker and his party crossed the Black Hills. Fourche Bois River was 4 miles from the North Platte.

77. Deer Creek has been described as a large stream that abounded with fish.

78. Joshua D. Breyfogle also noted them: "Saw a great curiosity today, a horned toad with a tail."

79. The ferry on the North Platte was kept by a Mormon family from Salt Lake. Dr. Boyle described the ferry as a boat made of two canvases fastened 6 feet apart by means of planks so that a wagon could stand on it. Joshua D. Breyfogle and the Delaware Company had arrived at this ferry on June 2. Breyfogle wrote: "He charges two dollars for each waggon and we have to swim our horses over." Decker records the ferry charge as $3.00, indicating the increase took place shortly after the Delaware Company had passed.

80. The last crossing of the Platte, known as "Upper Ferry" is the site of the present town of Casper, Wyoming. It was named for Lieut. Casper Collins, who lost his life there in an Indian fight. At the Upper Ferry the Platte turns northward, and here the Mormon and Oregon trails merge to strike 40 miles across country to the Sweetwater.

81. L. H. Sherman, Columbus California Industrial Association.

82. Independence Rock and the Devils Gate were two landmarks on the Sweetwater. The Rock was about 100 feet high and one mile in diameter. Presumably it was named by the fur traders in William Sublette's party, who are said to have celebrated the 4th of July, 1829, at this spot. The Rock has been described as a solitary pile of granite standing on the open plain. Names of those who passed it were inscribed with various media, such as paint, tar and knife. The Devils Gate, according to Dr. Boyle, derived its name from the profile of the rocks on either side of the stream, where it entered the Gates: "The outline of an enormous face may be seen. These are the petrified Genii of the Devils Gate."

83. M. N. Wambaugh, also spelled Wombaugh, Warnbaugh or Wambo. He was Camp-master of the Clyman, McCombs, Wambaugh Co. First arrived in California from Oregon in 1846. A First Lieutenant of Co. F, California Battalion. In the California State Legislature, 1852-53.

84. The Sweetwater River passed through the deep gorge. The canyon was 40 feet wide and the perpendicular walls from 300 to 400 feet high.

85. Captain William H. ("Owl") Russell headed the Howard Company from Missouri.

86. Perhaps Ed. Hurd, from Cincinnati, April 19, 1849.

87. Dr. Boyle commented on Decker's disposition — "Decker was in no very pleasant humor when he was relieved from the post of guard as there was no fire to warm his feet, and said several hard things to me about the impropriety of allowing the fire to go out."

88. The Iron City Rangers were mentioned in a letter printed in the New York *Herald,* April 22, 1849. The letter is dated April 7, 1849, at Independence, Missouri. The letter states that the Iron City Rangers were at Independence on that date, preparing to leave overland. The letter further states: "Pennsylvania has six companies in the field, equipped and ready to move. The first is styled the 'Iron City Rangers' and composed as follows [twenty-seven names are listed as members of the Company, all but six from Pittsburgh] . . . They are organized into messes of five, are provided with eight light wagons, to be drawn by mules, and each man, in addition, has a mule to ride and a mule to pack with. Their object is to seek for gold. In the company is an experienced chemist, and, with their outfit, all necessary mining implements. They are provided with everything necessary for expedition and comfort, and carry provisions for nine months. Like all other companies I have met with, they go loaded down with shooting irons of various kind."

89. The Delaware Company had traded with Louis Vasquez on June 9, according to an entry in Joshua Breyfogle's diary. The Delaware Company was in the vanguard of the 1849 overland emigration and at this point in travel was about six days ahead of Decker's party.

90. South Pass was about 300 miles from Fort Laramie and 980 miles from Independence. The Pass was from 15 to 20 miles wide, with an easy ascent. The summit was at an altitude of 7,550 feet. Thomas Fitzpatrick is said to have discovered the Pass in 1842. In 1849, 25,000 to 35,000 persons are said to have passed through this gateway to the west.

91. James Bridger and Louis Vasquez had been fur traders in the Rocky Mountains as early as 1842, when they formed a trading partnership. In 1849 they had set up a temporary trading post at the last crossing of the Sweetwater in order to trade with the California-bound emigrants. Diaries of 49ers indicate they were there from about June 9 to July 1, when they returned to Fort Bridger on Blacks Fork of the Green River. Breyfogle wrote of his meeting with Bridger: "I went over to the Fort and saw and conversed with Bridger. He is like other trappers . . . has an Indian wife and could not live anywhere else." From this last crossing of the Sweetwater it was about 115 miles to Fort Bridger.

92. Dr. Boyle referred to the malady as "Mountain Fever, probably caused by our great altitude, 7000 or 8000 feet. . . . The feeling is that of want of a sufficient amount of air." Breyfogle, having passed

through the same area some six days earlier, had commented: "Nearly half of our company are sick with a sort of mountain disease which attacked us as soon as we crossed through the pass. The other companies are in the same predicament. I am just taking a relapse after being nearly well. This is a hard place to be sick."

93. Pacific Springs, 2 miles west of South Pass. This was the first water flowing west. It was a marshy spot. The waters of Pacific Springs empty into the upper Colorado and are carried westward to the Gulf of California.

94. The Shoshone, or Snake Indians, occupied the territory immediately west of South Pass. Bryant says that their chief points of trade were Fort Hall and Fort Bridger. They were the most powerful tribe west of the Rockies, and their attitude toward the emigrants was always friendly.

95. The forks of the road, one leading to Salt Lake via Fort Bridger, and the other to the Greenwood Cut-Off, named after Caleb Greenwood who pioneered the route in 1844. This cut-off shortened the distance to Fort Hall. It was, however, a desert with no water between the Big Sandy and the Green River.

96. The Little Sandy, with the Big Sandy and the Dry Sandy, flows into the Green River southwest of South Pass, Wyoming.

97. The 35 Mile Desert from the crossing of the Big Sandy to the Green River. The road was level and easy to travel to within 15 miles of Green River. The last few miles were cut by deep ravines.

98. "Haystack Butte." This lone butte was undoubtedly the same described by Bruff who traveled this way August 10, 1849.

99. This ferry across the Green River was operated by French traders in association with some Snake Indians. Later in the summer the Mormons from Salt Lake would operate a ferry across the Green at the Sublette Cutoff. The fee for crossing the Green River at this point was $1.50 per wagon to do it yourself, or $3.00 for experienced hands.

100. D. C. Wood, Columbus California Industrial Association.

101. Fisk had shown signs of irritation before. On June 4th, Dr. Boyle wrote that Fisk had slashed his water bag in a fit of ill temper.

102. Thomas Forks of the Bear River.

103. Smith Forks of the Bear River.

104. The mountain man Thomas (Pegleg) Smith was born in Crabb Orchard, Kentucky, in 1801. He was in Santa Fe in 1824, and trapped on the North Platte and Green River with St. Vrain from 1827 to 1828. He is said to have amputated his own leg after an accident. He lived with the Shoshones much of the time and had an Indian wife. His trading post was on the Bear River, and in 1849 nearly every diarist taking this route mentioned "Pegleg." There is mention of the fact that Smith came west to California in 1852, and

it is a matter of record that he died in San Francisco's General Hospital in 1866, "from natural causes." There is a famous "Lost Pegleg Mine" story that appears in nearly every book dealing with California's lost mines. This mine was said to be located in San Bernardino County, and was the object of a search by a party headed up by Smith in 1854.

105. This might have been Isaac Brown, who had been associated with Pegleg Smith since the summer of 1848, and whose family was at the Fort on the Bear River.

106. Soda or Beer Springs, Idaho. The springs are now beneath the waters of the Soda Point reservoir.

107. This is probably an error on Decker's part. He meant Steamboat Springs, one-half mile below Soda Springs. He describes Steamboat Springs.

108. The rosters of companies departing overland from Missouri printed in the contemporary newspapers of the day do not show a Lexington Missouri Company as such. Inasmuch as Lexington was a point of departure—such as St. Joseph and Independence—it may be that this company Decker refers to was in fact from yet another point of origin, and that Lexington may simply mean the company departed from there rather than another jumping-off point.

109. Dr. Boyle describes this old Indian as "Captain Pontion." Boyle remarks that he could speak a little English and that he had been to St. Louis. "He told me a great many things of interest about the plants growing on the roadside, their names in Indian and their uses. He also told me the names of the different neighboring tribes and when he named the 'Shoo,' he added the sign, drawing his hand across his throat and then said, 'Me eat Shoo.' 'How many?' 'One Shoo!' 'Did you ever eat an American?' 'No eat'."

110. The Port Neuf enters the Snake River below Fort Hall. In the early days of the fur trade, it was a paradise of beaver.

111. Fort Hall was built by Capt. Nathaniel Wyeth in 1834 as a future trading post, and was sold in 1837 to the Hudson Bay Company who ran it until 1849. It was built of adobe bricks much in the style of Fort Laramie and in 1849 was commanded by Captain Richard Grant. The Fort was named for Henry Hall, partner of Wyeth, in the Rocky Mountain Fur Company. The site of the original fort was on the plain between Portneuf and the Snake Rivers. The Hudson Bay Company replaced the first buildings in 1839. In 1849 the Fort was a welcome sight to the overland emigrants starved for the sight of civilization. The Mormon family Decker mentions was commented upon by other 49er diarists, nearly all of them mentioning the butter and cheese. Jasper Hixon, traveling with a company a few days to the rear of Decker, wrote: "There were a few Mormon women and children who seemed to be happy and contented. They were

evidently making money, for they had quite a large number of cows to milk, and between making butter and cheese and preparing meals for the emigrants, they had enough to do . . ." Dr. Boyle—along with Decker—also commented: "We halted at the fort for a couple of hours to regale ourselves on bread and milk. . . . A Mormon family had moved hither from Salt Lake City for the purpose of supplying emigrants with articles of this kind and had brought a large number of cows. Butter was very scarce and they sold it as fast as they could make it. . . ."

112. American Falls, on the Snake River. These Falls were only seen by those parties taking the Hudspeth Cut-Off. This was where the Snake River, which was 900 feet wide above the Falls, poured over the cliffs into a narrow canyon through which the river ran for many miles.

113. Raft River, also called Cassia, and Cajeaux Creek, is in Idaho. It is about 60 miles from Fort Hall, and was so named because of the early French traders who crossed it on rafts.

114. Decker here is describing the area that was to become known as the City of Rocks.

115. Breyfogle's group, The Delaware Company, had previously been in advance of Decker's group on the overland trail. But at this point, at about the junction with the Salt Lake Cutoff somewhat south of the City of Rocks, Decker's group had overtaken the Delaware Company. Decker's party had taken the Fort Hall road, whereas the Delaware Company had taken the Salt Lake Cutoff. In so doing, the Delaware Company fell behind in the order of procession. Breyfogle wrote in his diary for July 2: "We are now on a new route. Not a man in our company knows anything about the road nor are there any directions or descriptions of the route given by anyone so that we have to go by guess altogether. . . . To-day we came in sight of Salt Lake again." On the 5th, Breyfogle wrote: ". . . are now on the Fort Hall road with about one hundred and fifty wagons ahead of us and a host close behind us. This is a splendid road. Charles Breyfogle and Price just came into camp. Their company is a little ahead of us. They took the Fort Hall road and gained on us by our lying still this afternoon." The Charles Breyfogle that Joshua mentions in his entry of the 5th is his cousin.

116. In the fall of 1848 some members of the Mormon Battalion who were in California at the time of the gold discovery at Sutter's Mill brought back to Salt Lake considerable gold dust. As the dust was awkward to handle, the idea was conceived by the thrifty Mormons to start coinage. A Mormon from England was commissioned to prepare the dies. The first gold dust was coined Dec. 10, 1848, when William T. Follett, a member of the Mormon Battalion, left his dust to be converted into coin. John Kay, a minter, turned out

forty-six coins of $10.00 within a few days of the receipt of the dust. The mint, however, proved a failure due to mechanical difficulties and the Mormons turned to printing paper money. In September, 1849, the Mormons again undertook to coin the gold that was pouring in from California. Dies were prepared for denominations from $2.50 to $20.00. This coinage continued until 1851.

117. Breyfogle's entry of July 6th, states that they nooned on Rattlesnake Creek with the Columbus Company, "all mixed together."

118. The Humboldt River was named for Baron von Humboldt, by J. C. Fremont. Prior to this it had many names. It was called "Paul's River," after Joseph Paul, a trapper with Peter Skene Ogden, in 1828. The name "Mary" is said to have come from the Shoshone squaw whom Ogden had taken as his wife. There is some contention that it was named for the Virgin Mary. Whatever the source of its name, the source of its waters is in the mountains that edge the Great Basin. It was Thomas Fitzpatrick, the famous Mountain Man, who admonished the Bidwell-Bartleson Party of 1841, to "find the Mary's River and follow it west, ever west."

119. Breyfogle mentions Plotner in his entry of July 24th: "Plotner, myself and Barnes . . . are here on the broad desert." He was probably a member of the Delaware Company.

120. The companies were now in the vicinity of Gravelly Ford. In his entry of the 12th Breyfogle writes that they could not follow the river through a deep cut, probably Palisade Canyon, and had to detour over a mountain to join the river again. On the 14th the Delaware Company lightened their wagons and discarded one "as our horses were getting very poor and weak." On the 15th the Columbus Company was just ahead and Breyfogle noted that they too had discarded a wagon.

121. From Dr. Boyle's diary entry for July 16 we learn of an altercation that Decker chose to ignore in his entry for the 16th. Dr. Boyle wrote: "The Delaware's have not yet appeared. Today the most interesting occurrence was a chat between P. Decker and Fisk in which the derelictions from duty and propriety by the said Peter were duly discussed with many classical epithets found only in a lexicon, called the vulgar man's pocket companion, which has not yet appeared in print, but of which Fisk would be well qualified to be the editor. In addition to this discourse he intimated that he would 'maks' [mash?] the said Peter's face, which I resolved should not be done as I should have knocked the whole business on the head by hitting C. M. Fisk with the butt of a horse pistol which I held in my hand for that purpose. Fisk restrained himself to the classics, however, and most of us supposed that Peter needed some little reviewing, as he had been very glib tongued and had made and tried to make some mischief in the company, and as long as Professor

Cassius confined himself to the words of the lesson merely we were very well content."

122. See footnote 33.

123. Digger Indians, a name applied to the Shoshone-Paiute tribes, especially those in California. They gained the name from their habit of digging roots for food during certain seasons of the year. The Digger Indians along the Humboldt in Nevada represented a particular menace to the overland emigrants. It had been their practice for a number of years to prey upon the stock of the companies, shooting strays with arrows, or ambushing grazing oxen at night. Usually at this point in the overland journey the stock were exhausted and frequently depleted, and any further losses critical to the companies.

124. Capt. Winter's company is mentioned briefly in the New York *Tribune* for July 17, 1849, in an article copied from the St. Louis *Reveille*, in which it is stated that the first party out of Missouri westward was Capt. Paul's company, and immediately following him was Capt. Winter's company, organized at Independence, and composed mostly of members from the Southern States. There were several men by the name of Winter or Winters that traveled overland to California in 1849. While it is not possible to say with certainty that this is any particular one, the possibilities reduce themselves to two. There was a G. E. Winters who traveled overland in 1849, and who later became the proprietor of the Oriental Hotel in Marysville. William H. Winter, co-author of the guidebook *Route Across the Rocky Mountains,* Lafayette, Indiana, 1846, is also reported to have traveled overland to California in 1849. Winter had traveled to California first in 1843-1844, and returned sometime in 1844-1845 to Indiana. In the Introduction to the reprint of the guidebook (Princeton University Press, 1932) the editor comments: "After his return he remained in Indiana until 1849 when the lure of the newly discovered gold regions drew him again to California, where he engaged in farming near Mokelumne." Bancroft also says Winter returned to California in 1849. Bancroft further states that Winter died in Shasta county in 1879. In the Shasta county *Great Register of Voters* for 1876 there is listed a William Henry Winter, age 56, place of nativity given merely as United States, occupation listed as manufacturer, and residence at Fall River Mills. Winter is said to have been born in 1819, so the age given in the *Great Register* closely coincides. Decker's "Capt. Winters" is not mentioned in Dr. Boyle's diary, nor in the diaries of Bruff, Stuart, McNeil, Wistar, Breyfogle, etc., other forty-niners, thus compounding the problems of identification.

125. The Sink of the Humboldt is where the river loses itself in the sand. It is an area described as between 40 and 50 miles wide and 12 to 15 long. It was a series of stagnant pools and marshy land,

a most forbidding area whose aspect gave small comfort to the weary wagon trains that passed over it.

126. This was H. Ranney, a member of the Columbus California Industrial Association. In 1850 Lorenzo Sawyer, under whom Decker had studied, and who later became a prominent California jurist, speaks in his account of his overland journey (*Across the Plains in 1850,* N. Y., 1926) of a Mr. Ranney, of Delaware, Ohio, who was with Sawyer's train. This was undoubtedly a brother of the man who came with Decker's Company.

127. William H. McFarland, a native of Louisville, Ky., who started for California April 2, 1849.

128. The Forty Mile Desert was the route opened by Joseph B. Chiles in 1848 when he led his wagon train across this desert. Chiles had met a company of Mormons headed by Azariah Smith, at Martin's Forks of the Humboldt, as the North Fork was then called. This party of Mormons had emerged from the mountains at the present site of Genoa, Nevada. They followed the Carson River to its northern end, and then turning northwest set their course for the Big Bend of the Truckee River where they made a right turn and set their course for the Humboldt Sink and the Boiling Springs. However, Chiles, instead of following the Mormon route as laid out for him by Smith, struck across the Sink of the Carson, cutting the line that formed the base of the triangle followed by the Mormons. It was the Chiles route that became the accepted wagon trail of 1849. This is evidenced by the fact that a note for the emigrant trains left by James Gooding stated: "The travel is now all by the Cutoff to Carson River—45 miles." Further evidence is that the route was recommended in a hand-written guidebook prepared by Ira Willis of Salt Lake City in 1849, and sold or distributed to those emigrants passing that way.

129. On Sunday, July 22nd, Breyfogle mentions the great numbers of wagons about three days behind them, "all jambed together." They were yet three hundred miles from their destination, and the gloomy prospect of crossing the desert ahead was not pleasant, "we hope it is not so bad as represented." In a letter dated "Old Dry Diggings, Cal., Oct. 20, 1849," printed in the New York *Tribune*, December 28, 1849, V. Daniels states: "I came across the Plains this season in a Company headed by Capt. J. A. Gooding of Lockport, Ill. and made the trip in a much shorter time than it has been made by any wagon-train that has crossed the mountains since the route has been traveled. We started from the Missouri on the 10th of May last, and arrived in the Diggins, July 28, making the trip in eighty days traveling time, which we contend is the quickest trip ever made. We lost no men or animals on the route, but had a very good time among the wilds of America, and ourselves as well as our animals fared much better, I fear, than many of the immigrants will that are now on the road, many

of whom are still east of the Sierra Nevada. I hear there is much suffering on the latter part of the routes, many losing their teams by the Indians and many, whose teams are overcome by fatigue, are obliged to remain where they are, or pace themselves across the mountains with a little *grub* in their pockets." Three letters by J. A. Gooding are in the Missouri Historical Society Library, St. Louis. One is dated April 12, 1849, St. Joseph, Missouri. Another, April 22, 1849, no place given. The third is to Mrs. Eunice D. Gooding, describing the rush to California at St. Louis and Independence, with no place, no date.

130. Breyfogle mentions meeting the Columbus Company on the 23rd: "Left this morning without breakfast and went six miles to the foot of the sink where we found the Columbus Company preparing to pass the desert of 45 miles, where there is neither grass nor water the whole distance. We have cut grass for our horses and are filling everything that will hold water. We started at four o'clock and drove all night. The Columbus Company started at 3 o'clock. We expect to lose some of our animals in crossing, but hope for the best. . . ."

131. Other diarists of 1849 also referred to this place as "Salt Creek." It was here that the overflow of the Humboldt sometimes spilled out upon the Carson Sink. It was at this point that the Forty Mile Desert began.

132. Crossing the Forty Mile Desert was one of the most difficult parts of the overland journey for many emigrants. At this point Decker and Dr. Boyle remained on the desert with part of the wagons of their company from the evening of the 23rd to the 25th. A short distance behind, Breyfogle of the Delaware Company, together with three companions—Plotner, Barnes, and Evans—was stranded on the desert with two of their wagons. It was not until the morning of the 27th that the rest of their company returned to take them to the Carson River. Meanwhile, Breyfogle and his companions had run out of water. Breyfogle wrote on the 26th: "This morning drank our last water and were disappointed in our boys bringing any from the river. Barnes and Evans have started for the river to have some sent to us, but we can't get it till some time after midnight as they cannot travel by day. . . . If the boys don't bring us water tonight, we shall be very thirsty at any rate. Sundown and no water yet. . . ."

133. The trail joined the Carson River in the vicinity of what would later be called Ragtown, Nevada.

134. The Desert Evening Primrose closes its petals at the first touch of the sun. As it opens in the evening the petals make a slightly snapping sound.

135. Carson River, over 100 feet wide and with only certain places where it might be forded. Named by Fremont for his scout, Kit Carson.

136. This would be in the vicinity of Carson City, capital city of Nevada.

137. Probably Eagle Valley.

138. Decker was evidently mistaken in thinking this small lake was Reed Lake.

139. Carson Pass was pioneered eastward in 1848 by members of the Mormon Battalion. The wagons of Joseph B. Chiles were probably the second train to negotiate the westward passage, in the same year. Chiles met the Mormons and exchanged Way Bills with them, thus learning of the route.

140. Pass Creek Canyon. This was the Carson Canyon through which flows the West Fork of the Carson River. The Mormons named this canyon in 1848, and it was so-called by the 49ers.

141. Other diarists remark these bridges were built by the Mormons in 1848.

142. James A. Pritchard also mentions a company of Utah-bound Mormons in his journal, in an entry of August 4, 1849. Some of these were emigrants of 1846, who came with Sam Brannan in the *Brooklyn.* Their leader was Thomas Rhoads. Mrs. Rhoads died in 1847 and her husband left for Utah in 1849. The meeting with the train is mentioned frequently in diaries of 1849. Bruff mentions meeting this company on the Humboldt. Rhoads was able to give the emigrants information about the mines.

143. Lorenzo Sawyer in his *Journal Across the Plains in 1850,* N. Y. 1926, says: "We passed . . . along a valley and through timber ten miles to Red Lake at the foot of the dividing ridge between the waters of the Pacific and the Great Basin."

144. Lake Valley.

145. Silver Lake.

146. This was the final ridge and the summit of the Sierra Nevada.

147. Lansford Warren Hastings had traveled to Oregon in 1842, then to California and back to the States. In 1845 he published his important guidebook, *Emigrants' Guide to Oregon and California.* He returned later that same year to California, purposely leaving St. Louis in late summer with a small party to prove that the overland crossing could be made at that late time of year. In 1846 Hastings was very active on the overland trail, as far east as South Pass, inducing the emigrants to travel to California via his new Cutoff to the Humboldt River. The Donner-Reed Party acted upon his advice, and Hastings has since been blamed by historians for a part in the great tragedy that befell that party in the Sierras. In later years Hastings had an interest in a store at Coloma, later developed ranching interests in the Carson Valley in Nevada. He was also active in mining in Arizona, and at the time of his death in the 1870's was involved in a colonization scheme in Brazil. In his usual expansive manner, Hastings told Decker

that there was enough gold in California to "last for a thousand years."
Such statements by Hastings were indicative of his passionate opti-
mism in California. Of Lansford Hastings' brothers there is the following evidence to set down. James A. Pritchard remarked in his
diary for August 6 that he too had talked with Hastings on the trail.
Pritchard wrote: "He was on his way to meet his Brother who was in
one of the back trains." Decker wrote on August 6: "who goes to meet
a train in which two of his brothers are." Dale Morgan, editor of the
Pritchard diary, says in his footnote 97 that the brother on the trail
in 1849 was probably Daniel Ephraim Hastings, listed in the Sacramento county census, October, 1852, as 23 years old, and that he died
at Sutterville from an accidental gunshot wound, September 1, 1867.
His obituary in the Sacramento *Union* Sept. 2, 1867, mentions a brother
then living at Latrobe, California, James Hannum Hastings, who
was also listed in the El Dorado County *Great Register of Voters* 1867
as born in Ohio, age not stated. Actually, there is evidence to suggest
there may have been three brothers. Mr. Newton Baird, of the Talisman Press, has found an obituary in the Sacramento *Union* of September 3, 1852, which reads as follows: "He is dead. LYMAN H.
HASTINGS died at Sutter yesterday morning, at half past 8 o'clock.
He was sick about 12 hours. He died as he lived—calm, honest and
careful. He arranged all his business and disposed of his property
as though nothing was the matter. When his brother L. W. Hastings
approached him in his dying moments, he said: 'Lansford, you have
arrived in time. I feel better, but I now know I shall soon die, and
have to tell you what I have already.' 'Hear me one moment,' said he,
'for I have a short time to live. You tell me I am better because you
think I fear to die, but I do not; I am prepared to meet death.' He
calmly made his requests in relation to the affairs of this world,
then extending his hand to his brother said 'God Bless you all,' and
with praise and thanks to God even up to the last breath—he died
lamented by all who knew him, and was buried by his friends with
due solemnity. He was amiable, modest and honest. He was born in
Sandusky, Ohio, in 1820." Thus from the information in the *Union*
obituary, Lyman would have been age 32 at his death. On the basis
of the chronology in this evidence, it would seem safe to assume that
Lansford was on his way to meet his brothers Daniel and Lyman, for
both were recorded in Sacramento in 1852, one in a county census,
the other in the *Union*. The third brother, James Hannum Hastings,
is not recorded until 1867, when he is mentioned in Daniel's obituary.
It may be that James came to California in later years, or it may be
that he came overland in 1849 with his other two brothers, and that
Lansford was in fact on his way to meet three brothers.

148. Pleasant Valley, not far from Placerville, where the Mormons
camped in 1848, waiting for the snow to melt in the Sierra. It was

an early trading post.

149. Weaverville or Weberville, on Weber Creek was the point where the road forked, the right leading to Sutter's Mill at Coloma, the left to Sacramento. Captain Charles M. Weber for whom the Creek was named, came to California in 1841 with the Bidwell-Bartleson Party. He settled at French Camp and later founded Stockton. In 1848 he mined on Weber Creek where he laid the foundation for his fortune.

150. Decker probably means the Cosumnes River.

151. Probably what later became known as Mormon Tavern, but which was constructed and in operation in 1849 at the time Decker passed through. It was enlarged in 1851 and later became a remount station for the Pony Express in 1860-1861. This historic building was burned to the ground by the Division of Highways in 1964 to make room for a new highway project.

152. Rancho Rio de los Americanos of William Leidesdorff. It was ten miles from Sutter's Fort. The house was built of logs and adobe. At the time that Decker passed there it was owned by a Mr. Kelly.

153. Rancho del Paso which was occupied by John Sinclair in 1841. There were also several other houses in this vicinity, one on the property of Joseph B. Chiles, another owned by A. S. Bayley. This property later was owned by James Ben Ali Haggin.

154. General John A. Sutter commenced the construction of his famous Fort in 1841. The Fort became the destination point of nearly all the overland emigrations to California after that year. In 1849, in the month of March, Sutter left the Fort to take up residence at Hock Farm. He leased the rooms of the Fort for various enterprises.

155. "Dr. Charles Hartwell Cragin (formerly of Washington City) respectfully offers his professional services to the citizens of Sacramento and neighborhood. Office at present at S. Brannan & Co." This was the advertisement carried by the *Placer Times* July 7, 1849. The *Alta* Aug. 4, 1849, mentions Dr. Cragin as being in charge of the hospital established at the large adobe building east of Sutter's Fort. Dr. Cragin died in Washington, D. C. in 1887.

156. The population in Sacramento prior to 1848 was 250. It rose rapidly after the gold discovery and approached 20,000 at the end of 1849. In 1850 the city began to develop a permanent population. Many business buildings and residences were built that gave a substantial appearance to the community, and the population became more permanent and less transient.

157. Some houses of a pre-fabricated variety were shipped to California around the Horn.

158. The first issue of the *Placer Times,* in Sacramento, was April 25, 1849. It was published by Edward C. Kemble near 28th and K Sts. Kemble gave up the paper because of ill health, in June of 1849,

and returned to San Francisco. The paper continued under another publisher.

159. This refers to Sutter's Mill at Coloma.

160. Probably this is a reference to Green Valley on the Coloma Road. The Green Valley House was an early hotel.

161. Mormon Island was above the present site of Folsom on the American River. The site took its name from the fact that it was extensively worked by the Mormons in 1848. It was one of the earliest diggings to be worked after the gold discovery at Sutter's Mill.

162. Work on Sutter's Mill commenced in the summer of 1847. Sutter had made a partnership agreement with James W. Marshall to supervise construction of the mill. It was Marshall who had discovered and recommended the site at Coloma as being satisfactory for operation of the sawmill. On the 24th of January, 1848, while making a routine inspection of the tailrace of the mill, James Marshall picked up the first flake of gold, signaling the discovery of gold in California.

163. Weaver, or Weber Creek.

164. The flag of the Columbus California Industrial Association was mentioned by Decker earlier in his Diary. It was given to him when he left home by his sisters.

165. On the Coloma Road, between Sutter's Fort and Coloma. In 1849 the road was heavily traveled by miners arriving in California via the Carson River route, and by traffic between Coloma and Sacramento.

166. Sutter had conceived the town of Sutterville as early as 1844. The townsite was laid out in 1846 by Sutter, Lansford Hastings and John Bidwell. One of the first brick buildings in California was built here in 1847 by George Zins. When Sacramento City began to develop as the commercial center adjacent to the Sacramento River, Sutterville went into a decline.

167. The Trinity River was named by P. B. Reading in 1845. The mines were discovered by him in 1848-1849, and were being worked extensively in the fall of 1849. To cross from Sacramento to the Trinity it was necessary to negotiate the Coast Range, a largely uninhabited and unmapped region in those days. The story was told that the Trinity River emptied into Trinity Bay, and was the reason the river was so named, where in fact the river emptied into the Klamath River before reaching the sea. There were many misconceptions and misrepresentations by miners as to the route to the Trinity mines. For additional information, see the letter by Andrew Bradbury printed in the Introduction to this volume.

168. Hinkle was with the Delaware Company. Breyfogle writes in his diary under entry of August 13 that he together with Israel Breyfogle, John Stimmel, and Hinkle withdrew from the company and divided the stock after reaching Sacramento.

169. The first ferry referred to was undoubtedly the ferry that had been instituted by Sutter and run by his Indians. It was located at what is now about the foot of K Street.

170. This ferry was undoubtedly the Chiles Ferry over the Sacramento River in 1849, in the vicinity of the present I Street Bridge. It was run from what later became the town of Washington, and then Broderick. Joseph B. Chiles and several of his family in partnership with Jerome Davis operated the ferry.

171. Joseph B. Chiles owned considerable land in the Sacramento Valley, some of it being a portion of the Rancho Laguna de los Santos Calles. He also had a house on a part of the Rancho del Paso in 1849.

172. Fremont, on the west bank of the Sacramento, opposite Vernon, was founded by Jonas Spect in 1849. He ran a ferry across the river. Fremont was the county seat of Yolo County in 1850. At the height of its prosperity it had a population of about 3000. Like its sister city of Vernon it depended upon the trade of the miners, and also suffered when the Feather River was opened to Marysville. Spect continued to live in Fremont long after its prosperity diminished.

173. Vernon, situated on the east bank of the Feather River where it joins the Sacramento. This was the natural site for a town, and Elisha O. Crosby, Sam Norris and Frank Bates joined forces to buy land from Sutter. They purchased 1800 acres and by the fall of 1849 the town had 700 population. It owed its prosperity to the fact that it was at the head of river navigation and therefore the outfitting point for miners bound for the gold country of the Yuba, Feather and Bear Rivers. Vernon was the county seat of Sutter County in 1851. By 1853 the town was almost deserted, for heavy rains had washed the sand bars from the river, and Marysville was to become the head of navigation.

174. Major Lawrence P. Graham of the 2nd U. S. Dragoons, in command of a Battalion from Mexico in 1848, had arrived in California in December, 1848.

175. The New York *Tribune* of February 7, 1849 lists a J. Morton Freeman sailed on the bark *Strafford* for California, Feb. 3, 1849, as secretary of the New York Mining Company. The *Tribune* for January 31, 1849 lists another person by name of Freeman—William Freeman, who sailed on the bark *Eudora* for California on Jan. 30, 1849, a member of Taylor's Mutual Association.

176. William Brown Ide came to California in 1845 with the Grigsby-Ide party. He settled in what is now Tehama county, and construction of the adobe house started in 1846. Ide helped organize the short-lived revolution against the Mexican Mandate requiring Americans to leave California, and was the first and only President of the California Republic, under the proclamation of the Bear Flag Party. The home was on the Rancho Barrancos Colorados, on the bank

of the Sacramento River, in 1849. This is now a State Historic Monument, near Red Bluff.

177. Lawson was described by William Kelly in *A Stroll Through the Diggings of California* (London, 1852) as "an unconscionable fellow who had established himself with a view of buttoning on his fellow creatures whose line of travel unavoidably passed his door." In all accounts he is merely called by his last name, but he may be the John Lawson listed in the Shasta County, California, Census, 1852.

178. Pierson Barton Reading came to California in 1843. His *Diary,* published in the *Quarterly* of The Society of California Pioneers, Vol. VII, Sept. 1927, tells of his trip from Fort Boise to Sacramento the same year. He worked for Sutter in 1844 and obtained a grant of 26,000 acres from Governor Micheltorena which he called *Buena Ventura.* His adobe house was built in 1847 and stood four miles east of Cottonwood Creek. In 1850 it was the County Seat of Shasta County.

179. This was Clear Creek Diggins later called Horsetown. Kelly described the country as follows: "The valley gradually expanded . . . widening into an enormous plain where we again struck the Sacramento thence it contracted as we approached Clear Creek. . . . There is a trading post at this point." It was in this area in 1848 that Reading first washed gold from the stream. It was a rich deposit and much gold was taken from it. On May 9, 1849, the *Placer Times* stated that the height and breadth of the gold region would not be believed.

180. This is a reference to Reading's Springs, so-called by the first emigrants in June, 1849. The name was changed to Shasta the following year.

181. Reading's Springs was the end of wagon transportation to the Trinity Mines. All goods had to be packed from this point and the last 90 miles to the river were over steep trails.

182. The New York *Tribune* of January 31, 1849 lists a Joel B. Barlow sailed on the bark *Philip Hone* for California on Jan. 27, 1849.

183. Reading's Bar, at the mouth of Clear Creek Canyon, where P. B. Reading first washed out gold in March, 1848. It was the following July that he found gold along the Trinity River.

184. From information printed in the New York *Tribune* in early February, 1849, it is clear that a company from Seneca County, New York, departed for California, composed of about 15 men. The *Tribune* does not print the names of the men, nor does it specify whether the company left by ship or struck out overland.

185. This was probably Judge Oliver P. Stidger, native of Ohio, who came to California in 1849. He kept a hotel at Sacramento and at Foster's Bar. He was editor of the Marysville *Herald,* practiced law, and finally went to North San Juan where he ran the San Juan *Press* in 1863. A year later he was in Nevada City where he was

publisher of the *Daily Gazette*. He died in North San Juan in 1888. He was famous for his fiery nature. A staunch friend and unyielding enemy, he espoused the cause of the Chinese and did much to aid them.

186. Shasta or Reading's Springs was six miles west of Redding. It was the gateway to the Trinity Mines. The first log house was built there in late 1849 and was owned by Milton McGee who came to California in 1843.

187. Ex-Governor William Shannon of Ohio. He opened negotiations to buy Reading's ranch but the deal did not go through.

188. Isaac L. Given was a civil engineer from Ohio. He came to California with the Workman-Rowland Party in 1841, but returned east, and came to California again in 1849, via Panama. He worked as a surveyor in the Sacramento River area.

189. The New York *Tribune* lists an "F. Campbell" in its issue of April 18, 1849, as belonging to a St. Louis, Missouri company of 66 men, referred to as the "Overland Company" about to depart on the overland journey to California.

190. A large oak tree standing alone on the plain served as a landmark for a pond of water that lay close by.

191. Thomas Cochran lived on the north bank of Cache Creek ten miles west of Fremont. This became known as "Cochran's Crossing." He set up a hotel which was later replaced by a larger building erected by James C. Hutton. It then became known as Hutton's Ranch or Travelers Home, and in 1857 was called Cacheville. County Seat of Yolo County, 1857.

192. Burke was very likely a member of one of two companies that left Columbus around the first week of April. The names of the persons in those companies were never printed in the *Ohio State Journal*. The editor of the newspaper wrote on March 31, 1849: "We have several times applied to members of the companies for a list of names of those who compose them, but have as yet been unsuccessful."

193. Benjamin Carpenter was a member of a small company that left Columbus the end of March, 1849, for California. See the Columbus *Ohio State Journal*, March 31, 1849.

194. Nicholas Demorest was a member of the Franklin California Mining Company from Columbus, Ohio.

195. According to the Breyfogle Genealogy no F. Breyfogle came to California. Those mentioned as being in California were: Joshua D., Charles C., Charles, Israel and Solomon.

196. John Walton, Captain of the Columbus California Industrial Association, became a member of the State Legislature in 1850.

197. Dr. Barnes was a member of the Delaware Company. Joshua Breyfogle mentions him frequently in his diary.

198. Joseph W. Booth and F. A. McCormick were members of the Franklin California Mining Company, captained by Joseph Hunter.

Decker frequently refers to this party as the "Hunter Company."

199. John Rogers, son of Williamson Rogers. Decker, hereafter, refers to the former as J. R. and the latter as Mr. R. or Mr. Rogers. In 1888 John Rogers published in the Nevada City *Miner's Transcript* some recollections of his early years in California, and Decker is mentioned in connection with some mining adventures. An excerpt of this is published in the Introduction to this volume.

200. The Sutter Buttes were known to all early travelers through the Upper Sacramento Valley. On the maps for the 1850's they are designated as Sutter's Buttes, los Picos de Sutter, Three Buttes, or Butte Mountains. Later the name of Marysville Buttes was used by the Whitney Survey Expedition and thereafter came into general use.

201. Nicolaus was named for Nicolaus Altgeier, who had a trading post on the Feather River. He established a ferry as early as 1843. In 1849 a government boat arrived at Nicolaus bearing supplies for the establishing of Camp Far West, which was to protect the settlers in the valley. The post only lasted until 1852. The site of Camp Far West is now marked by a monument four miles west of Wheatland.

202. There are several Bear Rivers in California. Decker is referring here to the Bear River that rises in the high Sierra in Nevada County, and runs through that county to the foothills, emptying into the Feather River in the area of Nicolaus.

203. Johnson's Ranch was the first habitation encountered by those who came into California from over the Sierra, via Donner Pass. The ranch was first a grant to Pablo Guiterrez. It was here that several members of the Donner Party found succor in 1846, and asked for supplies to be sent to those of the company who had not made it across the Sierra before the snows. After Guiterrez's death the property was purchased by William Johnson and Sebastian Kyser.

204. James Marshall, the gold discoverer at Sutter's Mill, is reported as the first man to pan gold on Deer Creek in 1848. See *History of Nevada County*, (Thompson and West, 1880), p. 52.

205. Deer Creek Dry Diggings was later called Caldwell's Upper Store, and later became Nevada. It was later named Nevada City to distinguish it from the Territory of Nevada. The route described by Decker was from the Dry Diggings to Blue Tent, north of the present Nevada City, then over the Washington Ridge to a point later known as "Central House." Here a steep trail descended into the canyon of the South Yuba. From Washington Ridge there is a magnificent view of the surrounding country. The old emigrant trail followed the ridge, which is now traversed by Highway 20.

206. Rock Creek is a tributary of the Yuba.

207. Washington Ridge.

208. John Epperson was born in Tennessee. He first went to Oregon, and later to the South Yuba and from there to Nevada City where

he is listed as a "Miner" in the 1852 California Census.

209. Named for J. H. Lippard, who came to California in 1849 with a company from Tennessee. Lippard left to return to the States in the summer of 1850, for Decker remarks in a letter to his sisters that he intended sending letters to the States with a friend, Mr. Lippard.

210. The point of descent into the canyon of the South Yuba is about 12 miles from Nevada City.

211. Ohio Bar was on the south side of the Yuba River one mile below the South Fork.

212. J. N. Turner, a commissioner of Nevada County, 1851.

213. Horatio Beach came to California with J. H. Jewett of Marysville in 1849. See also Decker's entries for April 2 and July 9 for additional information on Beach, including his murder.

214. The Delaware Company had traveled either closely ahead or behind Decker's party on the overland route to California. Its diarist, Joshua Breyfogle was also on the Yuba at about the same time as Decker, though not in the same vicinity. He arrived at the forks of the Yuba about March 6, and due to severe weather conditions did not start prospecting until about March 19. Other members of the Delaware Company were scattered along the Yuba River.

215. The Dayton, Ohio *Bulletin* for August 6, 1849, refers to an overland party—presumably from Dayton—as the "Clegg Company." The reference is in an article titled "News from the Plains." The possibility exists—but cannot be confirmed—that Decker's Mr. Klegg is the Mr. Clegg the *Bulletin* mentions, and that Ely and Ring may have been members of the same company.

216. Charles S. Decker.

217. These were two sisters of Peter Decker.

218. Perhaps the same Armstrong mentioned by Decker in his overland diary. (See index.) The "Hewleyt Company" may have been a mining company formed on the Yuba and not an overland company. Joshua Breyfogle in his diary entry for April 28 and March 1, 1850, mentions meeting Dutton and Armstrong while traveling up to the forks of the Yuba. Breyfogle also remarked: "I expect to see them up the river in a few days."

219. Charles Howard Shinn in his book on mining camps remarks that the mining courts of the gold camps were the first "assembly of free men in open council." All the miners participated and frequently there was a jury selected. A judge or presiding officer was chosen and he submitted the case to the assembly on a *viva voce* vote which was irrevocable. Joshua Breyfogle thoughtfully copied the laws of the Yuba Mining District as an appendix to his diary. There are 11 resolutions. Laws governing the river claims, as well as river dams, are included. The laws also provided for trials to settle disputes.

220. See footnote 198.

221. See footnote 32.

222. See footnote 59.

223. C. E. Bowers was a member of the Franklin California Mining Company.

224. See footnote 27.

225. Decker later refers to this man as F. L. Oats of Tennessee and tells us that he left California for the States on August 25, 1850.

226. Negroes were not uncommon in California during the gold rush. They were frequently brought to California by their owners. Titus Hale of Missouri brought his slave, Alvin Coffey, to California in 1849, and gave him his freedom. He became a most respected citizen of California and the only 49er Negro member of The Society of California Pioneers. The word appears in many place names. On the south fork of the Yuba, there was Negro Bar. In El Dorado County, there was a Negro Hill. In Nevada County there was Negro Canyon, etc.

227. In the spring of 1850 Indian depredations in Nevada County were a source of grave concern. A sawmill four miles south of Grass Valley, on Wolf Creek, was burned and the Holt Brothers were killed. Several volunteer military companies were formed for the purpose of protecting the miners and other settlers.

228. When a store was set up in a mining camp it took on the aspects of a town in a very short time. Washington, first known as Indian Boys Camp, on the South Yuba, was one of these early trading centers, and has survived to the present time.

229. Both Howard and Epperson had been members of an Oregon company that arrived on the South Yuba in the spring or summer of 1849. Decker remarks in his entry for May 26 that Howard's little girl was from Oregon. It was not uncommon for Oregonians to bring their families to California in 1849. See also footnote 208.

230. Gold Run, a small stream that runs into Deer Creek in Nevada City. Capt. John Pennington built the first cabin on this creek in 1849.

231. Dr. E. E. Gardner, alderman, Nevada City 1851, died same year.

232. W. C. Bradley, '49er living in Nevada County, Census of 1852.

233. Barton Lee came to California from Oregon in 1848. He was successor to the Sacramento banking house of L. Priest & Co. He failed for a large amount in 1850 and went to live in the Sandwich Islands.

234. The St. Louis *Republican* of April 21, 1849 prints a letter from Independence in which it is reported that a company from Hamilton, Ohio, is preparing to leave overland. Names of the party are not published, but it is stated that the company will be guided by a Mr. Pommell. Alcaldes were usually elected by the community. The *Alcalde* was representative of one of the types of early Cali-

fornia mining camp government. He often made up his own laws as
he went along. He issued writs, some of which were copied from law
books, but in many cases were written by him without reference to
established law.

235. F. J. Hoffman was one of the early expressmen of California,
organizing his first express in 1849. In 1850 he went into partnership
with a man by name of Page, which was short-lived. He later took
on a new partner, Robert Little, and the firm was called Hoffman &
Little. The original express route was between Sacramento and
Placerville via Webberville. After his partnership with Little, the
company extended as far as Grass Valley, Nevada City, and the South
Yuba. After two or three years, Hoffman retired and sold his interest
to C. C. Beekman, his son-in-law, who was to later become a prominent
expressman in the Northern part of California and Southern Oregon.
[The editor wishes to thank Mr. M. C. Nathan, San Rafael, California,
for biographical details.]

236. Poor Man's Creek, a tributary of the South Yuba, was a rich
area, and heavily mined in 1850. J. J. Rogers states that he and
Decker were among the first, if not the first, to explore the possibilities
of Poor Man's Creek. "At least there was not a man working on it
as far as we went." (Letter, *Miners Transcript,* Nevada City, 1888,
see Introduction.) Decker worked with a rocker for two days and
made about $10.00 a day. However, Irishman's Bar seemingly had
a richer yield and he abandoned the Creek and never went back even
though it later became one of the richest bars.

237. This refers to the widely publicized trial of Dr. John W.
Webster for the murder of Dr. George Parkman. The murder took
place in or near Boston Medical College, about Nov. 23, 1849. Dr.
Webster was found guilty and sentenced to be hanged. A news item
about the trial was carried in the *Alta* on May 21, 1850.

238. Rumors of rich strikes were constantly being circulated.
Decker is referring to the famous Gold Lake expedition made by
J. R. Stoddard who sought a lake whose shores were allegedly lined
with gold. The legend of Gold Lake originated in Coloma in the
spring of 1849 with the mountain man Old Greenwood, who said the
legend was told him by an Indian chief in that area. Old Greenwood
continued to spread the story so that the miners organized an expedition in June of 1849, to be led by John Greenwood, Caleb's eldest
son, to seek out the famous lake whose shores were lined with gold.
The expedition ended in failure and the miners returned to Coloma.
The legend was revived the following year by J. R. Stoddard. Stoddard recruited a large expedition from the towns of Marysville and
Nevada City to seek the Gold Lake. It was much ballyhooed in the
press. From what Decker says in his Diary it is clear Stoddard's
expedition passed near Decker's camp on the South Yuba, at the time

Decker decided to join the expedition. It is unfortunate that Decker's Diary does not give detailed entries of the wanderings of the expedition. The expedition broke up after it became clear that Stoddard had no clear notion of where to find the Gold Lake.

239. There were many preachers in California in 1850, the majority of them without parishes. They were only too glad to visit the mining camps to conduct whatever services might be desired. The Rev. Jolly was probably one of these itinerant preachers.

240. T. P. White, member of a Cincinnati Company, in Nevada City and on the South Yuba.

241. Sheriffs were frequently elected to assist the alcalde in carrying out his duties.

242. Decker had first met Beach on the Yuba on April 2, 1850. See also Decker's entry for July 9, 1850.

243. Jonas Spect, founder of Fremont, was a member of the firm of Spect and Winston. He mined in California in 1848, and was a member of the first State Senate. He died in Colusa in 1883.

244. White Oak Springs, six miles below Nevada City, was a trading post kept by David Bovier, in 1849.

245. This mention of "Pilot Breyfogle" refers to Charles Breyfogle, who had come overland with Decker to California in 1849, and who was a cousin to diarist Joshua Breyfogle and Charles C. Breyfogle. The reference to "Pilot Breyfogle's Company being in and splitting up on the road" means that Charles had journeyed back to Columbus, Ohio sometime late in 1849 or very early in 1850 and had there brought together a party of Ohioans to leave for California. It is that party referred to in Decker's entry for September 1, 1850, having a few days before arrived in California. The following evidence points to Charles as being "Pilot Breyfogle." In the *Ohio Statesman* for April 6, 1850, there is an article announcing the departure of a company "under the leadership of Captain Breyfogle of Columbus." Family tradition also tells us that Charles returned to Ohio by a long and tedious journey around Cape Horn. On his way to Columbus, he stopped and visited with Joshua and Charles C.'s brother, Jacob Breyfogle, and showed him specimens of gold he had brought with him from California. Further evidence that indicates that this is Charles—not Charles C.—is that the *Statesman* notice refers to him as "of Columbus." Further, in Decker's entry for September 28, Decker says they had a pleasant conversation about home and old times. Home, to Decker, would be Columbus, not Delaware, where Charles C. was from. Charles Breyfogle's early days in Columbus are outlined in the family genealogy, "What I know About the Breyfogle Family," by Lewis Breyfogle, Chanute, Kansas, 1963. And finally, it could not have been Charles C. for the simple fact that Joshua, his brother, who was on the Yuba from July 4, 1850 through September,

1850, mentions Charles C. in his diary on both July 4 and again on September 1. In both references, Charles C. is placed on the Yuba by Joshua.

246. Mrs. Penn's was the first boarding house in Nevada City in 1849. However, Luzena Stanley Wilson also set up an eating place for miners under a tree, in 1849. The Augustines were later arrivals.

247. Captain G. C. Addison was associated with Fall and Company in Marysville, and also in Park's Bar on the Yuba. Later he was with the firm of Shaffer, Addison & Co. in Marysville, jobbers and grocers.

248. Coyoteville was at the end of "Lost Hill" in the northwestern corner of Nevada City. Rich fields of gold in gravel started a boom in 1850, and led to a small community known as Coyoteville. Within two years, millions of dollars had been taken from these gravel deposits. When the gold ran out, so did Coyoteville. John Rogers says that he and Decker went down to Nevada City and sank a few shafts. They also hauled dirt for "those who struck it rich," using a mule and wagon purchased from an emigrant. However, neither Decker or Rogers had any luck. (Letter from Nevada City *Miners Transcript,* 1888.)

249. Mr. Stamps was elected Alcalde in March of 1850. Further information on Mr. Stamps is sketchy and incomplete. None of the contemporary sources give his first name. Bean's *History and Directory of Nevada County* (Nevada City, 1867) and Brown and Dallison's *Directory . . .* (San Francisco, 1856) both describe in similar his election as first Alcalde. Stamps served only for two or three months as Alcalde, having been elected in March, 1850. The term of the Alcalde's office expired in May by limitation, and a Justice of the Peace under the Constitution was elected.

250. This is Charles Breyfogle, who had just recently arrived in California from Columbus, Ohio, having brought out to California an overland party. See also footnote 245. Decker reports Breyfogle said "they had much harder times crossing the plains than last year." This refers to his recent crossing of the plains in 1850 and his crossing the year before, 1849, as a member of Decker's Company. Family tradition has it that Charles later returned to Columbus a moderately wealthy man, bringing back with him some $20,000 in gold.

251. H. C. Riordan, who left Columbus with a small company in April, 1849, is listed in the *Ohio State Journal,* March 31, 1849.

252. H. L. Morgan, who headed the small company Riordan traveled with overland. See the *Ohio State Journal,* March 31, 1849.

253. Rough and Ready was named after a company of gold seekers made up of men who had served under Zachary Taylor during the Mexican War. The company was headed by A. A. Townsend of Iowa. This mining community once had the distinction of seceding from the United States. An unverified story concerning this incident relates

that Rough and Ready never bothered to apply for reinstatement into the Union. This was discovered when Rough and Ready made application for a Post Office, many years later.

254. This Bar was two miles below present Oroville, and was worked first by the Long brothers in 1849. It is said that the first pan washed yielded $400.

255. In September 1850, the Rev. Isaac Owen arrived in Nevada City to lay the foundation for the First Methodist Episcopal Church. The Rev. Owen was from Indiana and came to California in 1849. He was the first regularly appointed minister for the M. E. Church in California. The Rev. Pollock from Missouri was sent to Nevada City in the fall of 1850 to organize the M. E. Church South.

256. Probably a misspelling of Epperson. See footnotes 208 and 229.

257. Sacramento had its first cholera epidemic in the late fall of 1850. A detailed description is given in Dr. John Morse's *History of Sacramento County*, 1850. According to his account the first case was detected when a man was found on the levee, far gone from the disease, Oct. 30, 1850. He had just arrived from San Francisco where the epidemic was already raging. Within six days the cholera had made inroads in Sacramento's population and it was impossible to keep up with the burials. An unsigned letter printed in the *Alta* of November 5, 1850, written from Sacramento City gives the following comment on the cholera epidemic: "Three of the large gambling resorts have been closed, the streets are deserted, as frequented almost solely by the hearse, and nearly all business is at a standstill. . . . The daily mortality is so great (60 per day) . . ." The letter goes on to list 126 deaths in Sacramento during the week previous. The cholera was also present in the mines, but to a lesser degree.

258. William H. French, miner, Nevada City.

259. J. L. Peters, carpenter, Nevada City.

260. The term "black-leg" was used derisively to refer variously to villains, vandals, pranksters, gamblers, ne'er-do-wells, etc.

261. Lafayette Lodge was the first organized Masonic Lodge in Nevada City. It was formed November, 1850, by dispensation of the Grand Lodge of Wisconsin, and was chartered in California in 1857.

262. A. W. Potter had a stationery store on Main Street, Nevada City.

263. "Seeing the Elephant" was an expression used by the miners who had been in the California gold region. Lettersheets, the forerunner of the picture postal card, often depicted a drawing entitled "Seeing the Elephant." Its first such use appears to have been in the pictorial lettersheet, "The Miners' Ten Commandments."

264. Samuel Colt obtained his first U. S. patent August 29, 1839. He manufactured his revolving arms in Paterson, N. J.

265. See footnote 260.

266. In Sierra County, along the ridge between the North Fork of the Yuba River and the South Fork of the Feather River. The area was first prospected in the spring of 1850 by an old sea captain by name of Sears.

267. Broad Street is still the main thoroughfare of Nevada City.

268. James S. Tolles started a one man express December 7, 1849, and continued it until January, 1852. Mountain Cottage was kept by Tolles, and was located eighteen miles above Bidwell's Bar on the road from Slate Creek to Marysville. Tolles' *Diary* is published in the Marysville *Appeal Democrat,* Feb. 5 - March 11, 1930.

269. Nelson's Creek appears on Gibbes' Map of California, 1852. The creek empties into the Middle Fork of the Feather River.

270. Bidwell's Bar on the Middle Fork of the Feather River, where gold was discovered by John Bidwell in July, 1848. The Bar will be inundated when the Feather River Dam is completed. The lodge at Bidwell was not formally recognized by the California Grand Lodge until 1855, when it became California Lodge No. 47.

271. According to Bean's *History and Directory* . . . (Nevada City, 1867) the lodge was named Oustomah after the Indian appellation for the site of the town of Nevada. In 1851, Bean continues, the first association was formed, and met in a log cabin. "Most of the members of the association were ancient Odd Fellows whose feet could not pass the portal of any well regulated lodge, but they kept warm in their hearts a love for the Order, and years after, when the great reform worked by the non-affiliated law went into operation, they renewed their regular connection with the Order. The association had many pleasant meetings, and finally led to the organization of a regular lodge in November, 1853, Oustomah Lodge, No. 16." Decker was to continue his interest in lodge activities in later years. He was instrumental in organizing Corinthian Lodge No. 9 in Marysville, F.& A.M. (Masons) in 1852, and was also in 1855 listed as Chief Patriarch of District No. 6, Marysville, Yuba County, of the I.O.O.F. (Odd Fellows).

272. The Sidneyites or Sidney Ducks were largely discharged convicts from Australia's penal colony.

273. This was probably the Diary—or a manuscript copy of the Diary—kept by Decker on his overland trip to California.

274. Dr. Lennox, of Missouri, was shot in his own house in Nevada City in December, 1850. The murderer, it has been indicated, was never apprehended. However, Decker infers that suspicion was thrown on a man named Bess, of Nevada City, with whom the doctor had had an altercation in the past.

275. Zachary Taylor, President of the United States in 1849-1850. After his death in July, 1850, Millard Fillmore succeeded to the

Presidency.

276. Thomas Freeman of Freeman's Crossing on the Middle Yuba.

277. Gold Bluffs, Humboldt County, about fifteen miles south of the mouth of the Klamath River. This was the scene of much excitement in 1851, when it was thought gold could be extracted from the black sands of the ocean beach. Decker was correct in assuming it to be a humbug.

278. California was truly a magnet for all the races, and indeed a great melting pot of humanity. A number of special studies have been published on the various nationalities in California during the gold rush. Some of these are: *A French Journalist in the California Gold Rush,* by A. P. Nasatir [French]; *The Irish Race in California,* by Hugh Quigley [Irish and Welsh]; *California Inter Pocula,* by Hubert Howe Bancroft, 1888, pp. 561-581 [Chinese]; *Gold Fleet for California,* by Charles Bateson [Australian], etc.

279. The Rock Creek Ditch was projected in 1851 by John and Thomas Dunn in company with C. Carroll and C. Marsh. The water was brought nine miles to Coyote Diggings. It was the first large ditch in successful operation. Prior to this a ditch had brought water a mile and a half from Mosquito Creek to Coyote Hill, and another short ditch ran from Little Deer Creek. In November, 1850, two rival companies constructed ditches to bring water from Deer Creek into Nevada City.

280. Rush Creek, a few miles northwest of Nevada City.

281. Erysipelas, an infectious disease caused by a wound or lesion in the skin. Today easily cured by the sulfa drugs.

282. Sol & J. Kohlman, clothing store in Nevada City.

283. A Mr. Berry and his wife built a log cabin in 1849, and called it The Mineral Hotel. It was not far from the present town of Smartsville and was maintained until 1851.

284. H. C. Stambaugh, alderman in Marysville, 1851.

285. The *Captain Sutter,* a side-wheeler built in 1849 and abandoned 1868. The *Tehama,* a stern-wheeler, built in 1850 and abandoned 1885. The *Governor Dana* was the first steamer to run up the Sacramento River. It was built in the east and was originally intended for a run on the Penobscot River. The builder, Gen. Veazi, had an injunction served upon him which forbid his using the boat on the Eastern rivers. So it was dismantled and placed upon the bark *Rio Grande* and shipped to San Francisco where she was reassembled at Pittsburg. All her officers came with her. (*Reminiscences* of Henry Hiram Ellis, Los Angeles, 1959.)

286. L. H. Babb, member of the firm of Eaton, Babb and Hawley, Marysville, 1853.

287. William Shannon, former Governor of Ohio. Shannon had come to California in 1849 with a company from St. Clairsville, Ohio,

sailing around the Horn to San Francisco. See also footnote 187.

288. Levi Hite became Decker's business partner in Marysville. An advertisement in the Marysville *Daily Evening Herald,* August 5, 1853, informs that Decker and Hite are successors to Packard and Woodruff wholesale dealers in provisions. Hite, unfortunately, is not listed in the 1852 Census of California, though he was in Yuba County at the time. Nor is he listed in the Marysville area directories for the period. There is a brief mention of him in the *History of Yuba County* (Thompson and West, 1879) where he is referred to as a charter member of Yuba Lodge, I.O.O.F. No. 5, organized July 27, 1853. He is also listed as among the founders and first president of the Odd Fellows Hall Association, formed in Yuba County on March 24, 1860.

289. Long Bar on the Yuba River. The longest Bar, and was worked longer than any other in the vicinity. The first miners were there in November, 1848. There was a postoffice in 1850, and a ferry in 1851 that ran between Long and Kentucky Bars.

290. Parks Bar, on the northeast side of the Yuba River, fifteen miles above Marysville. The first miners were there in June, 1848. They were Major Cooper of Benicia, Nicolaus Hunsacker, and Dr. John Marsh of the Rancho Los Meganos in the San Joaquin Valley. David Parks arrived in September, 1848, and established a store at the Bar.

291. Rose's Bar, on the south side of the Yuba, twenty miles above Marysville. On June 2, 1848, Jonas Spect made the discovery of gold on the Yuba River. John Rose opened a store there with William Reynolds in the fall of 1848. By 1850 there were 2000 men mining on Rose's Bar.

292. Barton's Bar, on the South Yuba, two and one-half miles below the junction of the north and south forks.

293. The steamer *West Point* ran twice a week from San Francisco to Marysville, touching at Sacramento enroute. In 1850-1851 her captain was Joseph R. Swift.

294. Judge F. Barnard, who arrived in California from New York early in 1851. Judge Barnard survived the stabbing Decker described. The *History of Yuba County* (Thompson and West, 1879) states that Barnard died at Park's Bar in 1857.

Appendix

I

Columbus *Daily Ohio State Journal,*
Thursday Evening, February 15, 1849.
Columbus and California Industrial Association.

The following are the officers and constitution of an association formed in this city for operating in the gold regions in California:

JOHN WALTON, *Pres't.*
J. G. CANFIELD, *V. Pres't.*
P. DECKER, *Secretary.*
G. Q. McCOLM, *Treasurer.*

Directors — G. Walton, T. J. Price, H. Moons, C. Breyfogle, and James Bryden.

WHEREAS, the undersigned parties have agreed to associate themselves together, for the purpose of prosecuting and conducting mining operations, and procuring gold and other minerals in the territory of California, and on and about the shores of the Pacific Ocean; and whereas, an undertaking requiring our presence at a point so remote from our homes, and from those whom we most cherish, and whose happiness we most desire, subjects us to many privations and hardships, and calls for cordial and united efforts for our mutual welfare; and whereas, we cannot hope for success in our labor without the guidance and blessing of an All-wise Creator, and a due observance of his laws; now, therefore, in consideration of the premises, and in order more efficiently to manage the property and prosecute the business of said company, the parties hereunto severally and individually, and each for himself, his heirs, executors, administrators and assigns, respectively agree that the following shall be the articles of mutual agreement and association, forever binding upon each of the said parties, his heirs, executors, administrators and assigns, to wit:

ART. 1. This association shall be known by the name and style of "The Columbus and California Industrial Association."

ART. 2. The officers of the Association shall be a President, Vice President, Secretary, Treasurer and five Directors, who shall be elected by ballot, and serve for three months, and until their successors are elected. A majority of all the votes shall be necessary for a choice. Each mess shall nominate one of their number as a candidate for Director, who (if elected) shall enter upon the discharge of his duties. The Board of Directors thus elected shall have a general supervision of all affairs of the Association, and shall perform such duties as may be required of them by the by-laws.

ART. 3. It shall be the duty of the President to preside at all meetings of the Association, and to preserve order and decorum. He shall decide all question of order, (subject to appeal to the Association, by 2 members.) He shall sign all orders on the Treasurer for moneys appropriated by the Association, and perform such other duties as may be prescribed by the by-laws.

ART. 4. In the absence or disability of the President, the Vice President shall perform the duties of the President; and in the absence or disability of the President and Vice President, any member of the Association may be chosen to preside.

ART. 5. The Secretary shall keep a correct record of all the proceedings of the Association, in a book provided for that purpose. He shall receive all moneys that may be paid into the Association, pay them to the Treasurer, and take his receipt for the same. He shall countersign all orders on the Treasurer, and perform such other duties as may be prescribed by the by-laws or by resolution.

ART. 6. The Treasurer shall receive all moneys from the Secretary, and receipt to him for the same. He shall keep a just and accurate account of all the receipts and

disbursements. He shall pay all orders, signed by the
proper officers, on presentation; and for the faithful per-
formance of his duties shall give a bond of $3,000, with
security to be approved by the Association.

ART. 7. The Association shall consist of thirty men,
with an equal capital of two hundred and twenty-five
dollars. They shall be men of good character and sound
constitutions.

ART. 8. This Association shall continue to exist for
one year and six months from the time of leaving Columbus, unless two-thirds of the Association determine otherwise. But in no case shall the Association be dissolved,
or a dividend declared, until the return of the Association to the city of Columbus, without the unanimous consent of the members present; nor shall such vote be taken
without notice to each member of the time and place at
which such vote will be taken. Provided, however, that
this article shall not be so construed as to prevent the
Association from granting an honorable discharge to any
member, upon his own application, two thirds of the
members concurring in the discharge. The member so
discharged shall be entitled to an equal division of the
gains of the Association to the time of such discharge.

ART. 9. This Association shall be united to share each
others fortunes, and render assistance in time of danger;
and if any member of this Association shall be deprived
of his health, or any way injured, so as to be unable to
aid in advancing the interest of the Association, he shall
not, for that reason, be deprived of his interest in the
property and effects of the Association; but he shall, at
all times, be regarded as a full partner in all things, and
entitled to the kindness and watchful care and protection
of every other member of the Association, and under no
circumstances shall he be deserted or permitted to suffer
for want of proper attention; and in the event of the
death of any member of the Association before the expira-
tion of the time limited for the continuance of this Association, his legal representatives shall receive his full

share of the property and effects of the Association, the same as though he had lived and faithfully labored through the whole period required by these articles.

ART. 10. No gambling of any kind shall be indulged in by the members of the Association, either among themselves or with others. Nor shall any member be allowed to use any kind of intoxicating drink, unless administered under medical advice. And any member who shall violate the provisions of this article shall be advised with by a committee appointed by the board of directors for that purpose, and if afterwards, he shall persist in it, he shall from that time forfeit his interest in the Association.

ART. 11. Any person who shall become a member of the Association, and shall pay in any part of, or the whole amount required by this constitution, and shall be removed by death or be disabled before starting, the amount paid in by him shall be paid back to him, his heirs or assigns. Should he fail from any other cause, he shall forfeit the amount paid in by him unless otherwise ordered by the Association.

ART. 12. Neglect of duty and disorderly conduct shall subject the offender to such punishment as the Association may determine by a two-thirds vote; but in no case shall a member be expelled without the concurrence of three-fourths of the members.

ART. 13. It is further agreed that any person or persons, who shall be detected in secreting or embezzling gold or other property for his or their own use, which he or they are bound to take charge of or collect for the benefit of the Association, on conviction thereof, after hearing the accusers and accused before 9 members of the Association—to be drawn by ballot—he or they shall be expelled from the Association, and forfeit all the stock he or they may have invested originally in said Association, and all his or their interest in said Association. The accused and accusers may each object to any three persons, who shall be drawn to try the accused.

ART. 14. It is further agreed that there shall be no

personal or individual interest, trade or traffic whatever; but that any article of individual interest disposed of shall be credited to the member at cost and the proceeds go into the general fund.

ART. 15. As religion is a matter of private opinion, the members of this company would not seek to enforce, by restrictive laws or penalties, the observance of any particular worship, or belief of any particular doctrine, yet we would earnestly recommend to every individual member of the association the observance of the Sabbath day—to cease from all unnecessary labor, and to engage in such worship as the judgment shall dictate and the conscience approve.

ART. 16. A copy of these articles shall be made and signed and duly executed by each member of this company, and said executed articles of agreement shall be deposited in the Recorders Office of Franklin county, Ohio, for safe keeping, and a certified copy taken with the company; and the said original articles of agreement shall not be withdrawn from the place of deposite unless by the unanimous consent of all the members of the association.

ART. 17. These articles of association are hereby declared to be unalterable.

II

COLUMBUS *Ohio State Journal,* APRIL 2, 1849.
THE BOYS ARE OFF FOR CALIFORNIA.

Two companies of adventurers, of thirty in each, residents of Columbus and vicinity, have this day taken leave of their fellow citizens, and started for the *El Dorado* of the Sacramento Valley. The first company, whose name has not been furnished,* is composed of the following persons: John Walton, President; J. G. Canfield, Vice President; Peter Decker, Secretary; G. Q. McColm, Treasurer; S. J. Price, H. Moores, G. Walton, and C. Breyfogle, Directors; C. E. Boyle, Physician. The other

---

*Columbus and California Industrial Association.

members are D. Bryden, E. Barcus, Jr., E. E. Canfield, G. Chadwick, W. Cain, A. B. Crist, C. Dewitt, J. S. Demgan, T. Davis, L. A. Denig, C. M. Fisk, J. Krumm, J. C. Lunn, P. McCommon, H. Ranney, T. Rugg, D. Rugg, J. P. Stone, W. C. Stiles, C. D. Wood, L. H. Sherman.

The company has ten wagons and 40 mules, and is well supplied with equipage, provisions and arms. In organization it is divided into five messes, with one director in each. Leaving Columbus, they pass thro' Xenia to Cincinnati, thence by water to Independence, in Missouri, beyond which the particular route is not determined upon.

The other band is called the "Franklin California Mining Company." Its officers are—Joseph Hunter, Captain; John Coulter, Lieutenant; J. H. Marple, Secretary; F. A. McCormick, Treasurer; O. S. Hunter, Quartermaster. The other members are Chester F. Colton, J. Robey, Joseph W. Booth, Geo. Woodward, Samuel Price, Matthew Williams, Alexander Robertson, John Spaythe, V. R. Smith, John Uncles, Charles A. Robertson, John McCartney, J. K. Barr, R. J. Hunter, C. M. Shaw, C. H. Myers, Jacob Armitage, Samuel Myers, A. M. Hunter, Jona. Bobo, Anderson Cornwall, J. W. Coulter, Nicholas Demorest, O. S. Walcutt, E. Gaver.

The members are associated upon the joint stock principle, and are to remain in California 18 months from May 1, prox. They carry provisions sufficient for that length of time. Their train consists of 8 new and strong wagons, and 26 yoke of oxen. The route to be pursued is the same with that of the other companies.

III

PETER DECKER TO THE COLUMBUS *Ohio State Journal,*
SACRAMENTO CITY, AUGUST 21, 1849.
[PRINTED IN THE *Ohio State Journal,* OCT. 20, 1849.]
FROM THE GOLD DIGGINGS.

SACRAMENTO CITY, CALIFORNIA
August 21, 1849.

*W. B. Thrall, Esq.:**

DEAR SIR:—With pleasure I comply with your request to inform you of the arrival of our Company in
California—and although the journey was tedious and
attended with difficulties, we all came through safely, in
the enjoyment of good health and spirits. The main train,
with the wagons, arrived in "the diggins" on the 12th
inst. Mess No. 2, of which I was a member, *packed,* and
were sent in advance of the Company, from the *Cannon,*
in the Sierra Nevada Mountains, and arrived in this city
on the 9th—the former having been on the road 104 days,
and the latter 191 days from St. Joseph. We were fortunate in being among the foremost trains on a road, this
year crowded to an excess that must result in much suffering to some of those behind, on account of scarcity of
grass, which to emigrants is second in importance to bread.
From advices received on the road from packers who left
St. Joseph after all the wagons had left, I suppose the
number of wagons that started across the plains this season was from eight to nine thousand—and on an average,
at least three persons to a wagon. Our Company came
through as an Association, but since have dissolved by
unanimous vote. Nearly all Companies formed in the
States broke up on the road—even down to the number
of two or three. This may appear mysterious to many,
but those who have observed human nature as developed
on the plains, have no difficulty in solving this mystery.

Well, we have passed through the hardships and difficulties incident to rude life in the wilderness, and are in
"the land of gold and wealth," concerning which I might

*W. B. Thrall was co-editor of the *Ohio State Journal.*

say much, even after a stay here of but a few weeks—but I will briefly say that the golden reports which reached us from California, a year ago, were in the main correct. California is undoubtedly a vast gold mine, which will continue to pay reasonably good wages to the miner for twenty years to come. The time was when immense fortunes were made in a short time; but, owing to various causes, this state of things has in a great degree changed. At present money can be made here, but it requires more time and labor than many had anticipated. The consequences is, that some who arrive here and find that only tens, instead of hundreds, can be made a day, become discouraged and "leave without striking a blow."

Not having seen much in the mines, or labored at it much myself, I cannot give you a very definite idea as to profits. Considerable seems to depend on luck. Some make money fast, while others do but little and yet labor hard—for mining is hard labor. An ounce a day is considered doing tolerably well. Other kinds of labor is not always to be had. Mechanics and laboring men get from $10 to $20 per day, and prices in other respects range as follows: Flour, $8 to $10 per 100 lbs.; Ham, 40 to 45c per lb.; Mess Pork, $35 per bbl.; Coffee, from 12 to 20c, and Brown Sugar the same; Tea, from $1.00 to $1.50; Molasses, from $1.00 to $1.50 per gallon. Butter is almost out of the question here—some (which in the States would only be used in place of lard) sells at $2 per lb., and Saleratus is from $3 to $4 per lb. Watermelons sell at $4 to $6 apiece; Cheese at $4 per lb. Loaves of bread, that sell in your city at 5 cts, are 50 cts here. Boarding is $18 to $21 per week— with the privilege of selecting the *smoothest ground* you can find to sleep on, outside of the "shanty," and then, too, you have a nightly serenade from the wolves.

Lumber is in much demand, and sells at $600 per 1000 ft. Hay $100 per ton, and 55 miles up the American Fork, (at Culloma,) where the mill race first laid bare the wealth of California, they asked me 50 cents a lb. for barley—the only food I could get for my mule. Milk cows sell at from $50 to $150. The price of wagons, mules, horses, and oxen, is pretty high. A horse I bought in Missouri for $45—after bringing him here in bad condition (as may be supposed,) I sold for $75. By the way, a blacksmith who occupied a part of "all out doors" as a shop, asked me $16 to put two new shoes on. But few horses are honored with shoes in this country. On account of cost of transportation, &c., the price of everything is much higher in the mines than here. This place is a kind of miners' headquarters, where provisions, &c., are much in demand. Freight from San Francisco is $3 per 100 lbs.—a distance of 180 miles. But prices of everything here are very fluctuating. Dry goods sell cheap—perhaps not over 50 per cent. higher than in Ohio.

This is termed the "sickly season," and I presume it is healthier now than it usually is in summer season in the goodly city of Columbus. Cholera has not made its appearance in California. The city from which I address you is about *three months of age,* and has a population of from 4 to 5,000 inhabitants. The *houses* are mostly *tents*—though some good wooden houses are being built, for one of which I heard a gentleman offer $31,000 rent a year. The streets cross each other at right angles, where the trees don't interfere with such an arrangement. Lots sell from $1,000 to $30,000 apiece. Its location is on the east bank of the Sacramento, at the mouth of the American Fork—two miles below Sutter's Fort. Fifteen ships are laying in port here now, and steamers ply between this and San Francisco, giving quite a commercial air to this calico city. The Sacramento is perhaps the most beautiful stream in America, and is an outlet to commerce in importance to California, as is the Mississippi to the States.

A word as to the population of California: This country presents the singular anomaly of having no government, no laws, and no social organization; and yet perfect security is felt. Theft or quareling [sic] are crimes almost unknown. Property of the most valuable kind is exposed on every hand, and yet perfectly secure, which is astonishing to new comers from other parts of the world, where *bolts* and *bars,* in adition [sic] to *laws,* are necessary to secure property. This may be the result of two causes: one is, that nearly every one feels satisfied with what he is doing, and another is the summary manner in which punishment is inflicted.

In the States the adage has obtained that, "the march of empire is westward;" but here I find its limit. On the shores of the Pacific is the only country I have found where folks don't talk of "going to the West." Then a word to such as talk of coming to California, who are doing well and enjoy the advantage of comparative ease and comfort, the enjoyments of the social circle, and the endearments of home. To such my advice is, *stay where you are.* But if you are a young man, used to hard labor, and cannot restrain your spirit of adventure, you had better see for yourself. But take any other route than that across the plains and mountains.

Respectfully yours,
P. Decker.

P. S. I have had no news from home since I left your city. The reason is, that in California, no one will attend to a Post Office for the paltry compensation allowed by Government, and our postal arrangements accomplish no good.   P. D.

IV

Dr. C. E. Boyle to Dr. Smith,
Culloma, California, August 28, 1849.
[Printed in the *Ohio State Journal,* Nov. 17, 1849.]
Letter from Dr. C. E. Boyle.

CULLOMA, California, August 28, 1849.

DEAR DR. SMITH—Having at present an opportunity, I will give you a somewhat lengthy account of our trip, which you may trace on the map as follows: — From home to Cincinnati by land; thence to St. Joseph's by water, 1200 or 1400 miles; from St. Joseph's across the plains to Big Blue River; thence to Little Blue—along that several day's travel; thence to Main Platte at Grand Island; thence to Ft. Childs, on Platte, about 350 miles; thence on south side of Platte to ford of South Branch; from ford to North Platte 25 miles; along south side North Platte, till we reach the road to Laramie Fork and Fort Laramie, 750-800 miles from St. Joseph's; thence across Black Hills, to North Platte Ferry; across that, up north side North Platte, till we reach Sweet Water; follow Sweet Water through Devil's Gate, past Independence Rock, (four miles east of it,) and on to South Pass; thence to Green River Ferry, on which route there is 45 miles of Desert; thence to Thomas' Fork of Bear river; down Bear river to Soda Springs, Hot Springs, Smith's Fort, &c.; thence again across dividing ridge on to Fort Hall, 600 or 800 miles from Laramie, on the Lewis or Snake river; (this is in Oregon, near California line,) thence down Lewis river to Fall or Raft river, pass the American Fall; thence again across the dividing ridge to head of Humboldt or Mary river, (hot springs and sulphur springs and swamps); down Mary to Sink; across 45 miles salty, sandy desert, to Carson river, near Carson lake; up Carson river to its source in the Sierra Nevada mountains; across these, and down a small tributary of the Sacramento, to the American Fork, at Sutter's saw-mill, (now owned by Bailey and others,) 850 miles — some 3000 or 3600 miles.

Now the incidents of travel which occur in so long a route are too numerous to be crowded into a letter, and may be included in the following few words: — hunting buffalo, deer and antelope on the Platte and Black Hills, and guarding the wagons and animals from troublesome visitors at night, Indians and wolves. Our guard was strictly maintained, and we lost no animals; while others, more careless, lost in proportion to their negligence. We only once had occasion to fire at prowling Indians, and then they could not see the guards until very near them.

They usually kept out of sight, and stole animals which were not guarded. Then passing through the Snake country, we traded every day more or less with the Snakes, or as they call themselves, the Shoshonees and Pannacks. These are friendly and honest, and extremely filthy, eating their own vermin. They use a large black cricket as a common article of food, have an abundance of excellent horses, and live in tents or lodges made of buffalo hides well dressed—have as many wives as they can buy and support. One old fellow traveled with us several days— had been to St. Louis and could talk a little English— was a decided enemy of the Sioux, of whom he told me he had eaten one, and was consequently called Captain Poniteow. The whole nation is a kind, good natured, talkative, honest, proud and filthy set of fellows; not prone to begging as are the Sioux; nor stealing, like the Pawnees. Then at Ft. Hall we met quite a variety of Indians, in small numbers; Snakes, Pannacks, Creas, Flat-heads, Nezpierces, &c. When about the Sink, on Carson and on the Sierra Nevada, constant vigilance was required to keep the diggers from killing our animals. Some lost all their stock along here, having been killed by the diggers, the most degraded human beings I ever saw, subsisting on roots, insects, lizards, horned toads, marmots, prairie dogs or woodchucks, and stolen mules, and some entirely naked. On the western slope of the mountains game is not scarce, but to the east, as far as the Black Hills, it is by no means plenty.

We have had considerable sickness in our company, but very few and unimportant accidents. The diseases were diarrhoea, on the first part of the trip; and when crossing the Rocky mountains, mountain fever, as it is called, a very painful malady of the nature of bilious fever, to which emigrants are subject usually but once in their lives when crossing these mountains. The attack is usually sudden, always painful, and sometimes speedily fatal. Fifteen out of our 30 had the disease; of these, 5 were very seriously ill. I was ill of the disease myself two or three days—not dangerously, but very painfully. The proportion of those who had it, in most of the trains heard from, was even larger than the proportion in ours. Some deaths occurred from it in other companies. Nearly every man in the Delaware company had it, and at one time seven men only, out of twenty-seven, were fit for duty, but all recovered.

The country we passed thro' is quite diversified in scenery, and somewhat so in productions. The country is alluvial till we reach the black hills. These are volcanic, as in all the countries from that to Sacramento river, and probably to the Pacific, with small strips of alluvial land along the margin of the streams. Strong alkaline ponds are numerous, and some of these having dried up by evaporation, a mixture of saleratus and nit. prot. formed in some places an incrustation from 1 to 6 inches in depth, covering many acres of ground. The Soda Springs are a very remarkable natural wonder, and would almost pay for a voyage to them, for the mere purpose of seeing and drinking. One of them, called the Steamboat Spring, is strongly impregnated with iron, and the journey to it and residence at for two months, would be of more benefit in incipient consumption than half a dozen voyages to Madeira. The natural curiosities which attract attention are described by Fremont, Bryan[t], and others, quite accurately, and to these I must refer you for such description. When we cross the dividing ridge into the great basin, the traveler is much disappointed, having but little information on the subject, and Ware's guide book being very erroneous. The Humboldt mountains are nothing in all the parts of them seen by us, (and we traveled along their foot some 400 miles,) but bare burnt volcanic rocks, of reddish bricklike hue, piled up in the utmost confusion, with their peaks frequently capped with snow. Humboldt, or Mary river, is a pretty stream, arising in a swampy valley and fed by a few sulphur springs and by the melting snows, increases rapidly in size till its width is from 4 to 6 rods, and its depth 8 or

10 feet, with a current of 6 or 8 miles per hour at this season, and yet the evaporation is so rapid and the inbibition so great that in less than 100 miles from where it begins to decline not a particle of water is left in its channel, which at some seasons is full much farther than to the Sink, which is a large, reedy, strongly alkaline pond, which in the latter part of the summer becomes perfectly dry. The desert to be traversed between the Sink and the Carson river is nearly level, sandy, incrusted with salt in some places, the most dismal spot man ever trod; for miles there is not a living thing, animal or vegetable to be seen, except now and then a red wolf, which is hastening across from one mountain to another on the other side. Then again we arrive at a place where the desert plants, the sage and grease wood grow few and far between, and here we find lizards and scorpions, the former 10 or 12 and the latter 4 to 8 inches long, and a few desert insects. On this desert we started about 3 in the afternoon, and traveling all night reached a point within five miles of the river, where our animals, unable to draw their loads any further, were loosened and driven on to the river to recruit, and here Decker and I remained as wagon guard 36 hours, making in all about 85 hours that we were on this horrid desert, which has since been the scene of much suffering, both by men and animals, hundreds of animals and some men perishing for want of water. We, however, lost but one animal, which gave out after traveling about half across, and as he would go no further we shot him, and thus terminated his suffering. Along the road we saw quite a number of animals, dead and dying, which had been abandoned to their fate. Here for forty miles the road, so we learn from people who have since arrived, is strewed with the carcasses of animals, wagons, provisions, and other property, abandoned by the owners to save their own lives. Knowing what I do of that route, I would not like again to expose myself to its dangers and difficulties for the sum of gold any 5 men may chance to find in California, and when I

return it will be through Mexico or by Panama.

From the time we left the bottom land of the Missouri, until we reached the Sierra Nevada, we saw nothing that could be called a forest, and even groves of a diminutive size were few in number, and very far apart; sometimes we travelled for weeks without seeing a single tree on mountain or in the valley, and [line or lines missing in microfilm text] most luxuriant growth, many of the trees (various species of conifers) growing to the height of 250, a few 300 feet. The diameter of some of these is from 8 to 10 feet. There are cedars here which may well vie with the cedars of Lebanon, both for size and beauty. There is but little variety in the productions of the vegetable kingdom until we reach Carson river valley, which affords a great variety of plants, most of them, even the gooseberry, however, contain so much tannin as to be unfit for use. On this side the mountains there is at this time nothing green to be seen, except the oak, the pine, and a few shrubs—the grass and other plants, being all withered by the intense heat of the sun. As to inhabitants, look at the ceaseless toil and commotion of the busy world of an anthill, and you will have a fair idea of things here. All hurrying hither and thither, intent upon one object, but trying different ways to obtain it; here to-day, and gone to-morrow. Nearly every nation, civilized and savage, is represented, yet peace and good order reigns to a surprising degree. Property is perfectly safe without lock, bar or bolt; stores are kept in large tents, with no doors; people pass and re-pass, and nothing is missed, day or night. Liquors are plenty and cheap, yet people are sober and peaceable; yet every man goes armed, and it is as common to see a man with his bowie knife and pistols, as the soldier with his musket or sword, yet no one fears his neighbor, but goes and comes at all hours. When any one commits a breach of the peace, or laws of property or personal rights, his punishment is quick and condign; for petty thieving, 39 lashes; for robbery, cropping, whipping, and pillory, and banishment from

the mines, under pain of death; and for murder, a public
trial by judge and jury of miners, or other peaceable
citizens, fairly conducted, and upon conviction, hanging.
The first night we spent in the diggins, we slept beneath
a gallows tree, where, last New-years, three murderers
were hung. They were tried in the morning for robbery,
and were whipped, and on account of threats of ven-
geance, they were detained; while detained, they were
identified as the perpetrators of a murder which had taken
place some time before, and were then tried, condemned,
and executed before sundown.

As for gold there is a great deal of it, but it is thinly
spread over the country, through the ravines, with occasionally tolerably rich deposites in the crevices of the
rocks. The usual average for strong hard working men
is about $12 to $16 per day, and of this it costs about 3
to live, as prices are extremely high, although provisions
are plenty.

The company dissolved by mutual consent one week
after their arrival here, and the medicine chest, here somewhat valuable, fell to my lot; but the practice of medicine
here is not likely to be very profitable, as nearly every
company which came here had one or more Dr's among
their number. I shall therefore go to digging so soon as
the weather shall have become sufficiently cool to allow
it. The thermometer here has been as high as 105 in the
shade, (too hot for digging.) Dysentery prevails here
but is not generally of a fatal tendency. When our company dissolved they were all well and had been so for
some weeks.

The atmosphere is very dry here, dust abundant and
fleas innumerable. People slept in tents, on the ground,
in the open air, and in every way. There are a few women
and children here. Yesterday I saw the former Alcalde
of some little Mexican village here; he is as black as he
can well be, and as ugly as any negro you may see at
home. The Mexicans here are all about the complexion
of Poindexter, or even blacker. The Indians are scarce

and somewhat shy. Sandwich islanders I have not seen, but they are in the country.

Walton has just returned from Sacramento city, is well, as is also his brother and nephew. Canfield and brother, Decker and Price are well, and of the others all are well that I have heard from, except Moore, he has a slight attack of dysentery. I have not seen him but will this afternoon.

Preaching here every Sunday well attended.

Direct your letters in future to Sacramento City, California, as that is only 40 miles from here and I can get them from there. I am very anxious to hear from home, as nothing has reached me from there since April 2d. In my future letters I can give you more information than in the present. Write and send papers that all news possible may reach me here,

And believe me truly
Your friend and debtor,
C. E. BOYLE.

V

DR. C. E. BOYLE TO ARMSTRONG BOYLE,
CAMP 100, NEAR COLOMA, SEPTEMBER 16, 1849.
[PRINTED IN THE *Ohio State Journal,* DEC. 15, 1849.]

FROM CALIFORNIA.

The mails of Wednesday brought a large number of letters from the California boys to our citizens. In addition to the one published on Thursday we have been permitted to publish the following from a young man well known in this city. It will be seen that their health remains good, and that they have very fair returns for their labor.

CAMP 100, NEAR COLOMA, UPPER
CALIFORNIA, Sept. 16, 1849

Brother Armstrong: — According to promise I now write you a few items of travel to El Dorado. On the second of April we left the goodly city of Columbus, Ohio, (since found to be the centre of the world,) and arrived at St. Joseph, Mo., on the 16th. Here we remained until about the 1st of May, when we moved onward towards the Great West. About the 1st of June we reached Fort Laramie, at the foot of the Black Hill; on the 28th of June Fort Hall, a trading post belonging to the British Fur Company, situated in the Eastern part of Oregon, and found ourselves traveling up Carson river towards its source in the Sierra Nevada, on the 1st of August, and arrived in the diggings, Camp 100, on the 12th of August. A tolerably correct notion of the journey may be gathered from the works of Bryant and Fremont, but experience, actual experience alone, can picture the whole route in that panoramic manner which is requisite to a full appreciation of scenes, pleasant or unpleasant, which are of daily occurrence on the pilgrimage to the shrine of Mammon, taken by so many of his votaries during the past summer. I shall not, therefore, even attempt a description, but will merely say that the man who makes the trip once may consider it an achievement of such magnitude that he need not repeat it to establish his fame as a hardy adventurer, and may rest satisfied with the laurels gained in a single trip.

Contrary to my expectation, we arrived in safety and good health, although most of our company had been more or less indisposed during our toilsome march, and a few of them had been dangerously ill.

After our arrival here, it was deemed expedient to dissolve the company, and this was effected with the utmost good feeling, and without the occurrence of any thing to make the recollection of the meeting, called to effect the dissolution, unpleasant in the least.

The company, thus separated, went in small parties to different localities, to pursue the business of making money, by mining or otherwise, as might be best suited to their tastes and previous business habits. Ten of us remain in the neighborhood of Camp 100, near an excellent spring, and generally work at gold digging. This is very laborious business, but generally pays at the rate of from $8 to $25 dollars per day, although there is OCCASIONALLY a person who, for a few days, may obtain much more—hundreds and sometimes even thousands being obtained by a few days' labor, but the average amount obtained, so far as I can learn, is about one ounce per day for each laborer. This, it is true, is not so great as many expected, but it exceeds my anticipations, and I have some hopes of getting a nice little sum during my stay here.

The appearance of the country is quite peculiar, and not like anything I ever saw before. In all that part of California through which I have travelled, there is a constant succession of high hills, narrow valleys, and deep ravines. The soil is mostly of a reddish color, almost like brick dust, and this is intermingled, with quartz rocks, broken into variously sized fragments, granite, talc, and other rocks of similar character. The gold as found, and it is distributed in every direction, is usually in small scales, lying in contact with rocks which underlay the soil, and is most easily obtained from the bottom of ravines, and the beds of small winter streams.

The implements required are quite simple, and consist of ordinary digging tools; a pick, crowbar, spade, a knife or horn for scraping the rocks, a pan, and cradle for washing the dirt. The motion given to the dirt and gravel during the process of washing, is such as to allow the gold to find its way to the bottom, which it readily does by its gravity, and at the same time wash off the lighter portions of the soil. In the bottom of the pan or cradle, with the gold, remains a fine black metallic sand, which may then be washed out, blown out, or picked out with a steel magnet, this sand is itself rich in particles of gold almost invisible to the naked eye, which it yields up to mercury at the rate of 8 to 16 dollars per pound of mud.

The timber around here is principally oak, with a few gigantic pines, and various species of undergrowth. But all is peculiar; there are no trees or flowers that exactly resemble the same species in the United States.

Game of various kinds is abundant here during the rainy season, which sets in about the last of November, or earlier. It consists principally of grizzly bears, elk, black-tailed deer, antelope, California quails, &c.

Order prevails here to an *alarming* extent, and lawyers have nothing to do. An interference with the rights of others is promptly punished by a disinterested jury, and their executive officers appointed *pro tempore*. The punishment for stealing is cropping, whipping, banishment, or death, according to the article taken, and the manner of taking it.

I have not heard from home since I started, and feel considerable anxiety to know what has taken place in Columbus, and other parts of Ohio; and also, the political news of the day. I have just learned that the government has appointed a man to go out to meet emigrants still on the road, and render them any assistance they may need. There are very many who have not yet arrived. A fearful amount of suffering must result from their detention on the desert or Sierra Nevada. And my advice to all future emigrants is to start early and hasten through, but to go in preference by the Panama route. I must close. Write, and direct papers to Coloma, Sutter's Mill, Upper California.

Yours, &c.   C. E. BOYLE.

VI

JAMES G. CANFIELD TO HIS WIFE,
"GOLD DIGGINGS OF CALIFORNIA,"AUGUST 21, 1849.
[PRINTED IN THE *Ohio State Journal,* Nov. 19, 1849.]

INTERESTING FROM CALIFORNIA.

We have been permitted to make some extracts from a letter just received by a lady in this city, from her husband, now in California.

"GOLD DIGGINS" OF CALIFORNIA, AUG 21, 1849.

My Dear Wife—

It is with pleasure I once more seat myself on the

ground to address you. The last chance I had to write you was at Ft. Laramie, about the 1st of June. We arrived in the gold diggins nine days ago, being 132 days from Columbus, and travelled over thirty-five hundred miles, and for the last sixty or seventy days, nearly all the time in the mountains, and was only one week out of the sight of snow. Two weeks ago today I drove my team for a long distance over three feet of snow, on the top of one of the highest mountains on this continent. Our company all arrived in the diggins safe and sound, and every man in good health. We are as rough and ready a looking set of men as ever came across the plains, although we have suffered a great many things that you would hardly think a man could stand.

Yet our sufferings are nothing to compare with those that are behind us. There are probably thousands on the road that will never see California or home either. I would not be five hundred miles back and have those great sandy deserts to come over again for all the gold in California. I was three nights on one desert which we could not travel in the day time, and for a whole week all the sleep I got was about 14 hours, and worked day and night; but all these things have had a tendency to toughen me. Although I am not quite as fleshy as I was when I left home, yet what flesh I have is plump and hard, and I flatter myself that I can stand as many hard knocks as any man in the company. I have not had my clothes off but one night since I left Ohio. I can wrap myself in a blanket, and lay down under a tree in the mountains with bears, wolves, rattle-snakes and lizards for neighbors, and sleep as soundly as I used to in our pleasant little bed room. The nights are very pleasant, but the days are most outrageous hot, so much so that we cannot stand it so work only mornings and evenings. You can form some idea of digging gold, when I tell you it is very similar to digging cellars where the ground is full of rocks and large stones, and taking the dirt to the water and washing it in pans till there is nothing left in the bottom but small particles of gold, varying in quantity from one to twenty dollars in value, according to the richness of the earth. I have dug some gold but not much, though I have dug two and three dollars worth per hour —but after we get to work, and get used to the work, we can do well. When I say "we" I mean our mess, for the company has dissolved and divided the property, and have all gone their own way rejoicing. John Walton, Gideon Walton, Shade Dungan, Edgar and myself, and a young man by the name of Krumm, have formed a company of six that will probably stick together.

I calculate to work hard for one year and then take the quickest route home, and if I ever leave my little family again I shall have lost my senses. But I have no doubt but that I shall do very well in that time, for there is plenty of gold here and men are making money. I could get 16 dollars a day to drive team, or chop wood, or any other kind of labor, but I think I will run the risk of digging and get as much as I can. I sold my gun to-day for one hundred dollars in gold. Living is very high. Pork sells at 65 cts per pound. Flour 25, Sugar 45, and every thing else in proportion. Boarding is $21.00 per week and find your own place to sleep, and bed to sleep on. It is believed that provisions will be much cheaper in a few weeks, as soon as more ships arrive. Every ship that comes in is loaded with men and provisions, and every ship that leaves is loaded with disappointed men who came out here expecting to get rich without hard work, and they are the most of them from the eastern cities, that come by water, and have never done any hard work, and consequently cannot stand the hardships that men will have to undergo in order to make money. But the men that cross the plains are the ones that can stand it, as they have all seen the "Elephant!"

The mines are the most quiet places I ever saw. A man is as safe here as he would be locked up in a room at home. They deal very severely with a man for stealing or rob-bing in this country. For stealing any small article they tie him to a tree and whip him severely, and then cut off both ears and let him go. For robbing they whip in the morning and hang him in the evening. For murder they hang him on the first tree. The first night I arrived in the diggings I slept under the limbs of a tree where three men were hung for robbery a few weeks ago. A man can have any amount of valuable property by a tree or by the road side—go off and be gone for days, and return and find everything as he left it. In the towns the streets are full of property and provisions of all kinds, and they do not pretend to watch them, day and night, and they are as safe as they would be in the States under strong locks and bolts. There is no more danger in California than in the streets of Columbus. So you need not give you any uneasiness on that score.   J.G.C.

[JAMES G. CANFIELD]

INDEX

A. A. Vantine and Co., 26
A. S. Decker and Bros., 13
Abbott, Mr., 269-70
Acapulco, Mexico, 27
Adams and Co., 232
Addison, George C., 25, 38, 233, 234, 235, 236, 237, 240, 241, 243, 249, 258, 260, 295
Addison and Stambaugh, 26, 259, 262
Alabama miners, 229, 230, 244
Abert, Lt., 59
alcaldes, 217, 221-2, 233, 292-3, 295, 315
Allen, Bradley Ripley, 34
Allen, Jedediah, 14, 53, 266, 268
Allen County, Ohio, 213
American Falls, 110-11, 157, 278, 310
American River, 17, 151-2, 153, 154, 161, 162, 165, 307, 310
Anderson, H., 215, 217, 224, 225, 229, 230, 249
Anderson, Ore., 34
antelope, 16, 71, 72, 73, 77, 83, 85, 96, 121, 170, 171, 172, 173, 174, 175, 177, 189, 191
apricots, 139
Aristocracy Hill, 23
Arkansas emigrants, 177, 178
Armitage, Jacob, 305
Armstrong, (J. Elza?), 48, 207, 208, 220, 267, 291
Arnold, Mr., 251
Ash Hollow, 80-1, 118, 156, 272
Astor House, 28
Astoria, Ore., 154
Atlantic (river steamer), 267
auctions, 248, 252, 253, 256
Augustine family, 246
Augustine's Boarding House, 23, 232

Babb, L. H., 259, 298
Baden, Germany, 60

badger, 79, 90
Badger (miner), 230-1
Bailey, A. J., 310
Baker Library, 267
Baker (miner), 219, 244
Baldwin, Capt., 29
Bancroft Library, 10
Baptist Church, 28
Bar Rock, 202
Barcus, E., 58, 96, 98, 105, 111, 119, 118, 128, 132, 153, 161, 165, 192, 250, 269, 305
Barlow, Mr., 180, 181
Barnard, F., 265, 299
Barnes, Dr., 192, 289
Barr, J. K., 305
Barton's Bar, 261-2, 264, 299
basalt, 182
Bates, Frank, 287
battle of Cerro Gordo, 241, 271
Beach, Horatio, 203, 204, 222, 227, 228, 291, 294
Bear River, 105-7; *Smiths fork,* 105, 276; *Thomas fork,* 105, 276, 310
Bear River (Nev. county), 195, 196, 290
Bear River ferry, 106
beaver dams, 111
Beckville, Calif., 23
"Bed Rock" (Maine miner), 222
Beekman, C. C., 293
Benicia, Calif., 31, 32, 39
Berkeley Square, 37
Berry, Mr., 258, 298
Bess, Mr., 252
Bess's Hotel, 256
Bidwell, John, 35, 286, 297
Bidwell's Bar, 250, 297
Bidwell's Rancho, 35
Bieber, Ralph, 8
Big Blue River, 58, 66-7, 270, 310
Big Sandy River, 100-1, 156
Bingham, Mr., 37
Bitter Creek, 87